CAHIERS
D'ÉCONOMIE POLITIQUE

PAPERS
IN POLITICAL ECONOMY

Histoire de la pensée et théories
History of Thought and Theories

67

What Have We Learned on Growth Cycles Analysis?

Qu'a-t-on appris sur la croissance cyclique ?

2014

Publié avec le soutien du CNRS, de l'université de Paris Ouest
et de l'Institut d'études politiques de Lille

L'Harmattan

Depuis 1974, les *Cahiers d'économie politique* sont un lieu privilégié pour les discussions théoriques qui prennent en compte toute la dimension historique de la discipline économique. Considérant que l'étude des auteurs passés et les débats actuels en analyse économique peuvent mutuellement s'enrichir, ils publient des articles qui relèvent de l'histoire de la pensée économique, de la philosophie économique, ou qui se situent à l'intersection de l'histoire de la pensée et de la théorie économique contemporaine ou de l'histoire économique.
Les *Cahiers d'économie politique* publient deux numéros par an, généralement en juin et décembre. Un de ces deux numéros est thématique. Les numéros thématiques publient des sélections d'articles proposés dans le cadre de colloques ou de journées d'étude. Ces manifestations sont organisées par la revue ou par des institutions universitaires sur le principe d'un appel à communication. Pour envisager qu'un colloque soit publié dans la revue, il est nécessaire que le responsable prenne contact dès l'organisation de la manifestation avec le comité de rédaction des *Cahiers*.

Since 1974, *Papers in Political Economy* have published and participated to the main theoretical discussions by paying a particular attention to the historical aspects of economic analysis. Considering that the study of past authors and present debates are complementary, the PPE publish papers on history of economic thought, economic philosophy, or papers overlapping fields of history of economic thought and contemporary economic theory or economic history.
Papers in Political Economy is a biannual journal, usually published in June and December. One of the two yearly issues is thematic and includes papers presented at a workshop or conference and selected among responses to an open call for papers. For proceedings to be published in this form, conference organizers are invited to contact the journal's editorial board at a very early stage.

Adresse • Address

Site Internet : http://www.cahiersdecopo.fr/

Éditeur : Éditions L'Harmattan, 5-7, rue de l'École Polytechnique, 75005 Paris

Tél. : 01 40 46 79 10 – Site Internet : http://www.editions-harmattan.fr

Éditeur électronique : CAIRN, http://www.cairn.info/

Instructions aux auteurs • Notes for contributors

Les *Cahiers d'économie politique* acceptent les articles en français et en anglais. Normes de publication disponibles sur le site internet : http://www.cahiersdecopo.fr/

Papers in Political Economy accept papers in French and in English. For a full and complete guide for authors, please go to: http://www.cahiersdecopo.fr/

5-7, rue de l'Ecole-Polytechnique, 75005 Paris

http://www.harmattan.fr
diffusion.harmattan@wanadoo.fr
harmattan1@wanadoo.fr

ISBN : 978-2-343-05340-0
EAN : 9782343053400

SOMMAIRE

Michaël Assous, Muriel Dal-Pont Legrand	What have we learned on growth cycles analysis?	7
Kevin D. Hoover	Man and machine in macroeconomics	15
Niels Geiger	Cycles « versus » growth in Schumpeter – A graphical interpretation of some core theoretical remarks	35
Alain Raybaut	Modeling the interaction of cycles and growth in the fifties: two Schumpeterian attemps	55
Claude Diebolt	Kuznets versus Kondratieff. An essay in historical macroeconometrics	81
Amanar Akhabbar	Circulation du capital et explication du changement économique chez Marschak, Frisch et Leontief	119
Michaël Assous, Olivier Bruno, Muriel Dal-Pont Legrand	The law of diminishing elasticity of demand in Harrod's *Trade Cycle* (1936)	159
Johannes A. Schwarzer	Growth as an objective of economic policy in the early 1960s: the role of aggregate demand	175
Eric Nasica	Stabilization policies and banking behaviors: a rereading of Minsky's conception of business cycles	207

CONTENTS

Michaël Assous, Muriel Dal-Pont Legrand	Qu'a-t-on appris sur la croissance cyclique ? 7
Kevin D. Hoover	L'homme et la machine dans la macroéconomie 15
Niels Geiger	Cycles vs croissance chez Schumpeter. Une interprétation graphique de quelques remarques théoriques centrales 35
Alain Raybaut	Modélisation de l'articulation cycles croissance dans les années 1950 : deux tentatives schumpétériennes...55
Claude Diebolt	Kuznets vs Kondratieff. Un essai de macroéconométrie historique..................81
Amanar Akhabbar	Capital circulation and the explanation of economic change by Marschak, Frisch and Leontief 119
Michaël Assous, Olivier Bruno, Muriel Dal-Pont Legrand	La loi de l'élasticité de la demande décroissante dans le *Trade Cycle* (1936) de Harrod........................ 159
Johannes A. Schwarzer	La croissance, objectif de la politique économique au début des années 1960 : le rôle de la demande agrégée..................................... 175
Eric Nasica	Politiques de stabilisation et comportements bancaires : une relecture des cycles d'affaires chez Minsky.........207

WHAT HAVE WE LEARNED ON GROWTH CYCLES ANALYSIS?[1]

Michaël Assous
Muriel Dal-Pont Legrand[2]

Business cycles and growth are considered as independent fields for decades. Indeed, after the Second World War, when macroeconomics began to develop through an increased use of mathematical models, the problem of analyzing growth-cycles dynamics appeared as a real (and certainly also mathematical) challenge. Some economists accepted that dichotomy, concentrating their attention on specific questions which they considered as better addressed in models specifically built in order to capture either long-run or short-run issues. Two subfields appeared: on the one side were business cycle theories which focused on understanding detrended data movements; on the other side was long-run growth theory which analyzed the existence and the stability of stationary paths. Even if one can identify an increasing tendency among economists to accept such a 'division of labor' between cycle and growth theories, there were also economists who never ceased to consider this dichotomy only as a pedagogical organization. One can indeed identify economists who were fully aware of the restrictions imposed by such a dichotomy and then proposed to explore the various lines of research which could analyze how cycles and growth dynamics can intertwine. Although the intensity of research in that field fluctuated sometimes, interest of macroeconomists for that question never fully disappeared.

At least two major episodes exist for which the idea of cycles – and consequently of the interaction between cycles and growth dynamics

1. The present issue contains a selection of the papers presented at the 14th International Conference of the Charles Gide Association for the Study of Economic Thought, at the University Nice Sophia Antipolis and GREDEG CNRS, May 2012, in a revised version after having been submitted to the usual refereeing process.
The authors of this introduction benefited a lot from earlier discussions with Harald Hagemann, and which are developed in Assous, Dal Pont Legrand and Hagemann [2015] in an extended version.

2. Department of Economics, University of Paris I, Pantheon-Sorbonne, PHARE. E-mail: Michael.Assous@univ-paris1.fr
University of Lille 1 and Clersé CNRS. E-mail: muriel.dal-pont-legrand@univ-lille1.fr

– ceased to be in the priorities of the agenda: (i) in the late 1960s, when Bronfenbrenner [1969] emphasized the lack of interest of macroeconomists for cycle analysis and (ii) more recently, when leading economists spread the idea that the central problem of depression / prevention has been solved (cf. Lucas [2003]) and that such a statement was also confirmed by practitioners[3] for whom "[o]ne of the most striking features of the economic landscape over the past twenty years or so has been a substantial decline in macroeconomic volatility." [Bernanke, 2004][4]

After the obvious return of instability and depression,[5] interest for growth – cycle's analysis is emerging again, and though one cannot still[6] say that this question has been solved, it becomes more and more difficult to consider this (artificial) division as a scientific choice. Indeed, more than "just" the unsatisfactory understanding of economic fluctuations, this dichotomy has a second consequence: the two subfields became so independent that debates on potential beneficial effects of stabilization policies clearly disappeared from the forefront of the field.[7]

One can also notice that when nevertheless the modern literature addresses the question of the growth cycles interactions, it does it through models which deal with those issues in a totally new analytical framework which makes difficult to evaluate effective progress in our understanding of such complex issues. On the one side, one cannot deny that various modern approaches dealing with the influence cyclical fluctuations can have on growth, sometimes offering competing views,[8] have recently provided a strong revival for those issues (stimulating also a large amount of empirical investigations). On the other side, and despite the use of sophisticated mathematical or computational devices, one can doubt that those models

3. In 2004, Ben Bernanke was already the governor of the Fed.

4. In the early 2000s this opinion is shared by a large variety of economists.

5. If a great majority of theoreticians seem to have discovered again the instability of economic activity, one can also find some cleaver economists [Krugman, 2009], not only among historians of economic thought, who never forget the periodicity of crises, and who never ceased to argue in favor of modeling approaches which could allow to take into account (monetary and financial) economic instability.

6. Cf. Solow [1988] "The problem of combining long-run and short-run macroeconomics has still not been solved."[p. 310].

7. One notable exception occurs when endogenous growth models were used in order to deal with business cycles (see Stadler [1990] for one of the pioneering contributions).

8. See, for instance, the debate within the New Growth Theory between the literature based on learning by doing *versus* learning or doing mechanism on the impact shocks can have on growth.

are more relevant than their ancestors. We then believe that incursions in the field of history of economic thought not only reminds us forgotten topics but also helps to understand to what extent the way economists address those questions has been affected by the evolution of modeling.

The purpose of this special issue is try to shed light of the diversity of approaches and modeling and most touchy problems macroeconomists had to deal with.[9] More precisely, its purpose is to pay attention to different lines of thought addressing growth cycle connection. Since economists dealing with that question naturally came to identify the need (or not) for stabilization or for growth enhancing policies, this special issue will also include papers which addressed the potential necessity and the nature of the economic policies which should be implemented in order to guarantee growth.

Matthews already noticed in the late 1950s that "there is less agreement among economists about the relation between trend and cycle than about most other topic in the theory of the cycle" [1959: 253].[10] The selection of contributions which compose this special issue may help to have an idea of the variety of approaches which have dealt with that question.

The story of macroeconomics is traditionally explained as continuity or antagonism to Keynes's contribution. *Kevin Hoover* proposes in this first paper to show how the (hi)story of macroeconomics, far from being so simple, is characterized by different views, not only concerning the variety of competing analytical frameworks but also with regard to the true nature of economics. More precisely, Hoover emphasizes in his prologue that "the notion that an economy is an object to be controlled by policy is pervasive." One can then identify two dominant metaphors: the first considers economists as engineers in charge of controlling a "machine"; it represents a mechanical approach which was developed by the well-known Ragnar Frisch and Jan Tinbergen; the second sees the economy as an organic entity and economists as physicians, it is the so-called "medical" approach and corresponds to Keynes's vision. Behind those visions, there is an interrogation about the fundamental nature of the economy, an element which determines the way economists conceive economic policy and then articulate short and long-run analysis. After presenting these different notions of what an economy is, Hoover shows that recent new classical macroeconomics, which strongly

9. See Assous, Dal Pont Legrand and Hagemann [2015] for a more detailed survey of this literature.

10. Quoted by Alain Raybaut in the introduction.

attacked the macroeconometric models in the tradition of Tinbergen, is nevertheless based on an amalgam of the medical and mechanical metaphors. Indeed they were successful in combining human decision-making with the mechanical models but only because they "applied highly simplified microeconomic models to aggregate data", an obviously dangerous shortcut, especially when those models have to produce economic policy advices.

The next two papers are concerned with the contribution of Joseph A. Schumpeter who is a central figure of the growth cycles analysis. The first paper provides a theoretically grounded graphical interpretation of some of Schumpeter's core theoretical conclusions on economic development. *Niels Geiger* notes that if the necessity emphasized by Schumpeter to deal with a growth and cycles interactions is well known, the technical separation he operates between growth trend and cyclical waves in real-world economies is more rarely discussed. Starting from Schumpeter [1927], the author comes back to the distinction Schumpeter makes between static and dynamic conditions. The first ones characterize the circular flow of an economy in, or in close proximity of, equilibrium, and are compatible with growth factors. In this case, changes are gradual which means that they can be absorbed by adaptive behavior, and that the economy can be maintained in the neighborhood of the equilibrium. On the contrary, dynamic conditions are necessary to account for business cycles [Schumpeter, 1927: 289]. Finally this paper proposes an original figure which provides a graphical representation of Schumpeter's ideas combining both, the ideas of cyclical and growth movements.

After drawing a clear picture of the different ways cycles and growth dynamics can intertwine (or not), *Alain Raybaut's* paper proposes to examine two Schumpeterian models which were developed in the 1950s by Smithies [1957] and Goodwin [1955]. At that time Schumpeter was the leading exponent of the view which considers that cycles and trend are not only intertwined but indistinguishable. Smithies emphasizes the Schumpeterian vision that economic dynamics is characterized by a process of disruption which leads the economy from one equilibrium position to the other, and described it with a two states linear model, while Goodwin prefers to analyze the role of technical progress in a nonlinear framework. They nevertheless both failed in overcoming the fundamental difficulty already identified[11]: indeed Alain Raybaut shows that, despite his claim, Smithies does not provide a purely endogenous explanation for business cycles and growth,

11. See, for instance, Pasinetti [1960].

and Goodwin, pursuing a more promising perspective, did not succeed in connecting Schumpeterian with Keynesian insights about investment dynamics.

Schumpeter was also the economist who considered fluctuations as the superposition of different waves or cycles characterized by varying amplitudes. In that line of research, but focusing on the views of Kuznets and Kondratieff, *Claude Diebolt* offers a comprehensive presentation of what can be the contribution of cliometrics to our understanding of the nature of economic movements. Combining historical, statistical and mathematical methods, cliometrics can contribute to gain insights at a theoretical level. The author then examines various national series and concludes the existence of a single intermediate cycle, a Kuznets swing with 15–20 years frequency which contradicts, at least partially, previous contributions which gave support to the existence of long-term economic cycles. Such a result gives support for more concerted and cooperative economic policies at the international level.

The years of *High Theory* (1926–1939)[12] are known as the years during which macroeconomics but also econometrics and national accounting emerged. *Amanar Akhabbar* concentrates his attention on models based on a disaggregated macroeconomic production function: namely, the models of Marschak, Frisch and Leontief. The paper shows that these models share a common view on the growth cycles interactions. The three models based their analysis of growth–cycles interaction on the circulation of capital goods among producers examining two different causes: the first one is the spread of economic change through producers and the second is due to coordination problems between producers in the capital circulation process.

One of the pioneering authors of the growth-cycles analysis,[13] and of dynamics in general, is Roy Harrod. His seminal 1939 contribution is well-known – even if most of the time misinterpreted – but only few historians of economic thought have dedicated attention to his 1936 book, *The Trade Cycle*. *Michaël Assous, Olivier Bruno* and *Muriel Dal Pont Legrand* propose a closer investigation of the first hints Harrod provided for the dynamics he developed later.[14] Harrod initially emphasized the importance of imperfect

12. There is the well-known reference to Schackle's 1967 book *The Years of High Theory: Invention and Tradition in Economic Theory 1926-1939*, GLS Shackle, Cambridge University Press.

13. Cf. Bruno and Dal Pont Legrand [2014].

14. One can mention here the paper of Rodolphe Dos Santos Ferreira, Claude d'Aspremont and Louis-André Gérard-Varet "Imperfect competition and the trade cycle: Aborted guidelines from the late 1930s", *History of Political Economy*, 2011, 43(3): 513–36.

competition for trade cycle theory because of its compatibility with decreasing cost. The exploration of the implications of decreasing cost brought him to the conclusion that imperfect competition can provide an equilibrium approach to business cycles relying upon the existence of multiple long-period equilibria. Instability may then result from alternative producers (correct) expectations leading successively the economy in position of high and low equilibria. Relying on imperfect competition, Harrod later explains that turning points may result from changes in the value of the multiplier and the accelerator coefficients. It is in that context that the Law of Diminishing Elasticity of Demand (LDED) comes into play: changes in demand elasticity are likely to change income shares. This paper proposes first to clarify the precise role Harrod assigned to the LDED in the understanding of the trade cycle; secondly it shows how Harrod used the LDED in order to give microeconomic foundations to a non-linear saving function that may give rise to an endogenous countercyclical value of the multiplier. This paper sheds light on an element which has been undermined by most of the readers and which finally places Harrod as a pioneer of endogenous business cycle analysis before the seminal work of Samuelson [1939].

Johannes Schwarzer analyses a debate which took place in the early 1960s when the existence of an optimal level of demand, i.e. a level maximizing the rate of growth, was controversially discussed. The main idea was that "good demand management would dampen cycles, being then an efficient regulation tool for economic policy purpose. That regulation of the economy step by step, period by period, would allow the economy to follow a sustained growth path. Logically, the cycle became "a thing of the past" [Minsky, 1968: 45], and the attention of the economists became absorbed by short-term economic policies. There existed then a rather large consensus on the idea that sustained growth was the outcome of successful stabilization policies which, dampening business cycles, could maintain the economy at full capacity output. The author gives a survey of the debates which developed within this field and identifies three different views—the Keynesian, the Paishian and the skeptical one—the first two ones sharing the idea that high demand in the short and medium-run may foster growth, the last one providing arguments against this view. The conclusion outlines what we could learn from the debates of the 60's but also what may have been lost since Friedman's introduction of a "natural rate of unemployment" into the Phillips curve concept.

The last contribution follows the same line of research: without directly discussing the interaction between cycles and growth dynamics, the paper questions the efficiency of stabilization policies, which is a crucial issue. Indeed, all the discussions about the influence cycles can have on growth, or more generally about the impact short-run fluctuations can have on long-run (growth) dynamics, have *in fine* to decide whether there is a need for stabilization policies. *Eric Nasica* addresses this question in a Minskyan analytical framework. He starts showing the influence nonlinear business cycles models *à la* Hicks had on Minsky's own analysis of fluctuations. Minsky's financial instability hypothesis is then reassessed. The author explains how banks' behavior undermines the efficiency of stabilization policies and determines the nature of economic fluctuations. The author concludes by assessing the relevance this sort of approach can have in order to understand recent pre- and post-crisis stabilization policies.

References

Assous M., Dal Pont Legrand M. and Hagemann H. [forthcoming, 2015]. Business cycles and economic growth. In G. Faccarello and H.D. Kurz (Eds) *Handbook of the History of Economic Analysis, Volume I Great Economists since Petty and Boisguilbert.* Cheltenham: Edward Elgar Publishing.

Bernanke B. [2004]. The Great Moderation. 20th February. <http://www.federalreserve.gov/BOARDDOCS/SPEECHES/2004/20040220/default.html>.

Bronfenbrenner M. [1969]. *Is the Business Cycles Obsolete?* New York: Wiley Interscience.

Bruno O. and Dal Pont Legrand M. [2014]. The instability principle revisited: an essay in Harrodian dynamics. *European Journal for the History of Economic Thought* 21(3): 467–84.

Harrod, R. [1939]. An essay in dynamic theory. *Economic Journal* 49: 14–33.

Krugman P. [2009]. *The Return of Depression Economics and the Crisis of 2008.* New York: W. W. Norton.

Lucas R. [2003]. Macroeconomic priorities. *American Economic Review* 93(1): 1–14.

Matthews R.C.O. [1959]. Duesemberry on *Growth and Fluctuations. The Economic Journal* 69(2, part 1): 133–45.

Solow R.M. [1988]. Growth theory and after. *American Economic Review* 78(3): 307–17.

Stadler G.W. [1990]. Business cycle models with endogenous technology. *American Economic Review* 80(4): 763–78.

MAN AND MACHINE IN MACROECONOMICS

Kevin D. Hoover[1]

The potted histories of macroeconomics textbooks are typically Keynes-centric. Keynes is credited with founding macroeconomics, and the central developments in the field through the early 1970s, including large-scale macroeconometric models are usually termed "Keynesian." The story of macroeconomics is framed as support or opposition (e.g., by monetarism or the new classical macroeconomics) to Keynes. The real story is more complicated and involves at least two distinct threads. Keynes was important, but perhaps more important for the detailed development of the field were the early macroeconometricians – Ragnar Frisch and Jan Tinbergen. Frisch and Tinbergen adopted physical or mechanical metaphors in which aggregate quantities are central. Keynes's vision of macroeconomics is better described as "medical." It is based in human psychology and individual decision-making and sees the economy as an organic system. Whereas policymakers and economic advisers in Keynes view can operate only within the economic system, Frisch and Tinbergen laid the basis for an optimal-control approach to economic policy in which the policymaker stands outside the system. Recent new classical macroeconomics has adopted an uneasy amalgam of the medical and mechanical metaphors.

L'homme et la machine dans la macroéconomie

Les aperçus historiques des manuels de macroéconomie tournent généralement autour de Keynes. Keynes est crédité d'avoir fondé la macroéconomie, et d'être à l'origine de ses principaux développements jusqu'au début des années 1970, y compris les grands modèles macroéconométriques habituellement qualifiés de « keynésiens ». L'histoire de la macroéconomie est ainsi pensée comme un moyen de renforcer ou de contredire Keynes (par le monétarisme ou la nouvelle macroéconomie classique, par exemple). En vérité, la véritable histoire est plus compliquée et comporte deux fils distincts. Keynes fut important, mais les premiers macroéconométriciens, Ragnar Frisch et Jan Tinbergen, se révélèrent peut-être plus importants encore. Frisch et Tinbergen recoururent à des métaphores physiques ou mécaniques dans lesquelles les quantités agrégées étaient primordiales. La vision qu'avait Keynes de la macroéconomie était plutôt « médicale ». Elle s'appuie sur la psychologie humaine et les décisions individuelles et elle considère l'économie comme un système organique. Alors que les décideurs et les conseillers économiques ne peuvent opérer, selon Keynes, que dans le système économique, Frisch et Tinbergen posèrent les bases d'une approche de contrôle optimal de la politique économique où le décideur se situe hors du système. La nouvelle macroéconomie classique a réalisé un amalgame déconcertant des métaphores médicale et mécanique.

Keywords: Macroeconomics, Keynes, Frisch, Tinbergen, Klein, macroeconometric models, macroeconomic policy.

Mots clefs : Macroéconomie, Keynes, Frisch, Tinbergen, Klein, modèles macroéconomiques, politique macroéconomique.

JEL classification: B22, B23

1. Department of Economics and Department of Philosophy – Duke University – Box 90097, Durham, North Carolina 27708-0097 Tel. (919) 660-1876; E-mail kd.hoover@duke.edu

Plenary lecture delivered to the Colloque de l'Association Charles Gide pour l'Histoire de la Pensée Economomique, 7-9 June 2012, Université de Nice Sophia Antipolis. An earlier version was delivered in the New Directions in Economics, Public Lecture Series at Boston University, 17 November 2010;

Prologue

The Great Recession and worldwide Financial Crisis promoted soul-searching among economists and scapegoating among the public, from taxi drivers to heads of state: The Queen of England met with a gathering of economists at the London School of Economics to discuss the financial collapse: "Why," she asked, "did nobody notice it?" Despite our disappointing record as prognosticators, the public still expects economists to tell them how to extricate the economy from its current doldrums.

There is an element of magical thinking in these demands. In the United States, we see it in the notion that our president or the chairman of the Federal Reserve is directly responsible for the success or failure of the economy. Responsibility is more diffuse in the European Union, but I would be surprised if public's expectations of Brussels or Frankfurt are not similar. And I presume that one reason that the French President Sarkozy was not reelected was that he was held responsible for the ills of the French and European economies. I don't want to deny that leading politicians or central bankers are important players for good or ill; but, as I ask my students, if a president could set the economic dial as a matter of unfettered choice, why would the economy ever fare poorly? (Sometimes they would answer that George Bush was a bad man or that Vice President Richard Cheney benefited in some sinister way from bad economic times. But once Barack Obama became the American president and American economy still performed badly, I heard that less often.)

The notion that an economy is an object to be controlled by policy is pervasive. There are two dominant metaphors. The first sees the economy as a machine operated by the government: economists and policymakers as engineers. The second sees the economy as an organic entity. Bill Clinton campaigned for the American presidency in 1992 on a set of policies that he said would "grow the economy": economists and policymakers as farmers. Clinton's phrase is now ubiquitous; but it rings false in my ears – not, as I once thought, because it is ungrammatical, we naturally talk of farmers growing crops – but because, even if one accepts an organic metaphor, it seems like the wrong metaphor. Another organic metaphor that works better, perhaps, sees the economy as a body: economists and policymakers as physicians.

Esteem for John Maynard Keynes has ever ebbed and flowed. Since the onset of the Great Recession and the Financial Crisis, Keynes – never an obscure figure among economists – became ever more familiar to the general public. In the two years after the onset of the recession, Keynes was mentioned in print media more than three times more frequently than in the two years before the recession – the total number of mentions runs into the thousands per year.[2] Keynes, the economic hero; Keynes, the economic knave. Take your pick.

Reaching a nadir in the last heady days of the boom, Keynesian economics was again in vogue with the recession of 2007 and the financial collapse of 2008, only to become embattled with rising deficits and continued slow growth despite the stimulus. The *Wall Street Journal* often reminds us that Keynes is dead. In an article in the *New York Times*, N. Gregory Mankiw [2008], Harvard economics professor and former chairman of George W. Bush's Council of Economic Advisors, found a well worn passage from Keynes's masterwork, *The General Theory of Employment Interest and Money*, that speaks to our time:

> At the present moment people are unusually expectant of a more fundamental diagnosis; more particularly ready to receive it; eager to try it out, if it should be even plausible. But apart from this contemporary mood, the ideas of economists and political philosophers, both when they are right and when they are wrong, are more powerful than is commonly understood. Indeed the world is ruled by little else. Practical men, who believe themselves to be quite exempt from any intellectual influences, are usually the slaves of some defunct economist. Madmen in authority, who hear voices in the air, are distilling their frenzy from some academic scribbler of a few years back. [Keynes, 1936: 383; quoted by Mankiw, 2008.]

Keynes himself is now that defunct economist. *The Wall Street Journal* knows that he is defunct, but fears that – zombie-like – he won't stay down. Mankiw too knows that he is defunct, but sees Caspar, the friendly ghost.

Without diminishing Keynes's importance, I want to suggest that the story of macroeconomics is more complex than generally appreciated and that there are other economists from whom macroeconomists and policymakers – practical and mad – are distilling their frenzy and their wisdom.

2. Based on a search of the Lexis database.

The potted history of macroeconomics

Economists are typically both ignorant and unappreciative of the history of their discipline. Yet, economists, like the practitioners of other fields, convey a potted version of that history their students. The potted history is easily discovered through quick perusal of macroeconomics textbooks.

I don't need to recount the fine details of this potted history: we all know it. Broadly it goes like this: Once upon a time, economists were the champions of *laissez faire*. Then, along came the Great Depression. Keynes declared the end of *laissez faire* and provided us in his *General Theory* with an alternative. Thus, in creating the antithesis between microeconomics and macroeconomics, Keynes created a dialectical tension that Paul Samuelson then resolved with his *neoclassical synthesis*. And then Keynesian economics ruled the policy roost. But Keynes provided no theory of inflation. Phillips introduced his curve and provided policymakers with an instrument through which they could exchange inflation for unemployment. But Cassandra in the form of Milton Friedman presciently warned that the heady days of aggregate demand management would lead to the collapse of the Keynesian economists' Troy. The stagflation of the early 1970s blasted holes in the ramparts of Keynesian economic management, and Friedman's monetarism was there to fill the breach. But Friedman's monetarism did not get to the root of the problem with Keynes: real economics is microeconomics and – despite Samuelson's irenic doctrine of the neoclassical synthesis – Keynes failed to build on adequate microfoundations. Robert Lucas, Thomas Sargent and others introduced the new classical macroeconomics, which supported monetarists policies, but did so on a rigorous microfoundational analysis. Nostalgic for Keynesian policy conclusions, the New Keynesians adopted New Classical microfoundational methods while still addressing the problems of market failures. With that, we have reached the situation of macroeconomics today – at least as it is taught to undergraduate and graduate students alike.

I cannot begin to say all that is wrong with this potted history. But, love him or hate him, please note that Keynes stands at its center. And while no story maintains its currency for long if it is totally unconnected to the truth, this story is misleading or wrong in nearly every respect – not least in its *dramatis personae*. At a bare minimum, we must add the names of Ragnar Frisch and Jan Tinbergen to the history of macroeconomics.

Most of the pieces of the alternative story have been noticed by other scholars, but rarely have the pieces been put together. And I believe that they should be put together to craft a different history for macroeconomics – one in which Keynes remains important, but not preeminent, and one in which a tension between competing visions of macroeconomics is central. One result of this reappraisal will be to present Keynes as a substantially different thinker than he is regarded in our potted textbook histories.

The mechanical vision

The phenomena that we now recognize as macroeconomic – *inter alia* inflation, growth, mass unemployment, the balance of payments, interest rates, and exchange rates – are among the longest recognized and longest analyzed in the history of economics. Theories of the relationship of inflation to money clearly related to those of modern economics go back at least to the 16th century. But it was not until the 1930s that economists thought to address them through a special subdiscipline called *macroeconomics.* One problem that worried economists of the 1920s, even before the Great Depression, was the *trade cycle* or, as we now call it *the business cycle* – the alternation of good and bad times.

The puzzle was, how should we begin to think of business cycles. There were at least three options:

- First, they might be intrinsic to the structure of the economy;
- Second, they might be merely the cumulation of random influences;
- Third, they might be the complex implications of human actions in an unrepeatable historical setting.

The first two options could be regarded as analogous to physical dynamics – a pattern such as the tides or the amplitude of the string of a musical instrument.

The Norwegian economist Ragnar Frisch and the Dutch economist Jan Tinbergen were deeply influenced by such physical metaphors. Frisch and Tinbergen are not so well known as Keynes, even to economists. A search in the Econlit database for articles with their names in the titles produces 75 for Frisch, 117 for Tinbergen, and 1,978 for Keynes. Yet, they are not altogether uncelebrated. Strikingly, it was not Samuelson, but Frisch and Tinbergen who shared the very first Nobel Prize in Economics in 1969.

Frisch

Frisch was born in Oslo in 1895 and trained as a goldsmith. He entered university only at the age of 21 and chose economics as it was regarded as an easy subject and the path to a quick degree. He was drawn to mathematics and statistics and joined the then small group of mathematical economists.

As he saw it, earlier mathematical economists (e.g., Cournot and Walras) had satisfactorily analyzed exchange at a single period; so the key problem was to deal with economic decision-making over time. The first problem analogized to the problem of statics in physics; the second, to the problem of *dynamics*. And the physicists had already done the math. When Frisch began to analyze the business cycle, he began by thinking of pendulums.[3] The swing of a simple pendulum is too regular; so, he analyzed the movements of complex pendulums and worked out the mathematics of their cycles. In a famous paper, he analogized the business cycle to a rocking horse that is given a push from time to time. The rocking horse itself captured the intrinsic dynamics of the cycle (what he calls the *propagation mechanism*), while the irregular pushes (what he calls the *impulses*) corresponded to various random shocks to the economic system. In this metaphor Frisch ties together his interests in physical dynamics and statistics. Frisch was explicit: economics is social physics.

Frisch is a central, if neglected, figure in shaping modern economics. He was the moving force behind the Econometric Society – the group dedicated to promoting mathematical and statistical economics. Even today, to become a fellow of the Econometric Society is to join the elite of economics theorist and econometricians (a term which now has a narrower, statistical focus than it did in 1933). Frisch was the first editor of the society's journal, *Econometrica*, still reckoned among the top five economics journals.

Frisch was great coiner of neologisms. He originated not only *econometrics*, but the terms *microeconomics* and *macroeconomics*. Most people regard Keynes as the originator of this distinction. He certainly never used the terms, though he drew the distinction between the economics of individual or firm-level decisions, which we now regard as microeconomic, and the determination of output in the economy as a whole, which we regard as macroeconomic.

3 See, for example, Frisch [1933].

Frisch drew a similar distinction, earlier perhaps than Keynes, and clearly invented the terminology.[4]

Frisch thought that we should start with a macroeconomic model that worked with broad aggregates (GDP rather than an individual's income, for example) to determine the context for a microeconomic model of individual behavior. This is an inversion of the manner in which recent economists think. For them, the ideal is to start with microeconomic analysis and build up individual by individual to the behavior of the economy as a whole. Frisch rejected that idea. He conceded that we could imagine in principle a very complex economic model in which every individual and firm was represented. But such a model would be of no practical use.

Here again, he conceived of analogies with physics. To model the behavior of a single charged particle, the physicist conceives of it as being situated in a field that is the aggregate product of all the charged particles in a system.

Tinbergen

Tinbergen was born in 1903 in the Hague. He studied physics, and his doctoral supervisor, the eminent physicist Paul Ehrenfest, suggested that he apply physical analysis to economic problems. The result was a dissertation whose English title is *Minimization Problems in Physics and Economics.*

Frisch was primarily interested in the more theoretical problem of characterizing dynamics and the epistemological problem of discovering the right methods for working backwards from available economic data to the specification of an economic model. Tinbergen's interests were less detached from the beginning. He wanted to use economic models for policy. Tinbergen [1937] created the first econometrically estimated macromodel – a model of the Dutch economy – in the mid-1930s. On the basis of this achievement, the League of Nations, which had undertaken a larger project on the causes and cures of the business cycles – a response to the worldwide effects of the Great Depression – commissioned Tinbergen [1939] to create the first macroeconometric model of the United States, which was published on the eve of World War II. Tinbergen's model contained 48 equations and was estimated without the benefit of modern electronic computers. "It is

4. Frisch [1933] uses *microdynamic* and *macrodynamic* in a manner nearly equivalent to current usage of *microeconomic* and *macroeconomic.* At roughly the same time, he used their Norwegian equivalents, *mikroøkonomiske* and *macroøkonomiske* in a set of widely circulated, mimeographed lectures [Frisch 1933-1934]. Frisch's coinages appear to have spread through the early meetings of the Econometric Society.

strange," Keynes [1939: 568] observed, "that [Tinbergen's book] looks . . . to be the principal activity and *raison d'être* of the League of Nations" on the eve of the Second World War.

The medical vision

In contrast to Frisch and Tinbergen, physics did not animate Keynes's research strategy. He was not hostile to mathematics generally, having read mathematics at King's College, Cambridge and graduated 12th wrangler. His fellowship essay for King's was later published as his *Treatise on Probability*. Economics was not in Keynes's course of study; it was in his blood. When Keynes was student, economics formed part of the moral sciences tripos and was not an independent course of study. Keynes's father was himself a Cambridge economist; and Keynes absorbed economics both from formal study and from being dandled, as it were, on the knee of that Cambridge hero Alfred Marshall.

As an economist, Keynes is known so much in the caricatures of the potted history with which I began, that I want to state what seem to me to be the key points of his approach.

The fallacy of composition

Unlike the economics of Adam Smith, which focused on the wealth of nations, or the economics of 19th century neoclassical economists, such as William Stanley Jevons, which focused on markets, much of modern economics sees the most basic economic problem as the one faced by Robinson Crusoe: to do the best one can with scarce resources. For Jevons the game changes as soon as Friday arrives and opens up the possibility of trade. And for Keynes (and Smith), it's a new game altogether if we start to think about Friday's tribe – a whole economy.

For Keynes people are heterogeneous – each is situated differently, each has different tastes, different capacities, different beliefs. Yet, they form a society. And extending our reasoning from individual interactions to the whole economy is misleading. It commits a *fallacy of composition*. The quickest way for an individual from New Orleans to Baton Rouge is Interstate 10; but it is not the quickest way to get the whole population of New Orleans to Baton Rouge.

A key fallacy of composition in economics is a false analogy from elementary exchange to the economy as a whole. Robinson Crusoe's and Friday's different skills and different endowments give rise to mutually beneficial trade, and there is never any reason other than wanting to enjoy sleep or meal or a swim that they should be unemployed. But for Keynes, an economy as a whole is more like Mandeville's grumbling hive in the *Fable of the Bees* [1714]: private virtue (parsimony and restraint) produces public vice (economic collapse). A Mercedes sportscar or dinner at a fine restaurant is a dispensable luxury, but if enough of us dispense with such luxuries the autoworker and the busboy go without their dinners: as Keynes puts it, "the gay of tomorrow are absolutely indispensable to provide a *raison d'être* for the grave of to-day" [*General Theory*: 105–6]. Unlike Robinson and Friday, workers in a complex economy can be unemployed; the economy can operate at less than full capacity.

Keynes was keenly aware that the complexity of the economy depends on the institution of money, which allows us to obtains goods from people we'll never know, living lives that we can hardly imagine, in places we'll never see. Robinson and Friday may be selfish, but in an obvious sense they work for each other. If they save, they save by laying up stores. We too work for each other, but only indirectly. Directly, we work for money. And when we save, we save money, and do not demand the work of others. The process of my abstaining from spending leading to another's loss of income and his abstaining from spending, leading to still another's loss of income . . .and so on is Keynes's famous *investment multiplier*. The multiplier works the other way too – expenditure (yours or mine or the government's) gives some people income which, if they spend it, gives other people income . . .and so forth. The investment multiplier is the intellectual basis for President Obama's stimulus package.

Keynes's important analytical insight is that it just won't do to believe that the private sector will always and everywhere find and effect every valuable exchange. That would imply that the unemployed are dissembling: they say that they want to work, but really they are on vacation.

Uncertainty

The multiplier explains the process of getting into and out of trouble, but what started the trouble in the first place? Keynes's answer (surprisingly like that of the Austrian economists – often his most vocal opponents) is *time* and *ignorance*. The future matters to economic decisions, but we cannot know the future. Institutions have evolved to cope with time and ignorance – insurance, for example. As a chairman of two insurance companies and the author of a *Treatise on Probability*, Keynes understood *insurable risk.* The casino cannot predict each spin of the roulette wheel; the life insurance company cannot predict the day of each death; but the averages and their variability are known precisely. You take a chance on roulette; the casino calculates its return.

Keynes pointed out in 1937 that risk is not to be confused with uninsurable *uncertainty*.

> The prospect of a European war is uncertain, or the price of copper and the rate of interest twenty years hence, or the obsolescence of a new invention, or the position of private wealth owners in the social system of 1970. About these matters there is no scientific basis on which to form any calculable probabilities whatever. We simply do not know. [Keynes 1973: 113–4]

Keynes would no doubt see the onset of our latest financial collapse in the unfounded valuation of mortgage-backed financial derivatives as the result of an intellectual error – confusing insurable risk with uninsurable uncertainty.

How are we to cope with such radical uncertainty. For Keynes [1973: 113–4] a conventional response is better than paralysis: "the necessity for action and for decision compels us as practical men to do our best to overlook [uncertainty] and to behave exactly as we should if we . . ." could calculate the prospects and the risk. Such a calculation requires a view of those prospects; yet they too are uncertain, and "sanguine temperament and constructive impulses" determine our positive evaluation of them:

> If human nature felt no temptation to take a chance, no satisfaction (profit apart) in constructing a factory, a railway, a mine or a farm, there might not be much investment merely as the result of cold calculation. [Keynes, 1936: 150]

Elsewhere Keynes refers to "the spontaneous urge to action rather than inaction" as *animal spirits.* (Contrary to what many economists believe, Keynes did not coin this term – now revived in George Akerlof's and Robert Shiller's [2010] book of the same name: it is originally a term from now obsolete biology, which was already in common usage when Jane Austen's describes the frivolous Lydia Bennett of *Pride and Prejudice* as having "high animal spirits.") The conventional response to uncertainty is sometimes not enough:

> if the animal spirits are dimmed and the spontaneous optimism falters, leaving us nothing but mathematical expectation, enterprise will fade and die; – though fears of loss may have a basis no more reasonable than hopes of profit had before. [Keynes, 1936: 161–2]

He doesn't put it this way, but there is an *expectations multiplier* as well as an investment multiplier that can turn a boom into a bubble or a slump into a rout.

The most common convention of financial markets – stick with the herd – exacerbates our troubles: "Worldly wisdom teaches that it is better for reputation to fail conventionally than to succeed unconventionally" [Keynes, 1936: 158]. When expectations all point only one way, the herd follows and the market booms . . . or crashes. Keynes was himself a speculator, albeit an unconventional one who made a deal of money for himself and for King's College betting against the herd. But Keynes thought that a more conventional America was especially vulnerable:

> Americans are apt to be unduly interested in discovering what average opinion believes average opinion to be; and this national weakness finds its nemesis in the stock market . . . [A]n American . . . will not readily purchase an investment except in the hope of capital appreciation . . . he is, in the [this] sense, a speculator. Speculators may do no harm as bubbles on a steady stream of enterprise. But the position is serious when enterprise becomes the bubble on a whirlpool of speculation . . . [T]he best brains of Wall Street have been . . . directed towards [speculation rather than directing investment to its most profitable uses]. [Keynes, 1936: 159]

English chauvinist that he was, Keynes nevertheless thought that instability was the "scarcely avoidable outcome of our having successfully organised 'liquid' investment markets." And elitist that he was, it was popular access to financial markets that made the problems worse:

> the sins of the London Stock Exchange are less than those of Wall Street . . . not so much [because of] differences in national character, as [because of]. . . the fact that to the average Englishman Throgmorton Street is, compared with Wall Street to the average American, inaccessible and very expensive. [Keynes, 1936: 159]

Keynes was by no means an irrationalist; the market may *ultimately* conform to what rational calculation dictates. Yet, he is reputed to have remarked, "Markets can stay irrational longer than you can stay liquid."

Individual choice

In stressing the fallacy of composition and uncertainty – aspects of the economy that traditional economics had largely neglected – Keynes by no means rejected traditional economic analysis. His *General Theory* is constructed out of a series of functions describing the behavior of labor, investment, money holdings, and consumption. For most of these functions, his analysis is built on the a careful analysis of individual choice in a manner familiar to all students of Marshall and all modern microeconomists.

Take one example, his analysis of the demand for money (or as he calls it, "liquidity preference"). Keynes suggests that each person has an expectation of what interest rate is normal. Anyone whose expectation is below the market rate is a "bull" – one who expects rates to fall and, therefore, expects to take a capital gain on long-term bonds. Anyone whose expectations are above the market rate is a "bear" – one who expects rates to rise and, therefore, expects to take a capital loss. The bulls want to hold bonds; the bears want to hold money (which, for Keynes, includes short-term bonds, often counted as "cash" by financial-market players). The market rate is that rate that balances the bulls and the bears.

The point of this example is not the details, but to notice that Keynes appeals to profit-maximizing behavior exactly as any microeconomist would. What's more, Keynes does not follow Frisch or Tinbergen in aggregating. He does not look at the average behavior of individuals, nor does he add up all the supplies of money or all the demands for the money. Instead, the market rate of interest turns out to be what some particular individual believes the normal rate to be. In principle, we should be able to pick out the particular individual whose normal rate in fact defines the market rate. Keynes's object is macroeconomic analysis, but unlike Frisch and Tinbergen, he does not appeal to data that abstract from individuals, but to relationships that are fundamentally grounded in recognizable individual behavior.

Keynes's analysis of consumption is different. It is still deeply grounded in individual choice. But unlike the other functions, Keynes appeals not only to maximization of obviously economic factors, but also to a wider range of human behaviors and motivations: precaution, foresight, calculation, improvement, independence, enterprise, pride, avarice, enjoyment, shortsightedness, generosity, miscalculation, ostentation, and extravagance [Keynes, 1936: 108]. This is the Keynes who was the intimate of Lytton Strachey, Virginia Woolf, Duncan Grant and the other writers and artists of the Bloomsbury Group: patterns of consumption are not merely instrumental, but are a closer reflection of the ultimate human values than are returns on a financial portfolio. All these factors are deeply connected to individual values and individual choice; they are not considerations that are easily reflected in the national accounts.

Keynes's method of analysis keeps individual people and understandable human behavior front and center. Frisch's and Tinbergen's methods do not. But Frisch's and Tinbergen's methods allow for quantification and for making sense of economics. Keynes's method did not.

A medical metaphor

Keynes's approach to economics is richly social and deeply practical. Keynes is not as clearly committed to a metaphor as Frisch and Tinbergen are to the metaphor of the machine. I want to suggest nonetheless that there is an implicitly organic metaphor in his approach. Keynes's teacher, Alfred Marshall, had himself toyed with analogies between economics and biology. But it seems to me that medicine – a sort of applied biology – provides a closer analogy to Keynes's approach. I don't know that Keynes ever explicitly frames any biological metaphor, although he does, at least once, point to a minor medical specialty as a model: "If economists could manage to get themselves thought of as humble, competent people, on a level with dentists, that would be splendid." [Keynes, 1931[1972]: 332]

Keynes does, however, clearly reject the mechanical metaphor:

> The object of our analysis is, not to provide a machine, or method of blind manipulation, which will furnish an infallible answer, but to provide ourselves with an organized and orderly method of thinking out particular problems . . . [Keynes, 1936: 297]

And he ties that rejection specifically to policy analysis: He endorses

> [t]he reasonable doubts of practical men towards the idea that the Federal Reserve System has the power to raise or lower the price level by some automatic method, by some magic mathematical formula. [Keynes, 1930b (1971b): 305]

We don't understand the economy in the same manner as we understand a mechanical system:

> [t]he possible varieties of the paths which a . . . cycle can follow and its possible complications are so numerous that it is impracticable to outline

> all of them. One can describe the rules of chess and the nature of the game, work out the leading openings and play through a few characteristic end-games; but one cannot possibly catalogue all the games which can be played. [Keynes, 1930a (1971a): 253]

Keynes's metaphor is here not specifically organic, but he is alive to the complexity of even the relatively simple situations of games; and, as we shall see, his attitude to towards policy is that of a physician rather than an engineer.

Birth of modern macroeconomics

I don't want to exaggerate the divide between Keynes and Tinbergen and Frisch. Keynes's approach keeps individual human behavior at the center. Frisch's and Tinbergen's approach supports practical data-collection and quantification. The tension between these approaches is the mainspring of the history of macroeconomics after World War II.

Keynes famously attacked Tinbergen's [1939] econometric model of the United States, based in large measure on the presumed requirement that Tinbergen's statistics should capture a complete list of causes and that the relationships among the variables to be quantitatively stable – in his view an utter impossibility. Klein [2004: 156] later characterized Keynes's treatment of Tinbergen as "shabby," and he praised Tinbergen's good nature in expressing "no ill will toward Keynes." Tinbergen indeed took inspiration from the *General Theory* for his later work. As Tinbergen went, so did the profession. Within a few years of Keynes's untimely death in 1946, Keynesian economics became less associated with a direct acquaintance with the *General Theory* than with Sir John Hicks's [1937] simplified, aggregate reconstruction of its main functional relationships, known to generations of economics students as the IS-LM model.

The IS-LM model deals with aggregates. One can no longer, in principle, pinpoint the individual people. But then, one never could in practice. The IS-LM model licensed a fully aggregated version of Keynesian economics and gave free rein to the mechanical metaphor, which was made flesh in A.W.H. Phillips's machine – a model of the economy built from pumps, reservoirs, plastic tubes, and colored water.[5] While Phillips prefers hydraulics to oscillating pendulums, the metaphor is mechanical just the same.

5. Phillips [1950]; see also Boumans and Morgan [2004].

The American economist Lawrence Klein published his doctoral dissertation under the title *The Keynesian Revolution* (1947). Like Hicks, Klein tried to connect Keynes's principal insights to the older economic tradition, now largely encapsulated under Frisch's heading of microeconomics, to form the basis for a sound aggregate macroeconomics. Klein worked briefly at the Cowles Commission, which was developing macroeconometric modeling in the Tinbergen mold. The Phillips machine was an analogue model and used mainly as a teaching device illustrating macroeconomic principles. But just at the period that Klein began to work, the digital computer was invented. Macroeconometric modeling developed in lockstep with computing technology. Macroeconometric models grew increasingly complex: Tinbergen's model of 1939 contained 48-equation models; Klein's Brookings Model of 1965 contained 150 equations; later models were still larger.[6]

These models were referred to as "Keynesian." But, in truth, they owe considerably more to Tinbergen and to Hicks than to Keynes.

Policy and policymaking

Just as mechanics in physics is the basis for the applied science of engineering, macroeconometric models were created with policy applications in mind. From the beginning of his studies, Tinbergen conceived of his work in economics as supporting economic planning. In the 1950s, he wrote three books on the methodology of economic policy [Tinbergen, 1954; 1955; 1956]. Tinbergen introduced economists to the distinction between the objects of policy (*targets*) and the means of influencing the path of the economy towards those objects (*instruments*). His distinction is regarded as fundamental among economists. And it is heard constantly in recent discussions of monetary and fiscal policy the press, in the American Congress, as well as in Brussels and Frankfurt, and among economists. For example, it is the frame for unconventional or nonstandard monetary policy – the so-called quantitative easing that is the talk of central banks around the world.

The targets-and-instruments approach is essentially the approach of an engineer: we can analyze rocket guidance in exactly the same way. With the targets-and-instruments approach, the economist as policy advisor stands outside the machine: he observes the behavior of the economy and tries to

6. Duesenberry et al. [1965] provide a contemporaneous description of the Brookings Model; see Bodkin, Klein, and Marwah [1991] for a general history of macroeconometric modeling.

capture it a macroeconometric model; he manipulates policy instruments (e.g., interest or tax rates) using the model to predict the results of his choices.

Keynes's strategy is different. To return to his analogy with chess, the economist does not stand above the game. Instead, the economist is just another player of the board – say, the king's bishop. The future is not determined by the predictions of a formal model. He faces uncertainty, just as any other player does. Yes, he possesses a chess manual, but it is one that has been written, not from the overarching perspective of the chess master, but from the ground-level view of the bishop. Acquisition of economic knowledge occurs within the game. It is necessarily partial, bound by particular perspectives, and subject to debate. Yes, Keynes and his fellow economists are the bishops. They argue and debate. They possess the arcane knowledge of the manuals of play; in that sense they know more than the other players. Their theories may be cast in an over-arching perspective, but this is merely a projection from inside the game, and not the product of a standpoint that they somehow occupy above the game. The test of their theories is largely the success of their policy advice: does their side win the game? But tests of that sort can be run only if the economists can convince the kings, queens, and even the pawns to follow their manual. Doubts, Keynes wrote, about the efficacy of policy cannot be dispelled merely by appealing to economic theory or models; "they can only be dispelled by the prolonged success of an actual attempt at scientific control" [1930b (1971b): 309].

Both Frisch and Tinbergen came to agree with Keynes that estimated macroeconometric relationships were not sufficiently stable over long periods of time to projected far into the future. They reacted to this realization as engineers would. There is even an apt political pun. In the depths of the Great Depression at a time when the American South was essentially an underdeveloped country, mired in poverty, President Franklin Roosevelt took a tour of the Tennessee Valley. What did he say when he saw the Tennessee River for the first time? "Dam it!" That is the engineer's vision: *If the world is not how we would like it be, change the world.* Both Frisch and Tinbergen advocated central planning. And Tinbergen even served in the Dutch Central Planning Bureau, starting in the 1950s.

Frisch rejected any biological metaphor. The problem of cycles was not some sort of "bacillius cyclicus" [Louçã, 2007: 131]. We should not look for a disease nor should we seek a cure. Rather than as a physician, Frisch saw the economist as a "social engineer" [ibid.: 296]. The economic problem was that there were too many independent agents [ibid.: 289]. The solution was to use economic planning to circumvent "the human obstacle to human progress" [ibid.: 297].

In contrast, Keynes rejected the Corps-of-Engineers approach. He did not want to channel the unruly streams of society along simpler, more rational paths. Unlike Frisch and Tinbergen, he was not a socialist, but a liberal; not a central planner, but a social doctor. The metaphor of the body politic and the body economic suit him better than the metaphor of the machine.

Keynes wrote about the socialization of investment; but, by this, he mainly meant that, when private demand was inadequate, the government should nudge it along through monetary and fiscal policy. It did not mean that the economy would be controlled comprehensively from the center. Recognizing the complexity of the economy, he tried to suggest medicine and, like any physician, advocated watching the course of the disease and adjusting the treatment empirically based on the current state of the patient.

Desperate times call for drastic action, so that Keynes was more willing to engage in comprehensive intervention during the Great Depression than at other times. Yet, it is striking that Keynes bucked the conventional wisdom and placed his faith in the private sector, the price system, and monetary and fiscal policy to rise to the challenge when he advised against rationing in Britain in World War II. Frisch rejected Keynes's mild interventions as too weak to met the fundamental economic problem.

The continuing clash of metaphors

It is outside the scope of my talk to address more modern developments in detail. But it is worth noting that recent macroeconomics can be seen as an attempting reconciliation of the mechanical and organic metaphors. The new classical revolution of the 1970s, although framed as "anti-Keynesian," was more directly an assault on macroeconometric models in the tradition of Tinbergen and Klein.[7]

New classicals called for models that placed expectations and optimal choice by individuals back in the center of macroeconomic analysis. They rejected the view that the policymaker stands outside the economic system. In these respects they stood closer to Keynes than they realized. But in

7. See, e.g., Lucas [1976].

stressing quantitative and mathematically closed models, they stood firmly in the mechanical tradition of Frisch and Tinbergen. For instance, in a famous passage, Lucas wrote:

> Our task . . . is to write a FORTRAN program that will accept specific economic policy rules as "input" and will generate as "output" statistics describing the operating characteristics of time series we care about, which are predicted to result from these policies. [Lucas 1980, p. 288]

Keynes could never have agreed.

Combining individual human decision-making with the mechanical models is difficult. Just as Frisch had observed in 1933, there are too many individuals in the economy. His solution was to invent aggregate macroeconomics. Keynes's solution was provide only a qualitative analysis of the connection between the individual and the economy as a whole and to adopt the pragmatic stance of the empirically minded physician in matters of policy. The new classicals and their fellow travelers, the new Keynesian, have instead applied highly simplified microeconomic models – models in which one or a few agents stand for, or represent, individual choice – to aggregate data. These are now the most popular models in economics and the ones that have been most vilified by those who believed that the economics profession failed us in the Great Recession.

References

Akerlof George A. and Shiller Robert J. [2010]. *Animal Spirits: How Human Psychology Drives the Economy, and Why It Matters for Global Capitalism.* Princeton: Princeton University Press.

Bodkin Ronald G., Klein Lawrence R., and Marwah Kanta [1991]. *A History of Macroeconometric Model-building.* Aldershot: Edward Elgar.

Boumans Marcel and Morgan Mary S. [2004]. Secrets hidden by two dimensionality: the economy as a hydraulic machine. In Soraya de Chadarevian and Nick Hopwood (ed.) *Models: The Third Dimension of Science.* Stanford: Stanford University Press: 369–401.

Duesenberry James S. et al. (ed.) [1965] *The Brookings Quarterly Econometric Model of the United States.* Chicago: Rand McNally.

Frisch Ragnar [1933]. Propagation problems and impulse problems in dynamic economics. In *Economic Essays in Honor of Gustav Cassel: October 20th 1933.* London: George Allen and Unwin: 171–205.

— [1933-1934]. *Forelesninger holdt 1933II og 1934I over Makrodynamik.* Mimeographed lecture notes.

Hicks John R. [1937]. Mr. Keynes and the classics. *Econometrica* 5(2): 147–159.

Keynes John Maynard [1930a (1972a)]. *A Treatise on Money, vol. 1: The Pure Theory of Money. The Collected Writings of John Maynard Keynes*, vol. 5. London: Macmillan.

— [1930b (1972b)]. *A Treatise on Money, vol. 2: The Applied Theory of Money. The Collected Writings of John Maynard Keynes*, vol. 6. London: Macmillan.

— [1931 (1972)]. *Essays in Persuasion. The Collected Writings of John Maynard Keynes*, vol. 9. London: Macmillan.

— [1936]. *The General Theory of Employment, Interest, and Money.* London: Macmillan.

— [1939]. Official Papers: The statistical testing of business-cycle theories. *Economic Journal* 44(195): 558–568.

— [1973]. *The General Theory and After, Part II: Defense and Development. The Collected Writings of John Maynard Keynes*, vol. 14. London: Macmillan.

Klein, Lawrence R. [1947]. *The Keynesian Revolution*. New York: Macmillan.

— [2004]. The contribution of Jan Tinbergen to economic science. *De Economist* 152(2): 155–7.

Louçã Franciso [2007]. *The Years of High Econometrics: A Short History of the Generation that Reinvented Economics*. London: Routledge.

Lucas Robert E. Jr. [1976]. Econometric policy evaluation: a critique. Reprinted in Robert E. Lucas *Studies in Business-Cycle Theory*. Oxford: Blackwell: 104–30.

— [1980]. Methods and problems in business cycle theory. *Journal of Money, Credit and Banking* 12(4, Part 2): 696–715. References to reprint in Lucas (1981): 271–96.

— [1981]. *Studies in Business-Cycle Theory*. Oxford: Blackwell.

Mandeville Bernard de [1714]. *Fable of the Bees: or, Private Vices, Public Benefits*.

Mankiw N. Gregory [2008]. What would Keynes have done? *New York Times* 28 November.

Phillips A. W. [1950]. Mechanical models in economic dynamics. *Economica* N.S. 17(67): 283–305.

Tinbergen Jan [1937]. *An Econometric Approach to Business Cycle Problems*. Paris: Hermann.

— [1939]. *Statistical Testing of Business Cycle Theories*. Geneva: League of Nations.

— [1954]. *Centralization and Decentralization in Economic Policy*. Amsterdam: North Holland.

— [1955]. *On the Theory of Economic Policy*. Amsterdam: North-Holland.

— [1956]. *Economic Policy: Principles and Design*. Amsterdam, North Holland.

CYCLES « VERSUS » GROWTH IN SCHUMPETER
A graphical interpretation of some core theoretical remarks

Niels Geiger[1]

Schumpeter's business cycle and growth theory encompasses two distinct types of superposition. The first one is well known from its graphical representation provided in Schumpeter's *Business Cycles* [1939], namely the superposition of different waves or cycles of varying magnitude. There already is an element of combination of growth (Kondratiev) and cyclical movements such as "ordinary" business cycles (Juglar) here, although the connection *between* these waves of different order is not elaborated. Another point which is much more rarely discussed in the literature is Schumpeter's strict technical separation between a growth *trend* and cyclical *waves* in real-world economies. It appears as if the general interpretation of Schumpeter's statement here has also been influenced by the aforementioned graphical representation. The argument for the distinction between underlying growth on the one hand, and cyclical elements on the other, is put forward strongly in two papers [1927; 1935] especially, but lacks a graphical sketch of the core ideas by Schumpeter himself. The present paper aims at proposing just this by interpreting Schumpeter's logic, thereby illustrating the model in more detail and hinting at a possible inaccuracy in the *Business Cycles* graph.

Keywords: Business cycle theory, superposition, cycle and growth interdependence.

Mots clefs : Théorie du cycle d'activité, superposition, interdépendance du cycle et de la croissance.

JEL classification: B15, B25, E32

Cycles vs croissance chez Schumpeter. Une interprétation graphique de quelques remarques théoriques centrales

Les théories des cycles et de la croissance de Schumpeter comportent deux formes de superposition distinctes. La première est bien connue. Il s'agit de celle exposée sous forme graphique dans l'ouvrage Business Cycles *[1939] correspondant à la superposition de différentes ondes, ou cycles, de périodes différentes. Bien que la connexion* entre *ces ondes d'ordres différents ne soit pas élaborée en détail, force est de constater qu'un élément de combinaison de la croissance (Kondratieff) et de mouvements cycliques, comme les cycles économiques « ordinaires » (Juglar), est bien présent.*

Un autre argument, plus rarement discuté encore dans la littérature, est la séparation technique stricte entre le trend *de la croissance et les* ondes *cycliques dans les économies réelles. C'est un peu comme si l'interprétation générale de l'énoncé de Schumpeter était fondée sur la représentation graphique mentionnée précédemment. L'argument permettant de distinguer entre croissance sous-jacente d'un côté, et éléments cycliques de l'autre, est notamment avancé par Schumpeter dans deux articles [1927 ; 1935] qui ne donnent pas de représentation graphique des éléments clés de l'analyse. Cet article vise à proposer une représentation graphique détaillée et conforme au raisonnement de Schumpeter, de manière à mettre en évidence une possible imprécision présente dans* Business Cycles.

---

1. University of Hohenheim, Department of Economics (520h), D 70593 Stuttgart, Germany; Niels.Geiger@uni-hohenheim.de

Paper presented at the 14th International Conference of the Charles Gide Association for the Study of Economic Thought, Nice, 7-9 June 2012: History of Macroeconomics: From the Years of 'High Theory' (1926-1939) to Modern Approaches. I thank Johannes Schwarzer for helpful remarks on the original version of this paper, as well as my discussant Iurii Bazhal for his comments. Additional remarks from two anonymous referees were crucial to honing this paper as well, and are also gratefully acknowledged. Of course, responsibility for all remaining errors remains with myself.

1. Introduction

On page 213 of his *Business Cycles*, Joseph Schumpeter [1939] provided a famous illustration of the superposition of different "waves" or economic cycles, varying in duration and amplitude. Along a linear, horizontal trend, Schumpeter drew three kinds of sinusoidal waves: long, intermediate, and short ones, with their amplitudes somewhat proportional to the respective wavelengths. Although each type of wave was pictured as a sine function, the result of adding up the three different curves onto one another—i.e. the superposition—results in a, although still symmetric, more complicated image. In accordance with Schumpeter's general argument, it was thus shown that even such movements as the "Kondratiev", "Juglar" and "Kitchin" cycles, postulated to be regular in their frequency, could be combined to form the more complicated time lines of economic variables that can be observed in reality.

However, in addition to conveying this message, the graph has also influenced later discussions in other ways. As virtually the only graphical representation of some of his theoretical ideas in Schumpeter's own work, the superposition figure may be found referenced in discussions of Schumpeter's theory of economic development in general, not just specifically the idea of superposition (see e.g. Hanusch and Pyka [2007b: 23]). In this paper, though, it will be argued that the idea of drawing a business cycle around a steady linear, especially horizontal, trend as the economy's gravitational centre (i.e. its equilibrium) is insufficient when referring to and trying to depict Schumpeter's core ideas about discontinuous economic development. While it is true that the superposition figure provides the reader with some idea of Schumpeter's thought on economic development, particularly regarding the central role cyclical fluctuations play in capitalist economies, it does not contain the whole theoretical argument. This applies especially to the relations between cycles, underlying growth trends, and growth on the whole, as well as to the question of the development of the equilibrium level of production. While Schumpeter's superposition graph does illustrate the theoretical idea of observable "complications" as a consequence of concurrent waves, used as an explanation to such phenomena as the Great Depression of the 1930s, it should not be interpreted as representing the theoretical movements and components of every constituent cycle at the same time.

The discussion in this paper will start by summarizing core theoretical remarks by Schumpeter and then, after a short account of Schumpeter's business cycle theory, demonstrate why the idea of linking Schumpeter's superposition figure directly to his central ideas concerning economic development meets with some problems. In Schumpeter's theory, if any cycle does occur, it is always accompanied by a marked shift in the equilibrium level of production, since this is the primary effect of innovation, the core driver initiating the cycle. Thus, in the absence of exogenous shocks, what is observed *ex post* as the general picture of economic growth or development, is really a combination of those cyclical shifts, the accompanying fluctuations around the respective equilibrium levels, and underlying trend factors which induce gradual growth. In order to contribute to the discussion on this issue, a graphical interpretation of Schumpeter's ideas on discontinuous economic development in general, deeply rooted within his theoretical considerations, will be provided in what follows.

2. Schumpeter on the underlying trend, cyclical movements, and the observed trend

2.1. The three factors constituting movements in economic variables

One of the core theoretical ideas in Schumpeter's writings on the business cycle and economic development in general is the strict distinction between cyclical movements and an underlying trend in economic variables. Even more separate from these two are those influences which fall into the category of exogenous shocks. The importance of this differentiation becomes evident from the repeated and meticulous mentioning of the issue, most notably in Schumpeter's papers on "The Explanation of the Business Cycle" [1927] and "The Analysis of Economic Change" [1935],[2] but also in many other publications, e.g., in an extensive review of Mitchell's [1927] *Business Cycles* [Schumpeter, 1930] and in Schumpeter's own *Business Cycles* [1939, 6-13, 72-87]. In fact, one may go back even further, for already in his earlier German writings, in accordance with the fundamental distinction between statics and dynamics, Schumpeter drew a clear demarcation line between those factors driving economic development and disturbing the static equilibrium which originated from within the economy on the one hand, and those stabilizing influences which lead back to the static equilibrium on the other hand (see e.g. Schumpeter [1910: 324-5]).[3]

2. Both of these articles are reprinted in the volume edited by Clemence [1951].

3. In Schumpeter's dynamic theory, the economy is in disequilibrium over the course of a business cycle. However, as Schumpeter [1935: 4; 1939: 69] points out, the notion of a Walrasian general equilibrium,

The theoretical identification and separation of the elements that constitute movements in economic variables over time was thus at the heart of Schumpeter's analysis of economic change in modern capitalist economies, within which the explanation of the business cycle was regarded as essential to a complete understanding of the whole process [Schumpeter, 1939: v]. Following Schumpeter, observed time lines in economic variables, especially aggregate production, are the result of three different factors driving the movement in various ways. The following list is a summary of Schumpeter's remarks on this topic [see especially 1935: 2-5; also 1927: 288]:

1. "Outside factors": to this category belong possible influences which have no immediate link to economic considerations, e.g. season- or "sunspot"-specific variations in agricultural production, natural disasters, or political events such as revolutions, wars, shifts in trade or exchange rate regimes, etc. In general, they may be referred to as exogenous shocks. They contribute to the historical uniqueness of every economic fluctuation, but do not originate directly from within the economy.

2. "Growth factors": these amount to gradual increases in economic output, driven by population growth, savings and consequent capital accumulation related to well-established methods of production, and continuous, small but steady, technical progress, such as gradual increases in labour productivity as a result of learning by doing. In general, thus, "growth factors" are such changes in the data which can be absorbed by the economic system in (gradually changing) equilibrium without notable disturbance. They constitute an economy's underlying trend, a path of equilibrium points along which the system would move in the absence of other influences.

3. "Cyclical factors": these refer to economic development through innovation, i.e. changes in the production function which cannot be decomposed into a continuum of infinitesimally small gradual improvements (such as those determining the underlying trend), and the thus ensuing creative-destruction part of a business cycle.

i.e. a situation where every single sector of the economy, and thus also the aggregate, is in equilibrium (see Schumpeter [1939: 42–3] specifically), is still useful for the analysis as a *reference* point or "theoretical norm" [Schumpeter, 1939: 38 ff.], towards which the economy will usually tend to gravitate. Actual economic states can then be defined relative to this equilibrium, more generally with regard to whether or not they are in a "neighbourhood" of it (since perfect equilibria cannot be expected to ever be realized, see Schumpeter [1935: 4; 1939: 69–71]). Schumpeter [1935: 5, 7; 1939: 138, 20] demarcates a cycle as the movement between two neighbourhoods of equilibrium.

To sum up, Schumpeter [1935: 4] may be quoted for stating that "[i]ndustrial change is due to the effect of outside factors, to the non-cyclical element of growth, and to innovation." There is thus no conflict in the sense of cycles and underlying growth opposed to one another in Schumpeter's theory, but, as will be shown more clearly in the discussion in subsection 2.3, they still need to be regarded and treated as separate influences on the whole of economic development—hence this paper's title. Nonetheless, it should be noted that economic growth *as a whole*, i.e. the whole general upward movement of an economy over a long period of time, is not captured by those gradual "growth factors" alone (a point Schumpeter [1947b: 7–8] criticized classical growth theory for), as the further discussion will demonstrate in more detail as well.

To Schumpeter [1935: 3; 1939: 72], exogenous influences are of lesser importance for the explanation not only of the business cycle, but economic movements in general, because they do not originate from the economy itself and lack common elements or regularity. While they played an important role in pre-capitalist societies, owing to the lower level of the division of labour and the high production share of agriculture, more modern economies with a sophisticated division of labour and trade networks as well as per capita production that substantially exceeds mere subsistence levels become increasingly independent especially of natural factors, such as the classic "sunspots". Even if political factors, such as wars or specific trade policies, still exert significant influence on modern economies, they are only of secondary importance for Schumpeter's pure analysis of economic development as a consequence of the economic process *per se*.[4] Exogenous, or "outside" factors, will thus, following Schumpeter, be left out of the further discussion in this paper. Instead, what really matters are the endogenous economic elements: especially cyclical fluctuations, but also the "growth factors", that, at least to some extent, may be regarded as endogenous to the economy too.

2.2. Schumpeter's theory of economic dynamics: a short summary

To elaborate on the crucial distinction between "cyclical" and "growth" factors, some general remarks about Schumpeter's theory of economic

4. To illustrate this, Schumpeter [1935: 3] draws a distinction between a businessman buying an additional machine, or alternatively lobbying for policies beneficial to him ("rent-seeking" in today's terminology)—both actions may be motivated by economic considerations, but the act of acquiring a new capital good is clearly closer to the, as it were, "economic core" or "part" within the whole system of society, and thus of generally higher interest for the theoretical economist.

development are appropriate. Schumpeter's whole body of theory rests on the fundamental distinction between what he originally called "statics" and "dynamics" and later, due to the specific use Frisch [1929; 1936] made of this distinction, referred to as the "circular flow" and "economic development" respectively (see for example Hagemann [2003: 55-6]). Corresponding to these two categories, Schumpeter [1927: 290 ff.] also describes two modes of behaviour: "static" behaviour consists in adaptively reacting to the environment, usually in small steps, while "dynamic" behaviour (also labelled "creative response", see Schumpeter [1939: 72; 1947a]) is the act of trying out something new. Whereas the first is always observed in reaction to every influence affecting the economy, the second need not ensue. For example, in Schumpeter's understanding, people will always react to an exogenous shock, or the outburst of a business cycle (which requires that somebody has already acted "dynamically"), automatically in an adaptive way, trying to reconcile their previous business plans with the new *status quo*—or they may come up with a new idea to restructure their own enterprise, which, however, occurs far less frequently.

Within this theoretical framework, Schumpeter [1927: 290] notes that static conditions, i.e. those that characterize the circular flow of an economy in, or in close proximity of, an equilibrium, are compatible with "growth factors". The changes are so gradual that they can be absorbed by adaptive routine behaviour without affecting the economy's reference equilibrium in a drastic, non-gradual way, or even causing the economy to temporarily leave the neighbourhood of equilibrium. If the economy was only moved by growth factors, it would continuously transition smoothly from one equilibrium to a nearby other. The business cycle, in contrast, cannot spring from these conditions themselves, it is an inherently dynamic, not static, process [Schumpeter, 1927: 289]. Thus, it becomes clear why Schumpeter would draw such a clear line between "growth" and "cyclical" factors and why he would separate them theoretically: one is compatible with the circular flow and does not require any kind of behaviour different from that in the circular flow, and the other demands economic agents to act differently, namely in a "dynamic" way.

To further illustrate this point, it is helpful to look a bit closer at Schumpeter's theoretical understanding of the business cycle. Central to this theory is the idea of innovation: an innovation occurs when a pioneering entrepreneur[5] picks up an invention (the mere technical capability to do

5. The traits of Schumpeter's heroic figure will not be discussed in any detail here, because its underlying

something) and transforms it into something marketable. This usually requires a bank loan (or other form of borrowed capital), because most entrepreneurs do not command the means to fund their business entirely on their own, see Schumpeter [1934: 102]. Here, Schumpeter differs especially from most of his classical predecessors not only by separating the roles of "entrepreneur" and "capitalist" (see, for example, [Schumpeter 1928a;1928b]), but also by pointing out that banks are not merely traders, but creators of purchasing power, because they can virtually create credit out of nothing, see Schumpeter [1934: 98]. It is, however, important to note that credit taken out for the sake of innovation is used in a productive manner, hence, even though it may not be "backed" by current savings, it will ultimately be backed by future savings when the credit is paid back from the revenues generated from the innovation [Schumpeter, 1934: 115 fn]. It is also important to add that, while Schumpeter basically sees banks playing a passive role, simply serving pioneering entrepreneurs' credit demand, he nevertheless acknowledges that, if they so will, they may influence the amplitude of a cycle by their credit policy, e.g. if they set off or intensify a second, speculative wave through easy credit [Schumpeter 1927: 307]. Such a speculative wave may turn a recession into a depression during the downswing [Schumpeter, 1939: 148 ff.].[6]

Once an entrepreneur is in command of the additional purchasing power bestowed upon him through credit creation, he may bid away resources from other firms (especially those acting in a "static" manner) to pursue his innovation, e.g. manufacture a new product or produce in a wholly new manner. The innovation (in a way, successful by definition) will increase the entrepreneur's profit. It is these rents, plus the fact that it is easier to follow in somebody else's footsteps, which draw imitators into the market, following the innovator in "crowds" or "swarms", (e.g. Schumpeter [1927: 297 f.]). Imitators are still acting in a dynamic manner, but somewhat less so than the first pioneer did. This will lead to increased economic activity as the economy explores the potentials of the innovation, and competition increases not just between "dynamically" acting firms and "static" ones,

features are of no immediate relevance for the discussion at hand, while innovation *per se* and the role of credit is.

6. Whereas in earlier writings, Schumpeter had regarded the cycle as a sequence of two phases, he expanded this view to a four-phase scheme in *Business Cycles* [Hagemann, 2008b: 154]. However, Schumpeter [1939: 150] still emphasizes that while a recession (i.e. the return to equilibrium after a boom) is a necessary element of a cycle, the depression (i.e. the overshooting of the new equilibrium in the downward direction) is not: The cycle therefore might end after the recession, and let the economy settle in its new equilibrium, but it is unlikely to do so.

but also between the innovator and imitators. Through this, the extra rents available from the innovation slowly disappear at the margin, which diminishes the core propagator of the cyclical upswing [Dal-Pont Legrand and Hagemann, 2007: 11].

Schumpeter then follows Clément Juglar in describing the crisis as a necessary outcome of the upswing, and as the "turning point" leading to the downswing [Schumpeter, 1931: 6]. The crisis sets in when more and more of the consequences of the innovation actually reach the market, extra profits diminish, and entrepreneurs start paying back their loans. The recession in particular is the necessary adjustment to the results of the innovation [Schumpeter, 1934: 231 ff.]. Just as the upswing saw credit inflation, the downswing sees credit deflation, when the pioneering entrepreneur and the imitators pay back their loans with revenue generated from the innovation. Whether or not the economy overshoots its equilibrium during the downswing, the adaptive forces will ensure that sooner or later, the economy reaches its equilibrium level, which had been originally determined by the new combinations introduced through the innovation, i.e. at the outset of the cycle. In any way, up until this new equilibrium level is reached, all the processes leading towards it through the cycle are out-of-equilibrium movements. To sum up, it is suitable to refer to Stolper [1982: 239] and describe innovations as changes in the economy's production function, which, fuelled by credit, draw the economy out of its old equilibrium level and cause cyclical movements—because it takes some time to introduce new processes, and for everybody to adjust to them [Schumpeter, 1934: 232 ff.].

2.3. Economic development as the product of different influences

Schumpeter's primary concern had always been cyclical fluctuations. Nevertheless, in the following discussion, as mentioned before, "growth factors" will also be considered, since they do not complicate the picture much, but enrich the argument. These growth factors manifest themselves in some kind of trend, which in the absence of cyclical fluctuations caused by innovations determines the continuous path of the economy's stationary equilibria through time. This *underlying* trend has to be clearly distinguished from the *observed* trend, which is a result of all of the three components listed in subsection 2.2 which drive the movement in observed variables, e.g. production. Therefore, the underlying trend is made up of these "growth factors", while the observed trend is what would be regarded as growth in a more general discussion, i.e. the "averaged" or "trend" movement of the economy over some longer period of time, and therefore a result not merely of the underlying "growth factor" trend, but also of the impulses coming from cyclical fluctuations (Schumpeter [1939, 206–7] uses the term "Result Trend"). To be sure, Schumpeter was well aware of this difference and the implications it bears for interpreting statistically determined trend lines. Thus, as he rightly notes [1928a: 374]:

> We could, of course, . . . fit trend lines through the facts succeeding one another historically; but they would merely be expressions of whatever has happened, not of distinct forces or mechanisms; they would be statistical, not theoretical; they would have to be interpreted in terms of particular historic events, . . . and not in terms of the working of an economic mechanism *sui generis.*

Schumpeter was, of course, not the only one to discuss this general argument, even in his time. To name just one noteworthy example, Frickey [1934] submitted five theoretical and methodological problems in determining a trend for an economic time series. Schumpeter [1930: 166-7] may be quoted again here, this time from his review of Mitchell's [1927] *Business Cycles,* a vast empirical work which thus obviously made use of trend analysis:

> . . . if trend-analysis is to have any meaning, it can derive it only from previous theoretical considerations, which must not only guide us in interpreting results, but also in choosing the method. Failing this, a trend is no more than a descriptive device summing up past history with which nothing can be done. It lacks economic connotation. It is, in fact, merely formal. We can apply the familiar methods just as well to e.g. a few successive years of a prosperity-phase, as to the whole of the material we may happen to have (as, again, to a period of political commotion). The result has the same claim in every case to be called a trend in the statistical sense, and may in each case be decomposed into component elements in an indefinite number of ways which have no rational connection to each other—unless it be supplied by the theory of the subject under research.

Now, however, nowhere in Schumpeter's published writings can a graphical representation of these theoretical ideas be found sketched into a figure. Nonetheless, there is one famous illustration which Schumpeter provided on page 213 of his *Business Cycles* [1939] and which is replicated in Figure 1 here. This "superposition" graph shows how adding up three highly symmetric movements—in Schumpeter's example, long "Kondratiev" waves, medium-run "Juglar" cycles (the "ordinary" business cycle), and short-run "Kitchin" cycles, with their respective amplitudes roughly scaling in proportion to their wavelengths—can result in a complicated overall picture.[7] Even if all of those constituent waves have the shape of sine curves, and even if every Kondratiev cycle is made up of six Juglar cycles, each of which in turn is made up of three Kitchin cycles, a symmetric, but highly volatile picture emerges. Within this framework, Schumpeter [2000: 184; in a letter to Arthur Spiethoff from 1931] argued that extreme events, such as the Great Depression of the 1930s, could be explained by the joint occurrence of simultaneous troughs in the Kondratiev, Juglar, and Kitchin cycles.

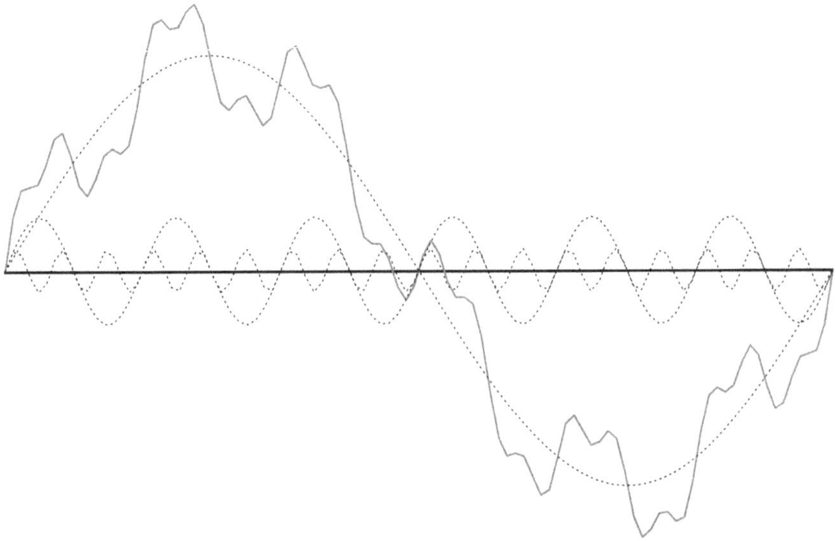

Figure 1. Replication of Schumpeter's original superposition graph from *Business Cycles* [1939]. The continuous black line displays the sum of the three dashed cyclical movements added up onto one another

There is, however, one major problem when trying to link Schumpeter's superposition figure to his core theoretical ideas about economic development as a process driven by cyclical movements. All cyclical movements in Schumpeter's graph basically evolve around an unchanged steady trend and end on that very same trend again as they complete. While this suffices to demonstrate the complications caused by different waves superimposed upon one another—for sure, it does not matter whether or not the trend is flat, or rising, to demonstrate this—it certainly does not incorporate the

7. A detailed discussion of this model, its original content and more recent interpretations, is beyond the scope of this paper. The interested reader is referred to Duijn [1983: ch. I] or Hagemann [2008a: 232 ff.].

core idea of economic development through innovation which shifts the equilibrium point, and consequently the path, of the economy upwards in a discontinuous manner, which is sharply different from underlying trend movements. If, in Schumpeter's theory, any of the cycles does occur, it occurs because some pioneering entrepreneur innovates (see especially Schumpeter [1939: 166-7, 171-2] on this monocausality argument). This, however, introduces new combinations into the economy. New combinations imply a different equilibrium level of production—usually higher—than before. Any underlying trend may continue, even at the same rate, but it will do so from a higher level.

This, now, is the core idea of the interpretation of Schumpeter's remarks this paper wishes to propose. Both "growth" and "cyclical" factors move an economy's equilibrium level upward, but they do so in a different manner. Growth factors appear in a gradual, steady way, and if they were the only one among the three factors responsible for economic fluctuations which were listed in subsection 2.1, one could think of both an economy's equilibrium and actual level of output as moving along the same line through time. An innovation, on the other hand, shifts the economy's equilibrium level in a notable way by altering its production function[8] far more than gradually (if it did not, then it would not be an innovation, but simply part of the underlying growth trend). In an economy affected only by this pure innovation effect, its output level through time would follow a flat line, except for every time an innovation occurred, where it would jump upwards. Adding an underlying growth trend to this, each of the fragment lines between points of innovations would be tilted upwards, with the shifts, too, appearing at higher levels.

So much about the movement of the equilibrium level. The actual, observed movement of this theoretical economy is more complicated though, because, as has already been pointed out, the business cycle arises as the effect of the dynamic innovation process. An innovation may shift the economy's equilibrium or reference level, but that, of course, does not mean that the economy will automatically reach this new level in an instant. Instead, when the innovation happens and the economy's equilibrium level shifts, the actually realized level of production at this point in time will in all likelihood be below the new, and close to the old equilibrium level. The new equilibrium level at this specific point will be more of a production "potential"

8. This focus of looking at the aggregates obviously abstracts from one core element of Schumpeter's creative destruction process, namely the fact that innovations also imply structural change. However, the argument put forward here is independent of this simplification.

provided by the innovation. For example in the case of a product innovation, the innovator may have already begun producing the new commodity, through which formerly latent demands for it have been activated. However, the full potential of the innovation could not be put to use so quickly, if only because the innovator would have needed a correspondingly higher amount of funding capital right at the outset—and, of course, the technical capability to bring it into being within a logical second.

The pioneering entrepreneur, however, will soon notice and reap the fruits of his success in terms of extra rents on his innovation. This will not only lead him to expand his production further and therefore bring the economy closer to its new equilibrium level, but also attract imitators. In any way, this will cause the actual level of output to rise further, and most likely faster than just before. The general story of Schumpeter's description of the cycle, as outlined in the previous subsection, ensues. It is only at the end of the cycle that the economy reaches its new equilibrium level on the shifted path (where, in the absence of exogenous shocks, it remains until the next innovation occurs), while until that point, there is overshooting both in the upswing and possibly in the downswing, the extent of which depends on banks' lending policies and the strength of the "secondary waves" of reaction to the original impulse and speculation they may provoke [Schumpeter, 1935: 5-6; 1939: 145 ff.].

Figure 2 displays the graphical version of these theoretical considerations. The bold black line depicts the time path of an economic variable's natural log level as it is actually observed—i.e. the overall course of economic development. To minimize on possible complications while still sticking to the spirit of both Schumpeter's ideas, and to what can actually be observed in empirical business cycle research, it can be thought of as an economy's production level. The blue line shows the economy's equilibrium path of production which follows an upward sloped trend (due to gradual expansions or improvements in production, namely the "growth factors"). This underlying trend, in turn, shifts (dashed blue line), or in Schumpeter's [1927: 297] own term *leaps*, every time a pioneering entrepreneur innovates. As already pointed out earlier, exogenous shocks are abstracted from. Finally, the dashed green line shows the *observed* trend, which as the result of the combination of both "cyclical" and "growth" factors, is different from the *underlying* growth trend.

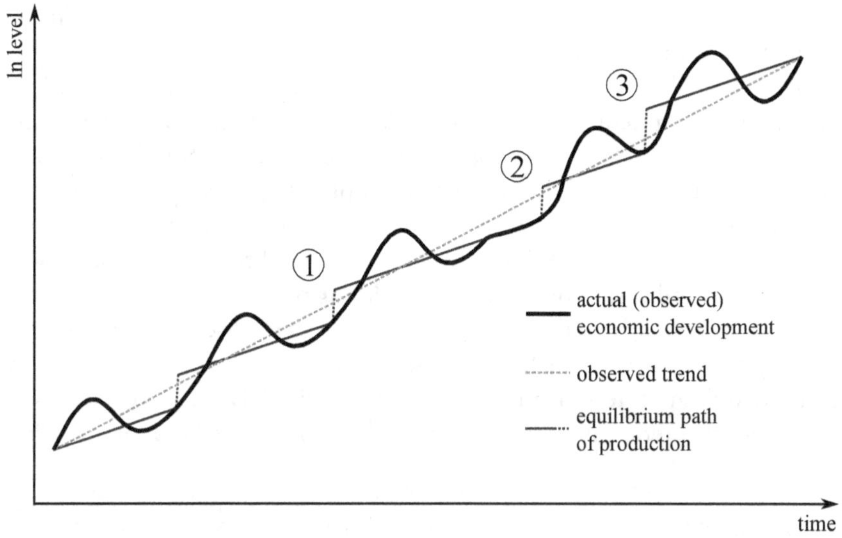

Figure 2. Graphical interpretation of Schumpeter's theoretical understanding of trend, cyclical elements, and resulting fluctuations forming a business cycle and economic development.

Own figure. The variable displayed is most apt to represent economic variables growing over time, and fluctuating during the cycle, such as gross domestic product. The numbers in the graph refer to a new cycle starting off (1) right after the previous cycle has completed (i.e. equilibrium is reached), (2) some time after the new equilibrium has been reached, (3) after the previous cycle has completed even before the new static equilibrium is restored, or at least without a depression having set in.

With the help of the picture, it becomes clearer once more why Schumpeter had been so eager to emphasize the difference between "cyclical" and "growth" factors (the underlying trend), and where his theoretical concerns with statistically determined trend lines from empirical data came from. Following Schumpeter [1928a: 374; 1930: 166–7], quoted earlier in this subsection, it is important not merely to estimate a statistical trend, but to embed this analysis in a theoretical framework—which then unveils possible problems, e.g. the difference between the underlying and observed trend. For example, one could, as is quite the frequent practice in theoretical and empirical work, take a time line, plot a trend curve, and use this as a reference point for determining at which points in time the economy realized activity levels above (positive deviation) and below (negative deviation) its presumed equilibrium level.[9] However, even in absence of

9. See for example the definition of the business cycle as "deviations . . . from . . . long-term trend" in Snowdon and Vane [2002: 64].

asymmetric shocks, this is only valid if cyclical components do not shift the economy's centre of attraction, that is, the equilibrium level, as in a highly stylised steady state growth model without Schumpeterian innovation. Otherwise, as in Schumpeter's case, which is illustrated in Figure 2, some serious misinterpretations are possible, especially when innovations are also accompanied by business cycles. For example, it can easily be seen from Figure 2 that, even though there are some obvious intersections, different intervals would be obtained for above or below equilibrium levels of activity respectively (and correspondingly for the timing of "turning points"), if these levels are taken to be reflected either relative to the observed trend, or the underlying trend. Since such estimates, e.g. of an "output gap" in economic activity, are central to much macroeconomic policy advice, it is evident that a different theoretical underpinning could lead to distorted economic policy.

The statistically determined, observed trend provides an account of average growth, but it does not distinguish between the cyclical and the underlying growth components. Thus, it cannot be used as an unproblematic reference point for economic policy, and it does not represent the movement which would be observed in the absence of exogenous shocks and cycles. If movements in economic variables are the result of both underlying growth and the cyclical component in Schumpeter's sense, then an observed trend which does not take their combination into account measures neither of the two factors accurately—indeed, it cannot. Therefore, the two have to be strictly separated theoretically for a precise analysis—exactly because the resulting, observed trend, is intimately linked with the movements connected to business cycles. Whereas the underlying trend and the business cycle are separate theoretical entities, the observed trend and the cycle are not. Unfortunately, while these arguments point to the necessity of careful analysis and the possible pitfalls when not following this theoretical road, they do not, by themselves, help with the practical problem of actually determining and disentangling the different components in the data.

On an additional note and for the sake of completeness, Figure 2 displays three ways in which two cycles can follow one another. This is of interest for one reason especially: while Schumpeter [1927: 294] emphasized the necessary connection between upswing and recession through the crisis, he did not seek to establish another causal link between recovery and boom. Indeed, Schumpeter [1927: 292] remarked that dynamic behaviour, i.e. exactly the kind of behaviour which produces cyclical movements, "cannot, with any certainty, be relied on to happen," and that it can only be expected to originate in a stable situation, i.e. in proximity of an equilibrium [Stolper 1951: 175; Böhm, 2008: 151]. This argument can also be found in Oskar

Lange's [1941: 191] review of *Business Cycles*, where Lange points to the lower risk of innovating which economic agents face in an economy in the neighbourhood of equilibrium (further see Schumpeter [1934: 235–6; 1939: 135]. In Figure 2, situation (1) depicts somewhat of an ideal case, where a new cycle begins right after the previous one has been completed, i.e. when the new equilibrium which had been established through the innovation is finally reached. As Kuznets [1940: 263] argued, Schumpeter never provided a comprehensive theoretical argument for this case, except for the small remarks mentioned just before. Nevertheless, this course of events may be regarded as a reference case. Case (2) depicts a cycle which only begins after the economy had remained in equilibrium for a while. Case (3) subsequently represents the situation which may occur if the downward movement does not shoot over into a depression, either because a new cycle starts early, or because the first cycle ends in equilibrium after the recession, whereupon a consecutive cycle may begin.[10]

The "observed trend" depicted in Figure 2 as the dashed green line is, of course, only one possible way of constructing and portraying the trend. But whether this trend is determined by linking the first point of the series to the last one, by calculating moving averages, by applying a Hodrick-Prescott-filter or by linear regression, one independent but important conclusion arises: the observed trend is different from the underlying "growth" trend. To solve this problem and measure the underlying trend, it will most likely be necessary to combine a trend analysis which allows for structural breaks with spectral analysis, but how exactly to calibrate these methods is, once again, a difficult theoretical question. Additionally, there have been some further simplifications made in drawing the graph which, however, are not a theoretical necessity and not explicitly described by Schumpeter—they were merely chosen for the sake of simplicity, but not making them does not change the core argument, it merely alters and further complicates the graph: (a) the growth rate behind the underlying trend is assumed to be constant, (b) which also applies to the discontinuous, "jumpy" growth resulting from innovations during cyclical processes, (c) only one "kind" of wave has been drawn, no superposition, (d) pictured waves have a fairly simple, sinusoidal shape, and (e) depressions do not alter the equilibrium level (see footnote 10).

10. Here, too, this need not happen immediately after having reached the equilibrium: compare cases (1) and (2). The distinction between cycles ending after the recession, and those which go through depression and subsequent revival as well, merits another remark, for Schumpeter [1939: 149] notes that a depression causes the underlying trend path to shift (downwards) once again due to "abnormal liquidation". However, since it does not change this paper's general message (overall economic development is the result of "growth" and "cyclical" elements combined, and every cycle also initiates a shift in the underlying growth trend), this complication has been abstracted from in Figure 2 for simplicity.

To further clarify this paper's message, a comparison with and distinction from some other graphical representations of Schumpeterian ideas, as well as similar graphs illustrative of different theories, seems appropriate. On the one hand, Figure 2 presented here corresponds to and goes further than the theoretical observation by Rühl [1994: 183]; on the other hand, it catches the essence of neo-Schumpeterian models of growth where innovations cause the income or production path of the economy to jump upwards (see e.g. Aghion and Howitt [1998: 60 or 248; 2009: 201]), but the business cycle is usually abstracted from.[11] Both components are combined, catching the essence of Schumpeter's idea that cyclical movements and overall economic growth are intimately entwined with each other. The graph provides a detailed illustration with explicit connections to Schumpeter's remarks, and especially, its focus is not limited to a gradual growth process, but it combines and integrates cyclical movements with trend components. In doing so, some of the core results in the general discussion on Schumpeter's theory of economic development are theoretically replicated, e.g. the fact that Schumpeterian growth cannot be understood as simple steady state growth. Figure 2 also bears some resemblance to possible depictions of Duesenberry's [1949] description of the trade cycle,[12] although the dynamics in this approach are clearly focused and based on the demand side, i.e. the consumption function, whereas the present paper, following Schumpeter's considerations, illustrates a supply-side perspective, with cycles driven by innovation and the consequent restructuring of the economy.

3. Conclusion

This paper has provided a theoretically grounded graphical interpretation of some of Schumpeter's core theoretical remarks on economic development. Schumpeter was quite explicit in pointing out that, in the absence of "outside

11. The figure found in Aghion and Howitt [2009] on page 201 is the same as the one that appears several times in their previous textbook of 1998. It displays a horizontal line, the time path of an economy's output, which shifts upwards whenever an innovation occurs, with the size of the shift depending on the power of the innovation. One of the instances where the figure appears is in the chapter on "Growth and Cycles", where otherwise, no illustration like Figure 2 here, or a detailed discussion of Schumpeter's theoretical concerns regarding the matter, appears. In general, though, it is surprisingly hard to find graphical representations of Schumpeterian modelling of the time path of production, especially with regard to the theoretical ideas underlying each model. In a search of volumes collecting different strands of the neo-Schumpeterian literature such as those by Magnusson [1994], Pyka et al. [2009] or the very extensive one by Hanusch and Pyka [2007a], which contains 70 different articles, no comparable sketch putting Schumpeter's theoretical ideas concerning the time path of production into picture was found.

12. Also see Smithies [1957], who explicitly builds on both Schumpeter and Duesenberry.

factors", movements in economic time lines consist of a steady underlying trend element compatible with static economic analysis, and the more jerky ups and downs caused by, as it were, "true" economic development through innovation and creative destruction. The observed trend is then a result of both these movements, and it is thus not what Schumpeter refers to as the gradual, steady, "underlying" trend movement. This can be pointed out in another way as well: Since it is described as compatible with the circular flow, the underlying trend can be seen as the time path of the economy's equilibrium, or in other words, its gravitational centre. However, it is the very nature of innovation through creative destruction to "lift" the economy's equilibrium path to a new, usually higher, level. This new state may still be characterized by a gradual upward trend. But the innovation causes this underlying trend line to break and jump at the point of innovation, i.e. when the new combinations are introduced—a shift which cannot be seen in the observed trend determined statistically, e.g. by linear regression, *ex post*. The figure proposed here bears some resemblance to graphical representations of Schumpeter's ideas in other works which were referred to as well, but, at least to the author's knowledge of the literature, it is new in the way it combines both the ideas of "cyclical" and (underlying trend) "growth" movements, incorporates not just the innovation element of cycles, and links the picture directly and intimately to Schumpeter's meticulous remarks on the matter.

As a concluding note, it should be remembered that Figure 2 provided in this article and Schumpeter's original superposition graph (replicated here as Figure 1), which served as the starting point for this discussion, are in no way contradictory. Rather, Schumpeter's *Business Cycles* [1939: 213] graph depicts the idea of explaining complex movements by a handful of quite simple underlying processes, while the graph presented in this paper aimed at drawing a single class of these cyclical movements more in accordance with Schumpeter's own ideas. The two figures can thus be complementary and combined:[13] obviously, the more one deviates from the simple sinusoidal shape of cyclical movements, and the closer one tries to integrate the three cycles along a respective non-steady underlying trend, the more complicated the resulting picture will become, although the basic ideas are, at least theoretically, still quite simple.

13. In this context, see e.g. Schumpeter's [1939: 172–3] remarks on how the equilibrium notion will have to be modified when connecting several types of waves to one another, as in the superposition graph.

References

Aghion P., and Howitt P. [1998]. *Endogenous Growth Theory*. Cambridge: MIT Press.

—, and — [2009]. *The Economics of Growth*. Cambridge: MIT Press.

Böhm S. [2008]. Joseph A. Schumpeter. In H. D. Kurz (ed.) *Von Vilfredo Pareto bis Amartya Sen*, Volume 2 of *Klassiker des Ökonomischen Denkens*. München: C. H. Beck: 137–60.

Clemence R. V. (ed.) [1951]. *Essays of J. A. Schumpeter*. Cambridge: Addison-Wesley.

Dal-Pont Legrand M., and Hagemann H. [2007]. Business cycles in Juglar and Schumpeter. *The History of Economic Thought* 49(1): 1–18.

Duesenberry J. S. [1949]. *Income, Saving and the Theory of Consumer Behavior*. Cambridge: Harvard University Press.

Duijn J. v. [1983]. *The Long Waves in Economic Life*. London: Allen & Unwin.

Frickey E. [1934]. The problem of secular trend. *The Review of Economics and Statistics* 16(10): 199–206.

Frisch R. [1929]. Statikk og dynamikk i den økonomiske teori. *Nationaløkonomisk Tidsskrift* 67: 321–79.

— [1936]. On the notion of equilibrium and disequilibrium. *The Review of Economic Studies* 3(2): 100–5.

Hagemann H. [2003]. Schumpeter's early contributions on crises theory and business-cycle theory. *History of Economic Ideas* XI(1): 47–67.

— [2008a]. Schumpeter on development. In Y. Shionoya and T. Nishizawa (ed.), *Marshall and Schumpeter on Evolution. Economic Sociology of Capitalist Development*. Cheltenham: Edward Elgar: 225–42.

Hagemann H. [2008b]. Schumpeters Konjunktur- und Wachstumstheorie. In R. Neck (Ed.), *Die österreichische Schule der Nationalökonomie*. Frankfurt am Main: Peter Lang: 149–76.

Hanusch, H. and Pyka A. (Eds) [2007a]. *Elgar Companion to Neo-Schumpeterian Economics*. Cheltenham: Edward Elgar.

— and — [2007b]. Schumpeter, Joseph Alois (1883-1950). In H. Hanusch and A. Pyka (Eds), *Elgar Companion to Neo-Schumpeterian Economics*. Cheltenham: Edward Elgar: 19–26.

Kuznets S. [1940]. Schumpeter's Business Cycles. *The American Economic Review* 30(2): 257–71.

Lange O. [1941]. Review: Business Cycles by Joseph A. Schumpeter. *The Review of Economics and Statistics* 23(4): 190–3.

Magnusson L. (Ed.) [1994]. *Evolutionary and Neo-Schumpeterian Approaches to Economics*. Boston, Dordrecht, London: Kluwer Academic Publishers.

Mitchell W. C. [1927]. *Business Cycles: The Problem and its Settings*. NBER Book Series Studies in Business Cycles. New York: NBER.

Pyka A. et al. (Eds) [2009]. *Recent Advances in Neo-Schumpeterian Economics. Essays in Honour of Horst Hanusch*. Cheltenham: Edward Elgar.

Rühl C. [1994]. The transformation of business-cycle theory: Hayek, Lucas and a change in the notion of equilibrium. In M. Colonna and H. Hagemann (Eds) *Money and Business Cycles. The Economics of F.A. Hayek*. Aldershot: Edward Elgar: 168–202.

Schumpeter J. A. [1910]. Über das Wesen der Wirtschaftskrisen. *Zeitschrift für Volkswirtschaft, Sozialpolitik und Verwaltung* 19: 271–325.

— [1927]. The Explanation of the Business Cycle. *Economica* 21: 286–311.

— [1928a]. The Instability of Capitalism. *The Economic Journal* 38(151): 361–86.

— [1928b]. Unternehmer. In *Handwörterbuch der Staatswissenschaften* (4. ed.), Volume: 476–87. Jena.

— [1930]. Mitchell's Business Cycles. *The Quarterly Journal of Economics* 45(1): 150–72.

— [1931]. The theory of the business cycle. *Keizaigaku Ronshu - The Journal of Economics* 4: 1–18.

— [1934]. *The Theory of Economic Development. An Inquiry Into Profits, Capital, Credit, Interest, and the Business Cycle* (4. ed.). Cambridge (1951): Harvard University Press.

— [1935]. The analysis of economic change. *The Review of Economics and Statistics* 17(4), 2–10.

— [1939]. *Business Cycles. A Theoretical, Historical and Statistical Analysis of the Capitalist Process.* New York, Toronto, London: McGraw-Hill.

— [1947a]. The creative response in economic history. *The Journal of Economic History* 7(2): 149–59.

— [1947b]. Theoretical problems of economic growth. *The Journal of Economic History* 7 (Supplement): 1–9.

— [2000]. *Briefe/Letters.* Tübingen: Mohr Siebeck.

Smithies A. [1957]. Economic fluctuations and growth. *Econometrica* 25(1): 1–52.

Snowdon, B. and Vane H. R. (Eds) [2002]. *An Encyclopedia of Macroeconomics.* Cheltenham: Edward Elgar.

Stolper, W. F. [1951]. Reflections on Schumpeter's writings. *The Review of Economics and Statistics* 33(2): 170–77.

— [1982]. Schumpeters Theorie der Innovation. *Ifo-Studien* 28: 239–70.

MODELING THE INTERACTION OF CYCLES AND GROWTH IN THE FIFTIES: TWO SCHUMPETERIAN ATTEMPTS

Alain Raybaut[1]

In post-war macroeconomics, economic dynamics generally refers to two distinct phenomena, economic growth and business cycles, which implies the existence of a strict dichotomy between short run and long-run analysis. In this paper we focus on two original exceptions to this prevailing view during the fifties: the attempt made by A. Smithies using ratchet effects, and the nonlinear approach initiated by Goodwin. Both explicitly refer to Schumpeter's view on cyclical growth combined with post-war macroeconomic advances. However, they did not really succeed to overcome the major difficulties of a unified analysis of cycles and growth, stressed notably by Pasinetti in 1960. On the one hand, the introduction of ratchet effects into consumption or investment functions does not provide, contrary to Smithies's claim, an endogenous explanation of cycles and growth. On the other hand, Goodwin's nonlinear approach provides a promising perspective, but, in the fifties his attempt to connect a Keynesian framework with Schumpeterian insights remains rather tentative.

Modélisation de l'articulation cycles croissance dans les années 1950 : deux tentatives schumpétériennes

La macrodynamique d'après-guerre, considère généralement les cycles et la croissance ,comme deux phénomènes distincts, ce qui implique l'existence d'une dichotomie stricte entre les analyses des dynamiques de court et de long terme. Dans cet article nous mettons l'accent sur deux exceptions des années cinquante: la tentative singulière de A. Smithies et l'approche de Goodwin. Ces deux contributions se réfèrent explicitement à la conception schumpétérienne d'une dynamique unifiée en termes de croissance cyclique modélisée à partir des avancées de l'analyse macroéconomique d'après-guerre. Cependant, elles ne parviennent pas à dépasser les difficultés inhérentes à une analyse unifiée des cycles et de la croissance, soulignées notamment par Pasinetti. D'un côté, l'introduction d'effet de cliquet dans la fonction d'investissement ou de consommation ne suffit pas, contrairement aux affirmations de Smithies à produire une explication endogène des cycles et de la croissance. D'un autre côté, l'approche non linéaire prônée par Goodwin ouvre une perspective prometteuse, mais sa démarche visant à combiner macroéconomie keynésienne et points de vue schumpétériens reste encore embryonnaire.

Keywords: History of macrodynamics, business cycles theory, growth theory, cyclical growth.

Mots clefs : Histoire de la macrodynamique, théories des cycles, théorie de la croissance, croissance cyclique.

JEL classification: B20, B16, B22, E12, E32

---

1. University of Nice-Sophia Antipolis/CNRS GREDEG – 250 Rue A.Einstein 06560 Valbonne France. E-mail : alain.raybaut@gredeg.cnrs.fr

1. Introduction

In post-war macroeconomic analysis, economic dynamics generally refers to two main phenomena: economic growth and business cycles. This view implicitly implied the existence of a strict dichotomy between short run and long-run dynamics. The convergence between some general dynamic equilibrium business cycles models and endogenous growth theory in the nineties has changed the relation between growth and cycles in modern macroeconomics. As Aghion and Howitt summed it up briefly, "one of the general implications of endogenous growth theory is that growth and cycles are related phenomena, with causation going in both directions." [Aghion and Howitt, 1998: 4] Two main approaches then emerged. The first corrects the short-comings of early RBC models, offering a more sophisticated analysis of technological innovations and of their economic effects. The second approach refers to creative destruction and establishes, in line with Schumpeter, "causal links from cycles to growth or the reverse causality." [Aghion and Howitt, 1998: 233] This new conception contrasts with those defended by the first modern business cycle model-builders and growth theorists. Thus, in 1960, Pasinetti characterized the various models combining multiplier effects and some form of the acceleration principle noting that "the situation is that, on the one hand, the macro-economic models which provide a cyclical interpretation of the economic activity cannot give any explanation of economic growth and, on the other hand, those theories which define, or rely on, the conditions for a dynamic equilibrium to be reached and maintained cannot give an explanation of business cycle." [Pasinetti, 1960, p.69] The origin of this "situation" is to be found in the treatment of investment and its consequences on business cycles. Business cycles had to be interpreted as a pure short period phenomenon disconnected to long run accumulation. Furthermore, this approach neglected the reverse influence of economic growth on business cycles [Arena and Raybaut 2003].[2]

2. This dichotomy between growth and fluctuations prevailed until the end of the sixties. Lucas's monetary equilibrium BC theory favored a completely new approach to fluctuations but maintained the idea that they were independent from economic growth. Even, the various generations of early RBC models did not improve this state of affairs.

However, the need to connect short-run and long-run dynamics did not disappear from the research agenda of post-war macroeconomic theory.[3]

On the contrary, the postwar extension of Keynesian concepts to problems of economic growth has been progressively accompanied since the mid-fifties by a shift from the investigation of the requirements for pure cyclical behavior towards the study of the interrelation of cycle and trend. The period under consideration in this paper is characterized by the emergence of various approaches of the problem, so much that Matthews [1959] could write that "there is less agreement among economists about the relation between trend and cycle than about most other topic in the theory of the cycle" [Matthews R.C.O,1959: 253].

A first difference refers to the conception of the growth process.

On the one hand, the approach developed by Duesenberry [1958] in *Business Cycles and Economic Growth* which combines the traditional ingredients of business cycle theory to yield steady growth instead of fluctuations. Fluctuations are due to causes exogenous to the process of growth and are separately explained. In particular, if speculation and financial disturbances are avoided, steady growth is possible without cycles.[4] On the other hand, the majority of the contributors adopt Harrod's view, trying to describe in terms of endogenous factors what happens when the economy is not on the steady growth path. In this perspective, the question is mainly to determine by what mechanism, if any, the rate of growth of effective demand and the rate of growth of productive capacity are brought into alignment.

A second difference refers to the very relation between cycles and growth.

3. As we may recall, early writers — such as Spiethoff or Tugan-Baranowsky — analyzed trade cycles stressing the essential role of investment and the accumulation of productive capacity in the genesis of both growth and fluctuations. They interpreted trade cycles as intrinsic components of the long-run process of growth [Arena and Raybaut, 2003].

4. The second characteristic of the model is its treatment of the relative importance of demand as the prime determinant of the rate of growth. Thus, "In normal circumstances factor limitations are held not to impose any significant constraint. Either there are plenty of resources or else the natural rate of growth adjusts itself to the requirements of demand." [Matthews, 1959: 750]

To begin with, a trend can be introduced into a model of the trade cycle or a trade-cycle theory can be used to "explain" the trend as well. This is in particular the case of Felner [1956] or of Tinbergen and his successors, notably Klein for the US economy. To some extend Kalecki is also in the same position. The cycle refers equally to a static or a growing economy. Certain variables, which were held constant for business-cycle analysis, are subject to long-run changes to produce a trend. Tough, "in his latest work, Kalecki has attempted to produce a separate theory of trend. But he has still not shown how the process of growth itself can generate fluctuations." [Smithies, 1957: 4]

Second, the trend can be conceived as an essential ingredient of the explanation of the cycles. Hicks'1950 trade cycle theory is representative of the this view. As we know, the trend is an essential element of his theory of economic fluctuations. Accordingly, Hicks insists on the necessity of dealing of the business cycle as a problem of an expanding economy. But the way he incorporated as a deus ex machina a linear steady state growth trend in an unstable multiplier/accelerator business cycle framework without changing its basic characteristics remains "quite unconvincing in spite of its brilliancy." [Ando and Modigliani, 1959: 502] This influential approach has given birth to several variants in the fifties. Among others, let mention the model of Minsky [1959]. Floors and ceilings in the linear multiplier accelerator framework are interpreted as imposing new initial conditions reflecting different effective supply constraints or institutional and financial environment. Another interesting reinterpretation of Hicks' model is due to Higgins [1955]. For him, "the relationship between cycles and growth is a two-way one." [Higgins, 1955: 595] One can conceive of economic growth without fluctuations and of economic fluctuation without economic growth. But, "At the same time, actual fluctuations will be markedly influenced by the growth factors, and the actual trend will be very much affected by economic fluctuations." [Ibid.] The models first considers briefly as to whether autonomous investment can conceivably produce smooth growth without significant fluctuations. Then, he analyzes more fully the effects of the autonomous trend on the amplitude and duration of economic fluctuations. The analysis relies on the role of expectations effects and Marrama's "rationality factor", showing notably that after the floor is reached, it may take a longer period for sustained increase in output to start induced investment and launch an upswing.

Finally for a third approach, cycles and trend are so intertwined as to be indistinguishable. Schumpeter was obviously the leading exponent of this view, but in the fifties his position is reasserted by younger scholars who try to reformulate the problem within the post-war macroeconomic framework. In the light of the recent Neo-Schumpeterian advances on cycles and growth mentioned above, we will focus in this paper on this view. Two main contributions are particularly representative of this approach. The first one is the attempt by A. Smithies [1957] to link more closely fluctuations and growth using ratchet effects. The second one is the nonlinear approach of cyclical growth initiated by Goodwin [1955].[5]

2. The ingenious contribution of Smithies

This interesting attempt which deserved a lot of attention in the period was developed by A. Smithies in a long article published in *Econometrica* [1957, 25(1): 1–52]. According to Smithies, the existing bridges between business cycles and growth theories of the post-war are rather "infrequent and by no means satisfactory." [Smithies, 1957: 1] For instance, Tinbergen and his successors made a clear separation between cycles and trends in the data, and the cycle is entirely analyzed as deviations from trend, "Thus the possibility of interaction between long-run growth and cyclical fluctuations is removed before the analysis even commences." [Ibid.] The position of Kalecki seems to him rather similar, since "his cycle works equally well in a static or in a progressive economy." [Ibid.] An attempt to produce a separate theory of trend exists in Kalecki's work, "But he has still not shown how the process of growth itself can generate fluctuations." [Ibid.] Concerning the growth issue, the suitable point of departure is obviously

5. Kaldor's position regarding cycles and trends is somewhat ambiguous. In his the trade cycle model of 1940 cycles are obtained without growth. He begins his 1954 article by insisting that it is possible to conceive economic fluctuations without growth and to introduce an independent trend explained by technical progress. At the conclusion of his article, he insists on the complex connection between cycles and growth. In addition, in his final paragraph he refers to Schumpeter's hero who is found to play "a key role, in the drama." Thus Kaldor seems to be in the end on the side of those who contend that economic growth and the economic fluctuations have a common cause, without ever referring explicitly to a process of cyclical growth. However, all the ingredients for building such a process are present in Kaldor's approach if we consider it in retrospect [Arena and Raybaut, 2003].

the contribution of Harrod. Indeed, "Harrod himself would agree that displacements from steady growth are more likely to generate further displacements than a return to the original position . . . One of my major purposes is to produce a theory that takes Harrod's steady growth as a path of reference, but describes what happens when the economy is not on that path." [Ibid.: 4] From this standpoint, Hicks's Trade Cycle is an important, although unsuccessful, attempt to link the explanation of growth and fluctuations. But, for Smithies there is no evidence at all that a full-employment ceiling is responsible for cyclical downturns, in addition, there is also no empirical evidence for the value of the accelerator during the upswing or the downswing. Finally, the trend is a deus ex machina. Indeed, "what motivates autonomous investment is entirely unexplained, and it has no influence in increasing capacity output. And since it is the factor that explains economic growth, it urgently needs explanation. The Hicks cycle may well be a trivial addition to the main phenomenon of investment which the theory does not touch." [Smithies, 1957: 5] It is thus necessary to take another direction which tries to overcome these difficulties.

In this perspective, according to Smithies the main reference in the field, which interrelates growth and cycles, is the theory advanced by Schumpeter in the *Theory of Economic Development* and in *Business Cycles.*[6] If the Schumpeterian concept of innovation has clearly won its place in economic thinking, for Smithies it is not completely the case for Schumpeter's conception of equilibrium in his theory of economic dynamics. Smithies refers here in particular to the idea that the phases of expansion are characterized by disruption of an initial equilibrium position and the depressions by convergence towards a new equilibrium. Consequently, a process of cyclical expansion is generated "whereby the economy moves through successively 'higher' equilibrium positions. [Smithies, 1957: 6] Smithies understands clearly that the crucial point is precisely the new potential equilibrium established in every cycle "holds the economy up, and prevents a return during the depression to the initial

6. As we may recall, Smithies was personally in touch with Schumpeter during the last eighteen years of his life. He published several article on Schumpeter, notably on the relation between Schumpeter and Keynes and wrote in 1950 Schumpeter's obituary in the *American Economic Review.*

(equilibrium) starting point. In this manner Schumpeter explains growth and cycles as part of the same dynamic process." [Ibid.]

As we know in *Business Cycles* Schumpeter argues that equilibrium may never be actually achieved, but that it exists a tendency towards it. This tendency refers notably to the concept of a normal business situation "present in the minds of businessmen-as evidenced by directors' reports which usually describe the affairs of the business or the economy by reference to a norm." [Smithies, 1957: 6] On this basis, Smithies contends that business men generally consider that "neither booms nor depressions will last forever but will make their investment and production plans with reference to a normal situation and that the normal itself will change as development continues." [Ibid.] However for him, Schumpeter's argument calls for additional considerations on the demand side since "Businesses will not increase production simply because they believe business is subnormal." [Ibid.] For Smithies, the suitable mechanism refers here to an extended use of the ratchet effects recently introduced by Modigliani and Duesenberry to explain the relation between consumption and income. To put the argument in a nutshell, consumption depends not only on the current level of income but also on the highest levels previously achieved. Consequently, if current income is lower than some previous level, that level will exert an influence on current consumption, and "in this way the theory recognizes that consumption standards and patterns once achieved are not lightly abandoned and the retention of those standards provides the demand needed to spark the equilibrium tendency." [Smithies, 1957: 7] Moreover, these ratchet effects may involve different aspects than the mere relation of consumption to income. In particular, Smithies believe these effects play an important role in investment decisions.

On this basis Smithies develops its own explanation of the interaction between fluctuations and growth "through the operation of endogenous forces." [Smithies, 1957: 1] The model consists of two interrelated parts. The first one relates to the dynamics of aggregate demand explained by induced investment and the multiplier. The second part is dedicated to the dynamics of full-capacity output.

The level of gross profits is the principal determinant of induced investment. The direct influence of profits is twofold. They provide a basis for expectations concerning the returns to be obtained from investment, and in line with Kalecki they influence the conditions on which firms can finance their investment. But additional factors are taken into account. First, investment also depends on the full-capacity output Y_F. Excess capacity will tend to reduce investment, while a general shortage of capital will encourage it. In addition, there exists a ratchet effect on profits captured by $\bar{Y}$, the highest level of GNP. Finally, "exogenous" trends may be introduced, in particular the rate of population growth. Smithies assumes that gross profits are proportional to GNP. Thus, the variable Y is used in the he investment function instead of profits. The investment function is linear with one period lags and writes:

$$I = \beta_1 Y_{-1} + \beta_2 \bar{Y} - \beta_3 (Y_{F-1} - \bar{Y}) + k^t \tag{1}$$

The first term captures the direct dependence on profits, the second one a ratchet level effect on profits and the third the capacity effect. The final term refers to the exogenous influence of trends, such as population growth.

Consumption C depends on disposal income and its ratchet value captured by GNP, Y, and ratchet GNP, $\bar{Y}$. All the relations are linear and the the consumption function is

$$C = (1 - \alpha_1)Y + \alpha_2 \bar{Y}. \tag{2}$$

Consequently, the long-run marginal propensity to consume when $Y = \bar{Y}$, is $1 - \alpha_1 + \alpha_2$ and the short-run one in a fluctuating economy is $1 - \alpha_1$.

Then, investment and consumers' expenditures determine in a standard way the level of Y at any particular time with $Y = C + I$ or $Y - C = I = S$ and "in that sense, the system is in short-run equilibrium" [Smithies, 1957: 18].

The model is completed by a relation depicting the effect of investment on full capacity. output Y_F. That is:

$$Y_F - Y_{F-1} = \sigma I_{-1} - D_1 - D_2 + l^t \tag{3}$$

where $D_1 = \delta_1 Y_{F-1}$ and $D_2 = \delta_2 (Y_{F-1} - Y_{-1})$ refer respectively to physical depreciation and extraordinary obsolescence. A trend factor l^t is introduced in order to take into account changes in capacity independent of the rate of investment.

On the basis of these simple set of linear relations, the core of Smithies' explanation of the interaction between fluctuations and growth lies in the distinction between two regimes, state 1 and state 2. In the first one the ratchet effect is discarded and $\bar{Y} = Y_{-1}$ in relation (1) and $\bar{Y} = Y$ in (2). This distinction results in two sets of equations, those that hold when the ratchets are operating and those that are in effect when the economy expands beyond the ratchet level of output. Consequently, the dynamics of the model consists of two simultaneous linear difference equations, one with actual output Y and the other with full-capacity output Y_F as the dependent variable. We have for state 1:

$$Y = aY_{-1} + bY_{F-1} + gk^t \tag{4}$$

$$Y_F = cY_{-1} + dY_{F-1} + l^t \tag{5}$$

where, $a = \frac{\beta_1+\beta_2+\beta_3}{\alpha_1-\alpha_2}$, $b = \frac{-\beta_2}{\alpha_1-\alpha_2}$, $c = \sigma(\alpha_1 - \alpha_2) + \delta_2$, $d = 1 - \delta_1 - \delta_2$, $g = \frac{1}{\alpha_1-\alpha_2}$.

When the ratchet effect is operative the system for state 2 is:

$$Y = a'Y_{-1} + b'Y_{F-1} + r\bar{Y} + g'k^t \tag{6}$$

$$Y_F = c'Y_{-1} + d'Y_{F-1} + s\bar{Y} + l^t \tag{7}$$

where, $a' = \frac{\beta_1}{\alpha_1}$, $b' = \frac{\beta_3}{\alpha_1}$, $c' = \sigma\alpha_1 + \delta_2$, $d' = 1 - \delta_1 - \delta_2$, $g' = \frac{1}{\alpha_1}$, $r = \frac{\alpha_2+\beta_2+\beta_3}{\alpha_1}$, $s = -\sigma\alpha_2$.

It is thus easy to solve these two linear systems in Y and Y^F. As well known, monotonous or oscillatory solutions may be obtained with real or complex roots of the corresponding characteristic equations. Indeed, if state 1 is a monotonous process of growth with Y continually increasing, state 2 never becomes relevant. On the contrary, if Y oscillates it may sometimes fall below $\bar{Y}$, and the economy enters into state 2 until Y again exceeds $\bar{Y}$. Smithies considers also the possibility that the economy may enter in state 2 and remain in this state without the capacity to return to to State 1 "a situation which did not seem an absurd idea in the 1930's." [Smithies, 1957: 34] Consequently, the first step is to examine closely the solution of state 1. To begin with, let us notice as Allen [1960] put it that Smithies's state 1 bears a close family relationship to Duesenberry's simplified model. It can be shown to be its formal equivalent if Smithies's Y_F is replaced by σK where σ is Domar's coefficient.

First, Smithies considers the conditions of existence of a continuous growth path in which $Y = \bar{F}$. This equilibrium path refers to Harrod warranted rate and "represents an orderly and simple state of the economy and is a useful path of reference for considering other situations." [Smithies, 1957: 23] The other noncyclical case that is economically interesting is the case where Y grows over time and "is or tends" to be greater than Y_F. This case is called "persistent exhilaration" by Smithies. The other noncyclical solutions, persistent excess capacity or continual decline in both, are dismissed since they "reveal unstable states of the model rather than significant economic possibilities." [Op. cit.: 36] Second, Smithies examines the possibility of cyclical solutions in state 1. The model in this initial state can exhibit cyclical solution if the characteristic equation of system (6) (7) admits complex roots. That is if $\frac{\beta}{\alpha} - 1 < \sigma\alpha - \delta_1$. The interpretation given by Smithies is that cyclical fluctuations arise from the influence exercised by the difference between Y and Y_F on investment such that, "if this influence is great enough (but not too great) in the model it will produce fluctuations rather than continued growth or decline."[Ibid.] However, the economy may fluctuate and remain in State 1 without never interring in State 2, then "we have a model of the conventional Tinbergen-Kalecki type where the cyclical process does not engender growth, and growth depends entirely on trends." [Op. cit.: 29] Consequently, the most interesting configuration for our issue is clearly that State 1 admits complex roots of modulus greater than the unity. This condition discussed in length in the mathematical section is simply $ad - bc > 1$. In addition, it is shown that the roots of state 1 are complex, those of State 2 are necessarily complex. Moreover, if the solution of State 1 are explosive, that of state 2 may be explosive or damped and if solution of State 1 is damped, state 2 is also damped. Finally, the period of the oscillations in state 2 are greater than in state 1, since $\frac{2\pi}{\theta_1}$, where θ' and θ are respectively composed of the coefficients of the model in state 2 and state 1. Thus, "Provided state 1 is explosive, the ratchet effects can be such as to meet the required conditions; and a process of endogenous fluctuating growth is possible." [Ibid.] In this case, the economy may alternate between states 1 and 2 in a process of fluctuating endogenous growth in which "each depression and each boom respectively occurs at a higher level of output than the preceding one." [Op. cit.: 42]

The crucial element is the difference between actual and full capacity output. The mechanism can be summarized as follows. A boom ends and a depression begins when Y_F has sufficiently increased relatively to Y such that that total investment is reduced, and this in turn reduces consumption. The depression continues until depreciation and obsolescence reduce sufficiently Y_F in relation to Y to produce a revival of investment, and consequently of consumption. In addition, the mere fact that during the prosperity Y_F increases faster than Y sets the stage for another depression. Smithies insists on the fact that if State 1 were the only state of the economy, such mechanism would simply describes a process of explosive or damped deviations from equilibrium growth, "it is therefore the existence of State 2 that opens up other possibilities." [Ibid.]

He adds that this process is obtained without the introduction of any exogenous trend. Finally, Smithies discusses the potential influence of the introduction of exogenous trends in the model. These trends are likely to play the role of exogenous shocks and may modify the endogenous dynamics described above. For instance, a downward or an upward trend in the investment function can offset the process of endogenous expansion, keeping the economy indefinitely in state 2 or conversely can push the economy outside this state even with damped solutions.

The different possibilities with fluctuations are illustrated on the following figure [Smithies, 1957: 30] reproduced below.

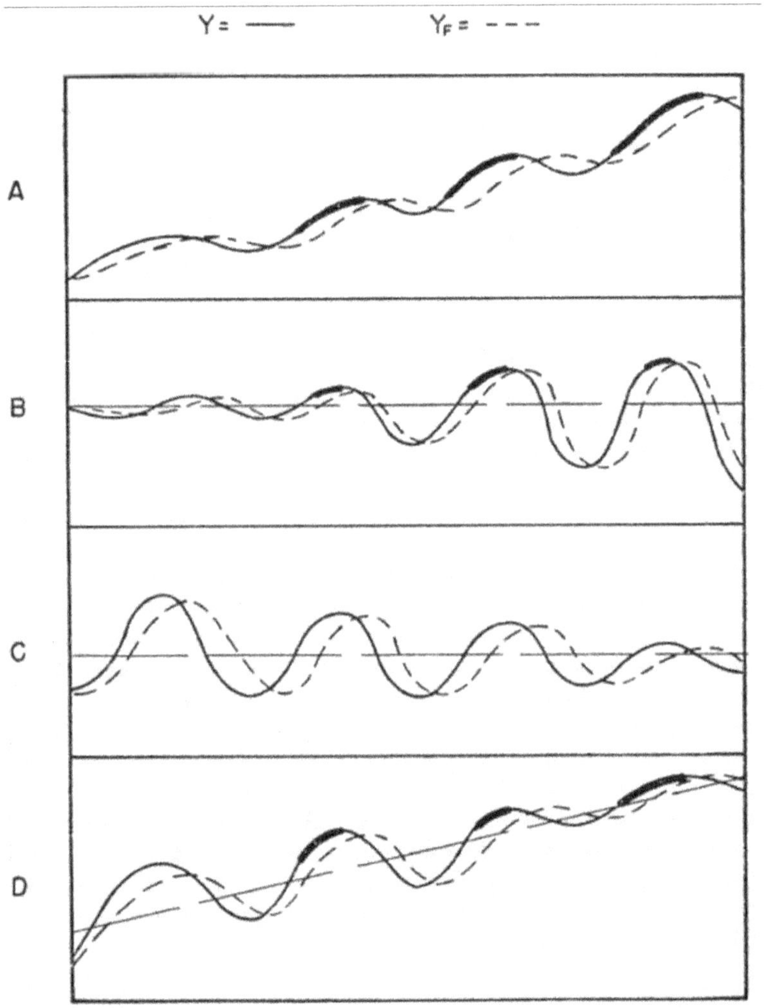

FIGURE 1

The solid lines refers to actual output Y and the dotted lines to Y_F. B represents the case where the ratchet effect is not strong enough to produce growth, such that the model exhibits explosive fluctuations without growth. In C, the endogenous forces for expansion are so weak that the economy remains perpetually in state 2. In D trend influences are superimposed on C, and are strong enough to bring the model into State 1 during prosperity periods. Finally, only A refers to a configuration in which the economy alternates between state 1 and state 2 leading to endogenous growth cycles in which each peak and each depression occur at a higher level of *Y* than the preceding one.

Smithies concludes: "Reasonable values of the coefficients of the model are consistent with continued economic growth or with fluctuations. Neither possibility can be excluded without specific knowledge of the economy under consideration." [Smithies, 1957: 23] In addition if we consider a specific country, these conditions may change from time to time, "so that in one decade a continued growth model may be appropriate while in another a fluctuating model is needed, depending on conditions outside the present frame of reference." [Ibid.] Smithies contends from the beginning of the paper that his framework is empirical in the sense that "any of the possibilities it suggests can be excluded by the available evidence" [op. cit.: 1], but this framework "is not numerical." [Ibid.] More generally, Smithies has doubt about the usefulness of time series to test a simple model of long run dynamics, since the structure of the model is likely to change within the period. This is precisely refers to one of the difficulties of providing a theory of both cycles and growth raised by Pasinetti [1960]. The outcomes of the models are generally obtained for a limited range of the parameters, which raises the question of their stability over time. These parameters are particularly sensitive to variations in expectations. Now, "if the parameters expressing the behavior of entrepreneurs in their decisions to invest are bound to assume different values in time, the situation certainly cannot be solved as trade cycle and growth theorists have practically done by choosing arbitrarily particular values of such parameters and then carrying on one's analysis on the assumption that such values remain constant." [Pasinetti, 1960][7]

Nevertheless, some attempts have been made to test empirically Smithies's model. Let us mention in particular the studies by Choudhry and Mohabbat in the early sixties. The authors notice that even if we overcome the initial reluctance of Smithies, "the manner in which Smithies puts together his equations and the variables he includes in them create some formidable methodological-conceptual problems in the construction

7. As we know, on the basis of these remarks Pasinetti draws the conclusion that we have to abandon the aggregated macroeconomic approach in favor of a different perspective looking more deeply behind the factors explaining the dynamics of the parameters themselves.

of time-series as well as in the estimation of equations. Our effort to cope with them may be deserving of interest." [Choudhry and Mohabbat, 1965: 90] Among these problems, two need special mention, the first one refers to the choice of the best method of estimation in view of the equations of the model. The second one is the problem involved by the construction of time-series on full capacity output. The authors are aware that a model as simple as this one can hardly capture the characteristics of the dynamics of a complex industrial economy, but the study confines to the Smithies's simplest case due in particular to limitations of data. The test consists first in estimating the parameters a, b, c, d, g in relation 4 and 5 and second in examining the time path of GNP induced by these values. A clear negative result concerning the fluctuating growth approach is obtained. The two roots of the difference equation are real and less than unity in absolute value, thus the system converges monotonically. This result does not really come as a surprise for the authors. Accordingly, "by now the knowledge that simple systems like these could evince the cyclical-growth characteristics of a modern industrial economy only under very special assumptions about the parameters therein is indeed hoary. And yet, to the extent that our findings lend support to the thesis that the economy is an essentially stable process relying chiefly on exogenous impulses and random displacements to account for its cyclical dynamics, they may deserve to be noticed." [Op. cit.: 96]. This conclusion directly refers to Duesenberry's view which, on this aspect, prefigures the approach of the eighties. In the same perspective during the seventies the study of Kromphardt and Döfner [1974] examines closely Smithies's attempt. The authors first recall that Evans had also shown numerically in 1965 that the range of parameters required to generate both cycles and growth in the model could hardly fit with their empirical relevant values. Then, they show analytically and numerically that it is actually impossible to found a set of relevant parameters compatible with the existence of cyclical solutions and endogenous growth with positive ratchet effects. Thus, they conclude that contrary to Smithies's claim, the mere introduction of ratchet effects on consumption or saving is not sufficient to explain endogenously both cycles and growth, an exogenous trend remains necessary.

These diriment criticisms confirm the logical difficulties to combined endogenously cycles and growth, even by using the ingenious solution developed by Smithies, in a linear framework. From this standpoint, let us now examine how the approach developed at the same period by Goodwin in a nonlinear perspective, may address these difficulties.

3. Interrelations of growth and cycles in a nonlinear perspective: the first models of Goodwin

Goodwin's idea to build a model which would fuse indissolubly the cycle and the trend was initially developed in the article "The problem of trend and cycle" [Goodwin, 1953], and began to take shape in 1955. According to Goodwin, the issue has been stated clearly by Harrod who "holds that the same theory must explain both growth and cycles, but it is, I think fair to say that few have been convinced that he has provided such a theory." [Goodwin, 1955: 123] Goodwin was initially convinced that the main difficulty was that Harrod did not develop a fully-fledged theory of the cycle.[8] Let us recall that Goodwin was very impressed by Tinbergen's formal judgment on Harrod. His theory could not emerge onto a cycle theory because of the impossibility to obtain self-sustained oscillations from linear first order differential equations. However, as Goodwin himself will clarify later [Goodwin 1982], he was convinced from the beginning that Harrod and not Tinbergen had the sounder view of economic dynamics. Indeed, as Harcourt put it, with the development of nonlinear dynamics Goodwin "had the answer as to why Harrod's intuition had been correct, that Harrod *did* have a cycle in his 1930s book." [Harcourt, 1985: 417] In the fifties, as regards the recent attempt made by Hicks in his trade cycle theory, the trouble for Goodwin is that Hicks "losses the theory of the trend in all but a trivial sense . . . his trend is unrelated to required capital or indeed to anything except the necessity to get a trend." [Ibid.] On the other hand, the decomposition of time series into cycles, trend and residual or the pioneer works on pure business cycles, including his own business cycles models, is "definitively not permissible." [Goodwin, 1955: 122] In a linear world, thanks to the superposition theorem it is always possible to decompose and add the different elements to obtain an adequate representation of the true dynamics. In a nonlinear world, this theorem does not hold and decomposition is invalid. It would remain of

8. For a modern restatement of Harrod's dynamic theory, see Bruno and Dal-Pont [2014].

course necessary to prove empirically that important nonlinearities exist, nevertheless "for the time being, we must, . . . , regard with grave misgiving the removal of trend, since we might remove much of the real problem." [Ibid.] As a consequence, the formal solution is to adopt a nonlinear framework, as Goodwin did previously in his business cycles models.

From an analytical point of view, the most fruitful source of inspiration in order to deal simultaneously with cycles and growth is obviously Schumpeter.[9] This theory is of course difficult to formulate in simple mathematical terms. Therefore according to Goodwin, him, "such use I shall made of it may seem rather a caricature," [op. cit.: 124] as regards Schumpeter's own theory and rich empirical illustration in *Business Cycles*. In addition, Goodwin contends that he cannot follow Schumpeter in his rejection of the Keynesian framework. From a theoretical point of view, there is no objection for him to combine Schumpeter's insights with effective demand analysis. On the contrary, Keynesian tools can be used to strengthen Schumpeter's system. Accordingly, "by incorporating effective demand it is possible to lessen the excessive strain that he put on his special theory on the innovational process. Essentially, he places *the* explanation of the cycle on the internal dynamics of successful innovation . . . It may sometimes be so, but that it has always been so over more than 150 years is difficult to accept." [Ibid.] In addition, the combination of the innovational mechanism and the role of effective demand makes more plausible Schumpeter's idea of clustering of innovations [see e.g. Goodwin, 1946].

Keeping these arguments in mind, Goodwin develops two simple models. The first one is a purely exercise which "is not designed to do justice either to [Schumpeter] or to economic reality." [Goodwin, 1955: 125] To begin with, Goodwin considers a curve $p(k)$ of present value of all capital projects as a function of the quantity of capital k. This curve shifts to the right at a regular rate due to progress. The simple purpose of the model is to show that the mere introduction of a nonlinearity (a hook) in the function of the supply price of new capital as a function of the rate of

9. As well known, Schumpeter was "one of Goodwin's heroes and towards the end of Schumpeter's life a close friend." [Harcourt, 1985: 414]

net output of new capital, opens the room to growth cycles. This process is analyzed graphically by Goodwin on the following figure.

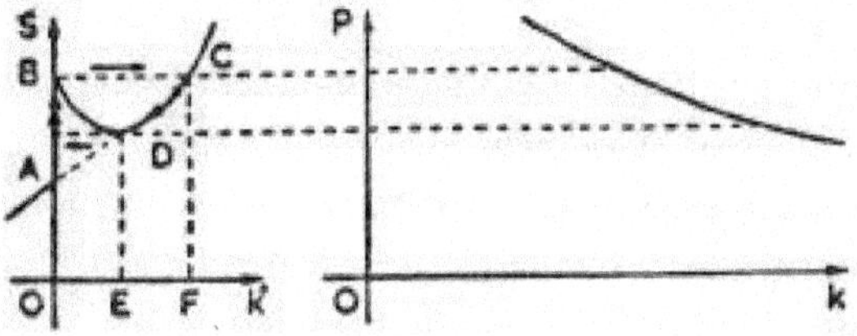

Due to "all the reasons which Schumpeter has widely describe" [op. cit.: 125], the range of profitable opportunities increases, but nothing is done until they are potentially so high, $B - A$, that an innovator may succeed. Then he is followed by many imitators with a burst of investment at a rate F declining to E. At this point net investment ceases, and again the economy slowly accumulate investment possibilities as p raises to B. At this point, the system jumps to C and so on and so forth. If progress is such as to require a rate of accumulation between 0 and E, this process is self-sustained. Consequently, in this simple framework, "the growth is the explanation of the cycle, and the latter would not exist without the former." [Op. cit.: 126]

The second model is based on more standard macroeconomic tools of the period.

To begin with, concerning the investment function, Goodwin considers a flexible nonlinear accelerator principle. From this perspective, investment will be undertaken as long as desired capital, ξ is greater than actual capital. Desired capital is determined by:

$$\xi = vy + \beta(t) \tag{8}$$

where v is the accelerator coefficient, y is output and $\beta(t)$ is a parameter associated with technical change. Consequently, the accelerator means that more capital is desired with increased output, while "innovation means that more capital is desired with a given output." [Op. cit.: 129] In addition, the pressure to expand is implicity reasons for proportional to the difference $\xi - k$. That is:

$$g(\dot{k}) = \xi - k \tag{9}$$

where g is an increasing linear piecewise function. In addition, Goodwin assumes that full employment of the capital goods coincides with "full employment generally". A related question discussed by Goodwin is whether or not innovations should raise the level of desired capital and the acceleration coefficient. Goodwin recalls that his "own inclination has always been to assume that the coefficient is increased" [op. cit.: 131], and that is due to the persuasive arguments of Harrod and J. Robinson that he changed his mind. The argument is that new methods of production require additional capital, but also destroy capital by obsolescence or by reducing replacement costs, therefore, "we may continually adding to our capital autonomously, but find that, after many years a routine addition to output requires the same addition to capital as before." [Op. cit.: 131]. It is thus simplest to assume that v remains constant.

Effective demand is introduced via the standard relation

$$y = f\left[\dot{k} + \gamma(t)\right] \tag{10}$$

where $\gamma(t)$ refers to public spending and the slope of f is the multiplier. Goodwin follows on saving the analysis developed by Duesenberry. Thus, concerning the slope of f, he assumes that "when going down, we follow the steeper slope, and only when we venture again into new high ranges of income does saving again grow only slowly." [Op. cit.: 132] It is interesting to note that Goodwin gives also another possible explanation of behavior referring to Marshall: The long period can be much longer in the downward than in the upward direction and "outlays expand easily but resist contraction to an extraordinary degree" [ibid].

Combining these equations and rearranging the terms, we obtain the following differential equation

$$k = vf(\dot{k}) - g(\dot{k}) + \beta(t) \tag{11}$$

Goodwin considers that in this rough approximation of the connection between cycle and growth, it is convenient to assume that all growth of the full employment ceiling occurs only during booms. Using the notation $\varphi(\dot{k}) = vf(\dot{k}) - g(\dot{k})$, an increase in $\beta(t)$ implies a shift of the curve φ to the right. As shown on the figure below, this means that the flat top to

$\varphi(\dot{k})$ slowly rises, "which raises the required capital and prolongs the boom." [Op. cit.: 135] Thus, the following diagram is obtained:

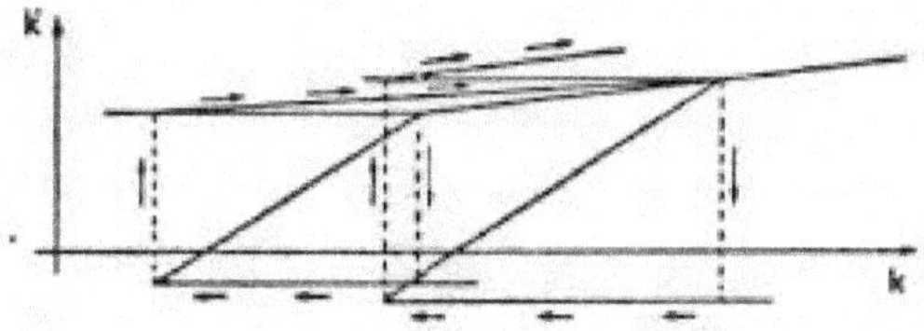

FIGURE 10.6

The dynamics follows a horizontal line which is steadily rising, "so that in fact we follows a slowly rising curve" [ibid.]. When a sufficient level of capital is accumulated, investment will slow down, which ends the boom. As a consequence, the model describes a process of cyclical growth in which "the economy surges forward and plunges down, but does not go back to its old low level" [Goodwin, 1955: 136], which captures one of the essential features of the Schumpeterian view on the connection between cycles and growth.

Accordingly, in this framework without lag it is assumed that "ordering new capital goods leads to immediate installation, and that the full effect of this on income also results immediately." [Goodwin, 1955: 138] As a consequence, the economy jumps instantaneously from boom to deep depression. Accordingly, in a second approximation, Goodwin introduces an average lag θ, which captures the lag between the decision to invest and its outlays. At the same time, he makes two simplifying assumptions. First, instead of $f(\dot{k}_{t+\theta})$, he writes $m\dot{k}_{t+\theta}$, where m is the constant multiplier. Second, he considers a linear investment function $\frac{\dot{k}_{t+\theta}}{a}$, where a is a constant, instead of $g(\dot{k}_{t+\theta})$. Then, he obtains the following linear second order differential equation:[10]

$$\theta\ddot{k} + (1 - amv)\dot{k} + ak - a\beta(t). \tag{12}$$

This linear equation gives rise to explosive oscillations if $amv > 1$. Goodwin assumes that the accelerator v and the multiplier m are both greater than unity and that $a < 1$. For example, with $v = m = 2$, the

10. By substitution into relation (11) and taking the two first terms of the Taylor series of $\dot{k}_{t+\theta}$.

solution will be unstable if $a < \frac{1}{4}$. Thus, in order to get an endogenous cyclical processes Goodwin combines this explosive linear oscillation with the floor-ceiling framework described above. Consequently, he draws the following picture:

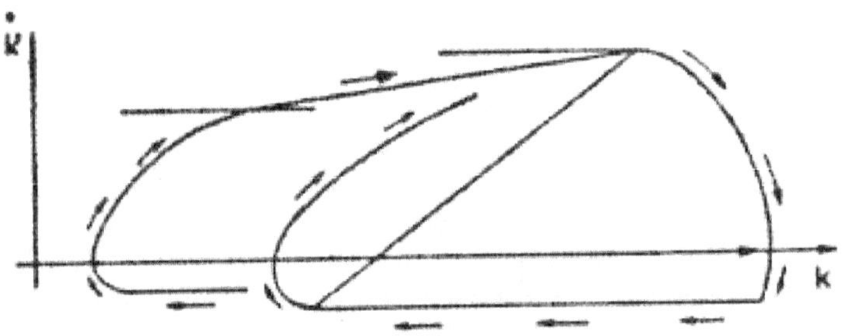

This figure depicts an endogenous cycle "made up of two simple routines, the flat top and bottom, and the outward spiralling ends . . . [where] the harshness of transition from boom to depression and back again is entirely softened." [Goodwin, 1955: 139]

However, we have not yet addressed the question of the evolution of the factor $\beta(t)$ capturing the Schumpeterian insights on innovative investment. Goodwin considers that in a progressive economy, $\beta(t)$ increases through innovation. These may occur slowly at some times and rapidly at others. Accordingly, the factor $\beta(t)$ is actually the product of many cumulated small events, but in a simple aggregated framework, it is likely to be continuous. However, Goodwin does not provide any explicit formalization of the dynamics of this factor in his 1955 model. In this perspective, it is interesting to refer to the relation introduced by Goodwin [1946] in an early contribution which has directly benefited from Schumpeter's critical and constructive remarks.[11] Accordingly, in this article dedicated to innovations and the irregularity of economic cycles, Goodwin develops one of the first formalizations of Schumpeter's ideas on clustering, in which the waves of innovation are simply modeled as a continuous periodic function of time. We have:

$$\beta(t) = L \cos \omega t + L \tag{13}$$

11. See notably Goodwin [1982] and Harcourt [1985].

where, L defines the amplitude and ω the frequency of the motion.

Let us now introduce this relation in a slightly modified version of Goodwin's model with delays, in which the linear accelerator vy is replaced by a continuous sigmoid shaped function $\Phi(y)$. We obtain:

$$\theta\ddot{k} + \dot{k} - a\Phi(m\dot{k}) + a(k - \beta(t)) = 0 \tag{14}$$

The equation becomes nonlinear and can easily exhibit endogenous closed orbits. We will not enter into the formal details,[12] and simply give below a numerical example of this type of solution with the forcing effect on $\beta(t)$ specified above.[13] The following results are obtained.

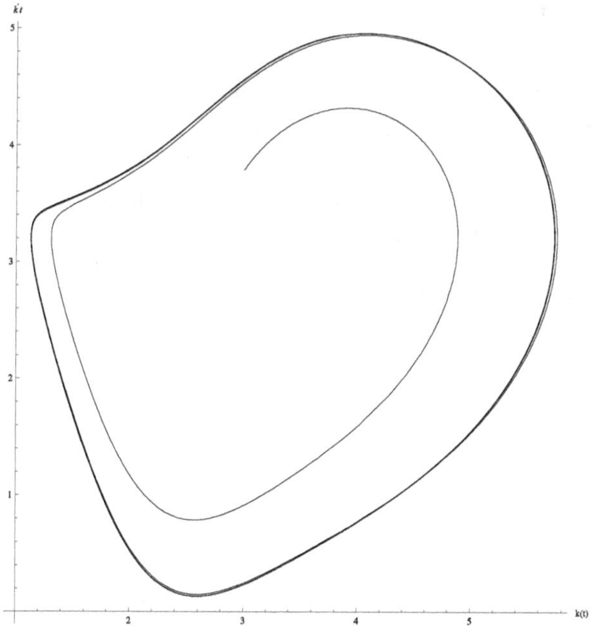

12. We obtain with a constant forcing effect β, a nonlinear second order differential equation of the type $\ddot{k} + f'(k)\dot{k} + g(k) = 0$, studied in length in the fifties, notably by Goodwin himself in his nonlinear business cycle models [see Goodwin, 1982], by the "Japanese connection" [Velupillai, 2008] and in France by Rocard and Allais [Raybaut, 2014]. See e.g. Lorenz [1987] and Sordi [2003] for a complete analytical and numerical analysis of this type of Keynes-Goodwin-Schumpeter model of growth and cycles.

13. The parameters are selected in Goodwin [1946] and Goodwin [1955]. We have, for example, $m = 2, \omega = .698$ and $a = 1.41$ and the sigmoid function is specified by $\mu + \tanh[x + v]$, where μ and v are two positive parameters greater than unity.

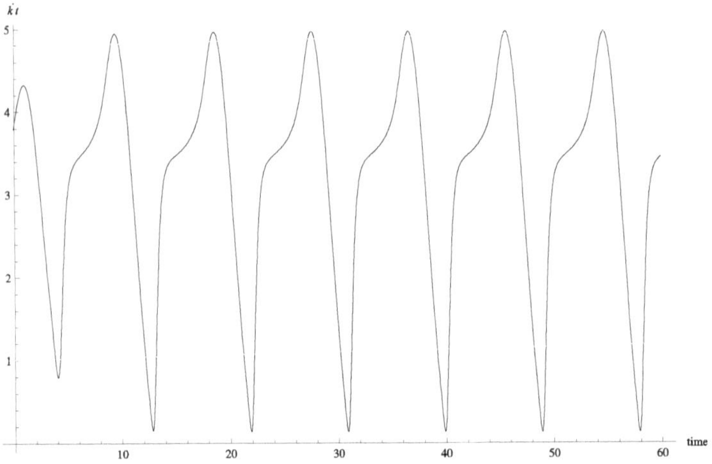

The first figure displays the phase diagram of the model in the k-$\dot{k}$ plane, showing the existence of a limit cycle. The second one displays the cyclical evolution over time of $\dot{k}$. The mere introduction in Goodwin's framework of a forcing effect modeled by a periodic function of time makes possible to explain the irregular shape of the growth cycles. Indeed, as suggested in Goodwin [1955], this example exhibits much shorter downswings than upswings.

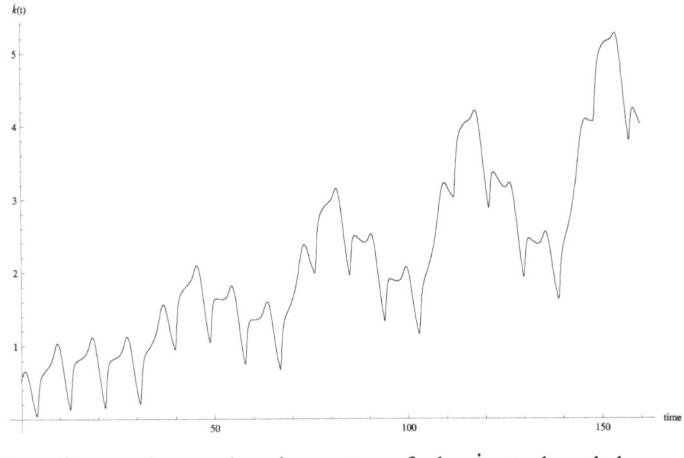

The last figure shows the dynamics of the $\dot{k}$, induced by a more complex forcing effect.[14] As noticed by Goodwin [1946], $\beta(t)$ is actually

14. Accordingly, the amplitude and the period are no more constant, but vary over time. We have $L = t\text{Exp}\left[\frac{.8\sin[0.25+0.698t]}{2-.8\cos[0.25+0.698t]}\right]$.

not sinusoidal and periodic as assumed hitherto. But, "the result of the simple case may be used however to study more complicated phenomena." [Goodwin, 1946: 99] In particular, $\beta(t)$ may be "approximately periodic" with an another shape. This makes possible, as shown on this example, to explain the irregular shape of the growth cycle.

In this perspective, the trend and the cycle should be regarded as fused indissolubly and "there would be no meaning to drawing any smooth trend line through the time series of national income." [Goodwin, 1955:136] Thus, this model extremely simple captures another Schumpeterian insight, the fact that steady accumulation is converted into bursts of development which eventually relax into depressions. Finally, as stressed by Goodwin [1946], this first approximation may also explain the existence of a short as well as a longer cycle, fitting with Schumpeter's formulation of the secondary wave.

Conclusion

This contribution focussed on two attempts to model endogenously cycles and growth in a unified framework during the fifties. An important aspect of these approaches lies in the fact that they explicitly refer to Schumpeter's view on cyclical growth combined with post-war macroeconomic advances. But they adopt two different perspectives. Smithies emphasizes Schumpeter's conception of economic dynamics as a process of disruption of an initial stationary state or regular growth path and convergence towards another one into his two states linear model, while Goodwin draws a stylized picture of the role of technical change in a nonlinear world.

These contributions lie at the cutting edge of the development of Post-War macrodynamics and constitute a first interesting Schumpeterian line of analysis of the issue before the modern neo-Schumpeterian advances. However they did not really succeed to overcome the major difficulties associated with the analysis of cycles and growth in a unified framework stressed by Pasinetti in 1960.

On the one hand, the introduction of ratchet effects into consumption or investment functions does not provide, contrary to Smithies's claim, an endogenous explanation of cycles and growth. The growth trend or the cycle can only be explained, as in other linear models of the period, by exogenous factors. On the other hand, Goodwin's nonlinear approach does of course provide a promising perspective to overcome these difficulties. But, in the fifties his attempts to connect a Keynesian framework with Schumpeterian insights remain rather tentative. In particular the models capture in a very rough way Schumpeter's conception of economic dynamics, reduced essentially to the mere introduction of an exogenous innovative investment function in a multiplier-accelerator model. [15] Goodwin's reasoning was mainly based on a graphical apparatus, albeit with an implicit analytical and numerical background, as explicitly shown in different modern advances inspired by his approach, combining a Keynesian framework with Schumpeterian ideas in a nonlinear perspective.[16] But, we have to wait his 1967 seminal model for a fully-fledged growth cycle model in which Goodwin adopts a different perspective.[17]

15. As we know, Schumpeter was very critical as regards the early developments of aggregated macrodynamic modeling.

16. For a complete treatment of the interaction of cycles and growth in this perspective, see e.g. Sordi [2003].

17. As well known, in this model Goodwin uses a prey-predator framework in a neo-Marxian background.

References

Aghion P. and Howitt P. [1998]. *Endogenous growth theory*. Cambridge, MA: The MIT Press.

Allen R.G.D. [1960]. The Structure of macro-economic models. *The Economic Journal* 70(277): 38–56.

Ando A.K and Modigliani F. [1959]. Growth, fluctuations, and stability. *The American Economic Review*. 49(2): 501–24.

Arena R. and Raybaut A. [2003]. Neo-Schumpeterian versus neo-Kaldorian approaches: two different views on learning, knowledge and cyclical growth. In Harald Hagemann and Stephan Seiter (eds.) *Growth Theory and Growth Policy*. London: Routledge: 65–83.

Bruno O. and Dal-Pont Legrand M. [2014]. The instability principle revisited: an essay in Harrodian dynamics. *European Journal of the History of Economic Thought* 21(3): 1–18.

Choudhry N.K. and Mohabbat K.A [1965]. Economic Fluctuations and Growth: Notes on Testing the Smithies Model. *Oxford Economic Papers* 17(1): 90–9.

Duesenberry J.S. [1958]. *Business Cycles and Economic Growth*. New York: McGraw-Hill.

Fellner W. [1956]. *Trends and Cycles in Economic Activity*. New York: Henry Holt and Co.

Goodwin R.M. [1946]. Innovations and the irregularity of economic cycles. *The Review of Economics and Statistics* 28(2): 95–104.

— [1953]. The Problem of Trend and Cycle. *Yorkshire Bulletin* 5(2): 89–90.

— [1955]. A model of cyclical growth. In E. Lundberg (ed.) *The Business Cycle in the Post-War World*. New York: Macmillan.

— [1982]. *Essays in economic dynamics*. New York: Macmillan.

Harcourt G.C. [1985]. A twentieth-century eclectic: Richard Goodwin. *Journal of Post Keynesian Economics* 7(3): 410–21.

Higgins B. [1955]. Interactions of Cycles and Trends. *The Economic Journal* 65(260): 594–614.

Kaldor N. [1954]. The relation of economic growth and cyclical fluctuations. *The Economic Journal* 64(253): 53–71.

Kromphardt J. and Dörfner J. [1974]. The capacity of the Smithies model to explain he growth trend by endogenous forces. *Econometrica* (4): 667–77.

Lorenz H.W. [1987]. On the uniqueness of limit cycles in business cycle theory. *Metroeconomica* 38(3): 281–93.

Matthews R.C.O. [1959]. Duesenberry on growth and fluctuations. *The Economic Journal.* 69(276): 749–65.

Minsky P.H. [1959]. A linear model of cyclical growth. *The Review of Economics and Statistics* 41(2 Part 1): 133–45.

Pasinetti L. [1960]. Cyclical fluctuations and economic growth. *Oxford Economic Papers* 12(2): 215–41.

Raybaut A. [2014]. Toward a nonlinear theory of economic fluctuations: Allais's contribution to nonlinear business cycle theory in the fifties. *European Journal of the History of Economic Thought* [Forthcoming].

Smithies A. [1957]. Economic fluctuations and growth. *Econometrica* 25(1): 1–52.

Sordi S. [2003]. The interaction between growth and cycles in macrodynamic models of the economy. In N. Salvadori (ed.) *The Theory of Economic Growth: A Classical Perspective.* Cheltenham: Edward Elgar.

Velupillai K. V. [2008]. Japanese contributions to nonlinear cycle theory in the 1950s. *The Japanese Economic Review* 59(1): 54–74.

KUZNETS VERSUS KONDRATIEFF
An essay in historical macroeconometrics

Claude Diebolt[1]

Spectral analysis has had limited applications in cliometrics to date. In this paper, it is used to determine, through international comparisons, the frequency of GDP series in the long run. A reminder of the spectral methodology (I) is followed by successive examinations of the series chosen, the treatment of these series and the results of the cliometric analysis (II). We show then the macroeconomic perspectives of this type of approach and we synthesise a new major result, i.e. the existence of a single intermediate Kuznets type cycle, in contradiction with the discourse around the dating of the famous cycles of Kondratieff type.

Kuznets vs Kondratieff.
Un essai de macroéconométie historique

L'application de l'analyse spectrale au domaine cliométrique a été jusqu'à présent restreinte. Dans cet article, elle est employée pour déterminer, en comparaison internationale, la périodicité des séries du PIB sur le long terme. Après avoir rappelé la méthodologie spectrale (I), nous examinerons les séries retenues, le traitement de ces séries et les résultats de l'analyse cliométrique (II). Nous montrons ensuite les perspectives macroéconomiques de ce type d'approche et synthétisons un résultat majeur, à savoir l'existence d'un cycle intermédiaire unique de type Kuznets, en contradiction avec le discours académique relatif à la datation des fameux cycles de type Kondratieff.

Keywords: Spectral analysis, economic cycles, comparison, cliometrics, GDP, OECD, Kuznets.

Mots clefs : Analyse spectrale, cycles économiques, comparaison, cliométrie, PIB, OCDE, Kuznets.

JEL classification: B15, B16, B22, B23, B41, C1, C22, C32, C82, E01, E32, N10

1. BETA/CNRS, University of Strasbourg Institute for Advanced Study, 61 Avenue de la Forêt Noire, 67085 Strasbourg Cedex, France. E-mail: cdiebolt@unistra.fr

Introduction

The dream of all cycle theorists has been to develop a general theory so good that it could serve as a code translating the meaning of present forces into terms of future movements. Imagine how simple the life of an economist would be if he could refer the symptoms of the past and current economic situations to a handbook, which would diagnose what was wrong with the economy and prescribe what should be done to restore it to health. This remains a dream. Our knowledge of the complex body economics is still too imperfect to be codified into a handbook. The best we can do is to synthesise existing theories of why the circular flow of socio-economic moves in the rhythms that we call long movements of the Kondratieff type, Kuznets cycles, Juglar cycles etc.

A cycle is a regular, self-repeating fluctuation of relatively fixed length and amplitude, often existing around some other trend. Economic cycles are not precise. They are self-repeating, but they vary in amplitude, and to some degree in length. An economic cycle consists of expansions occurring at about the same time in many economic activities, followed by a similar general recession, contractions and revivals which emerge into the expansion phase of the next cycle. The cycle is not married to a calendar. But there is a systematic, alternating sequence of cause and consequence that takes the economy through prosperity and depression.

The short-term and intermediate-term economic cycle noted by C. Juglar[2] and S. Kuznets[3] were easily perceptible fluctuations created by oversupply or excess demand for products, services, or money. C. Juglar was the first to correlate clearly perceptions of economics, statistics, and history to use them in the understanding of mechanisms of alternating prosperity and recession. C. Juglar analysed banking figures, interest rates, prices, marriage rates, and other evidence to support his notion of these major crises. He believed that he had discovered a single wave underlying the movements of world economies. More widely accepted in recent years is the 15- to 25-year swing in economic growth rates uncovered by Nobel laureate S. Kuznets. The cycle is more evident in the United States than

2. Juglar [1889].

3. Kuznets [1930].

elsewhere. M. Abramovitz recognises the Kuznets cycle as associated with population growth and immigration.[4] Most economists hold that this cycle was material only for the period from 1840 to 1914.

There is another type of cycle, less perceptible because its duration is longer, its dynamics less obvious, and its origins less well defined. Economists who refer to it as the long wave or long cycle of the Kondratieff type.[5] More than 160 years ago, H. Clarke described this longer cycle, which was different from others affecting the economies of Europe. In 1847 he published a paper in the British Railway Journal called *Physical Economy* describing fluctuations between 1793 and his own time. H. Clarke offered no explanations. He merely recorded the figures. At the beginning of the twentieth century, several economists suggested that a long economic cycle was identifiable: G. Cassel, J. van Gelderen, A. Spiethoff, S. De Wolff etc.[6]

Thus, the long cycle that bears his name was not originated by N. Kondratieff. In describing the origins of his theory, N. Kondratieff wrote that he arrived at the hypothesis concerning the existence of long cycles in the years 1919-1920. Without going into a special analysis, he formulated his own thesis for the first time in his study *The World Economy and Economic Fluctuations in the War and Post-War Period.* During the winter and spring of 1925, he wrote a special study, *Long Business Cycles,* published in Moscow by the Institute of Conjuncture in 1925. N. Kondratieff worked out his theories on the basis of wholesale prices, interest on British consoles and French rents, deposits at French saving banks, French trade, *per capita* coal, wage data of English farm and textile workers and French coal miners, pig-iron production in the United States, coal consumption in France, gold production, and other production series from 1780 to 1926.[7] He used regression analyses of quantified data and a

4. Abramovitz [1961].

5. As noted by one referee, "the empirical evidence of Kondratieff cycles (as well as of Kuznets cycles) has always been discussed controversially. This is already indicated by Georges Garvy (who was born in Russia as Georg Bronstein and therefore knew the early Russian literature very well) in his paper "Kondratieff's Theory of Long Cycles."

6. Woytinsky [1931].

7. Wagenführ [1929].

nine-year moving average to eliminate minor fluctuations.[8] With his development of a theory of investment cycles, N.D. Kondratieff was the first to put forward the idea that long cycles originated in the very functioning of the economic system. An increase in saving increases the possibility for investing available capital and causes the long upward period. Reduction in saving reduces investment and causes the downward swing.

J.A. Schumpeter[9] enriched the field of interpretation of long cycles by introducing the role of innovations. Grouped in time and concentrated in a few branches of industry, innovations govern regular cycles. They first tend to attract capital, and then the diffusion of the innovations throughout the economy modifies the economic balance and increases the risk of failure for the next innovations. The economy must use a recession process to assimilate the progress of the upward phase before the system approaches equilibrium again and allows for new innovations.

From 1945 to 1970, in spite of notable work by G. Imbert[10] and U. Weinstock,[11] less attention was paid to research on long movements of the economy because of the continuous growth observed in the economies of developed countries and the dominance of Keynesian thinking. With the change of this situation in the early 1970s and the renewal of research on long cycles, the theories resulting from the work of J.A. Schumpeter have been circulating more widely.[12] But, since that time, one of the greatest difficulties encountered in the study of long cycles remains: the main adopted statistical approach (trend-deviations and moving averages) includes the production of more or less artificial phenomena.

In this paper, I propose an alternative methodology: spectral analysis. Our method was first of all determined by the search for the greatest possible objectivity in the observation of time series and then by the

8. Kondratieff [1926].

9. Schumpeter [1939].

10. Imbert [1959].

11. Weinstock [1964].

12. Mensch [1977], Petzina & Van Roon Eds [1981], Kleinknecht [1987], Freeman [1996], Freeman & Louçã [2001].

possibility of applying it to a large number of series. This two-fold requirement was dictated by the need to anticipate the criticism generally aimed at statistical studies on long movements in the economy. It has had limited applications in cliometrics to date.[13] Nevertheless, in empirical macroeconomics we must mention some leading contributions, closely linked to our own research agenda.

D. Backus and P. Kehoe[14] study fluctuations in output, prices, and money in ten countries for which a century of data are available. They find especially a great deal of regularity in the cyclical behavior or real quantities.

B. A'Hearn and U. Woitek[15] establish stylized facts about business cycles in the late 19th century, using spectral analysis techniques which allow an intuitive description and analysis of cyclical structure in economic fluctuations. Analysis of industrial production data for 13 countries permits the following generalizations. In the advanced North Atlantic economies, a fairly regular long cycle with a periodicity of 7-10 years is identified in all countries. This component explains a substantial fraction of overall variation in industrial production. There is some evidence of a less regular, less powerful short cycle of 3–5 years duration. In peripheral economies experience is varied, but it is more often the short cycle that exercises greater influence. The long cycle component is shown to be highly correlated among the core economies, much less so between core and peripheral economies, and least of all among peripheral economies. The long cycle is more highly correlated among countries with important trading ties and those on a metallic monetary standard throughout the period.

A. Kose, C. Otrok and C. Whiteman[16] investigate the common dynamic properties of business-cycle fluctuations across countries, regions, and the world. They employ a Bayesian dynamic latent factor model to

13. Interested readers should see, in particular, Charles, Darné, Diebolt and Ferrara (in press), Ewijk [1982], Gerster [1988], Reijnders [1988] and Metz [2002; 2008], Diebolt [2005; 2012].

14. Backus & Kehoe [1992].

15. A'Hearn & Woitek [2001].

16. Kose, Otrok & Whiteman [2003].

estimate common components in macroeconomic aggregates (output, consumption, and investment) in a 60-country sample covering seven regions of the world. The results indicate that a common world factor is an important source of volatility for aggregates in most countries, providing evidence for a world business cycle. They find also that region-specific factors play only a minor role in explaining fluctuations in economic activity. Finally they document similarities and differences across regions, countries, and aggregates.

M. Uebele[17] analyzes international business cycles in Europe from 1862 to 1913 using disaggregated data and Dynamic Factor Analysis. In comparison with estimates of real national product, he came to the conclusion that there is more evidence for international business cycles in disaggregated data of Germany, France and Great Britain before World War I. This is because data used to construct historical national accounts are often not sufficient, and especially because little is known about general price fluctuations. Thus, national products in current prices show higher degrees of international correlation than deflated ones although price indices themselves are not very well correlated across countries.

Very recently, A. Karadimitropoulou and M. León-Ledesma[18] ask if sector-specific factors common to all countries play an important role in explaining business cycle co-movement. They address this question by analyzing international co-movements of value added (VA) growth in a multi-sector dynamic factor model. The model contains a world factor, country-specific factors, sector-specific factors, and idiosyncratic components. They estimate the model using Bayesian methods for 30 disaggregated sectors in the G7 economies for the 1974-2004 period. Their findings show that, although there is a substantial role for sector-specific factors, fluctuations are dominated by country-factors. The world factor appears to play a minimal role because, when using aggregate data, the world factor captures both the factor common to all countries and industries and the factor common to the same industry across countries.

17. Uebele [2011].

18. Karadimitropoulou & León-Ledesma [2013].

Methodology

Spectral analysis makes it possible to divide a particular category of long-term data sets into a set of oscillations with different periods (breaking down any time series into a sum of periodic functions) and then to show the links between the components with the same frequency in the various data sets examined. Each of these stages has obvious cliometric interest. The first, by showing all the frequency components of a data set and by isolating—if it exists—the most important frequency component (and its harmonics) reveals the cyclical behaviour of a time series and shows the frequency and amplitude characteristics of this cyclical movement. The second stage makes it possible to compare the periodic movements of two series and to establish a correlation between them. The latter stage therefore seems particularly suited to the aim of this article. The mathematical nature of the data sets to which the method is applied is analysed briefly before identification of the main estimators used.

1. The nature of the time sets: generating stationary and determinable processes

The spectral method is applied essentially to determinable stationary series. Understanding the reason requires an explanation of what I mean by generating, stationary and determinable processes.

1.1. Generating process

A given time series x_t ($t = 1, 2, .., n$) is assumed to be the accomplishment of a particular process:

$$X_t,\ t = -\infty, \ldots, -1, 0, +1, \ldots, +\infty$$

The generating process shows how the time series is formed at each instant. However, its stochastic nature means that the real value of the series at any moment cannot be determined.

Thus $X_t + aX_{t-1} = \varepsilon_t$ is a generating process, ε_t being a random term. This process is defined by its first and second moments. These are generally functions of time:

$$E\left[X_t\right] = m_t$$
$$E\left[\left(X_t - m\right)^2\right] = \sigma_t^2$$
$$E\left[\left(X_t - m_t\right)\left(X_s - m_s\right)\right] = \mu\left(t, s\right)$$

In which $\mu(t, s)$ is the covariance of X_t and X_s.

1.2. Stationary process

A very important class of series is that given by processes whose moments are not functions of time, that is to say:

$$E[X_t = m]$$
$$E[(X_t - m)^2] = \sigma^2$$
$$E[(X_t - m_t)(X_s - m_s)] = \mu(t - s) = \mu_\tau$$

where $\tau = t - s$ for all t, s.

Such series are referred to as being stationary of the second order. They possess excellent properties including the particularly useful feature of making it possible to estimate the different moments by means in time instead of overall means. In other words:

$$\bar{x} = \frac{1}{n}\sum_{t=1}^{n} x_t$$

$$s^2 = \frac{1}{n}\sum_{t=1}^{n} (x_t - \bar{x})^2$$

$$c_t = \frac{1}{n - \tau}\sum_{t=1}^{n-\tau} (x_t - \bar{x})\,(x_{t-\tau} - \bar{x})$$

provide efficient, unbiased estimators of m, σ^2, μ_τ respectively.

1.3. Determinable process

An important theorem developed by Cramer ensures that stationary series of this kind can be broken down into a set of separate sinusoidal oscillations whose characteristics, amplitudes and relative differences are random.

There will generally be a very large number or even an infinity of such oscillations, each of which is very small and the process is then said to be indeterminable. This contrasts with determinable processes consisting of a finite number of sinusoidal oscillations, each of which will have a finite non null amplitude.

2. Estimators: estimation of spectra and cross-spectra

2.1. Estimation of spectra

The amplitudes of the different oscillations (from the breakdown of stationary series) are random variables that can be defined by the scale of the values that they might have. A variance corresponds to each given period oscillation and this defines what is called the spectrum of the process envisaged. The differences between the various sinusoids are insignificant. The spectrum of a stochastic process $[X_t]$ is the function $f(\omega)$ defining within a multiplicative constant the expected value of the square of the amplitude of frequency ω in the Fourier decomposition. The spectrum thus describes the importance of the various frequencies in the process in question.

The calculations are as follows. For stationary processes, a bias-free estimator can be calculated from a single realisation of the process, that is to say from a particular time series X_t in which $(t = 1, 2, \ldots, T)$. This estimator is the periodogram and can be defined as:

$$I(\omega) = \frac{1}{2\pi} \sum_{\theta=-T-1}^{T-1} v_\theta \cos \omega\theta$$

v_θ being approximately the empirical autocovariance, and more precisely:

$$v_\theta = \frac{1}{T} \sum_{t=1}^{T-\theta} (X_t - \bar{X})\,(X_{t+\theta} - \bar{X})$$

($\bar{X}$ is the empirical mean of the series).

Although it has no bias, the periodogram is not a good estimator of the spectrum because it is not convergent. This is why the erratic function $I(\omega)$ is replaced by a more regular function representing the mean trend of variations of $I(\omega)$ with ω. This is referred to as the smoothing of the periodogram. The smoothed function is then:

$$f'(\omega) = \frac{1}{2\pi} \sum_{\theta=-m}^{m} \left(1 + \cos\frac{\theta\pi}{m}\right) v_\theta \cos \omega\theta$$

This formula is Tuckey–Hanning's estimation function (or window). There are other estimation formulas, especially Parzen's that causes less leakage in non-adjacent frequency bands but leads to higher correlation between the successive estimated values of the spectrum.

Finally, to improve spectrum estimation, the X_t series is generally filtered beforehand by subjecting it to a transformation in such a way that it is possible *a priori* to consider that the spectrum of the filtered series is more representative. In many of these practices, filtering thus eliminates the trend of the series in such a way that the hypothesis of the stationarity of the generating process seems less coarsely imprecise (especially for economic data series). The filter chosen here is that proposed by Hodrick and Prescott [1997], for several reasons. Firstly, it is easy to apply. Secondly, abundant literature shows that its statistical properties are satisfactory. Finally, it is commonly used in the literature and in the empirical analyses performed by national bodies and international organisations [Bouthevillain, 2002].

I thus take a series $[X_t]$ that has a trend (trend component g_t) and that fluctuates around the trend (cycle component c_t), that is to say:

$$X_t = g_t + c_t$$

The idea is then that of minimising the sum of the squares of deviations of $[X_t]$ in relation to its trend g_t while conserving a smooth trend, that is to say in which g_t does not vary too much between two successive periods:

$$\min_{g_t} \sum_{t=1}^{T} \left[(X_t - g_t)^2 + \lambda\big((g_{t+1} - g_t)(g_t - g_{t-1})\big)^2 \right]$$

λ (the multiplier related to the size of the constraint) is defined as the weighting awarded to the fact of having a 'smooth' trend. The choice of λ depends on the frequency of observation of the data; in general $\lambda = 100$ for annual data, 400 for half-yearly data and 1,600 for quarterly data. The series on which filtering is performed are usual the log of the series by level.

2.2. Estimation of cross-spectra

Cross-spectra examine the existing relations between the spectral components taken in pairs for two given time series. Generalising the case to a single variable, (X_t, Y_t) are stationary if their first and second moments are both independent of time. In this case, one of the results of the theory of stationary processes is that the component centred at ω_j is independent not only of the other components of the variable, but also of the components of any other variable whether or not it is centred on ω_j. A full description of the system of relation between two stationary processes just requires knowledge of the extent to which the frequency component ω of the process $[X_t]$ is correlated with the frequency component ω of the process $[Y_t]$ and knowledge of their phase difference.

This correlation between two frequency components in two processes is given by:

$$C^2(\omega) = \frac{c^2(\omega) + q^2(\omega)}{f_x(\omega) f_y(\omega)}$$

$0 \leq C^2(\omega) \leq 1$, $C(\omega)$ is called the cospectrum and $q(\omega)$ is the quadrature. $C^2(\omega)$ is the square of coherence at ω (equal to the square of the coefficient of correlation). The measurement of the phase difference between the frequency components of the two processes is given by:

$$\Phi(\omega) = \arctan\left(\frac{q(\omega)}{c(\omega)}\right)$$

It can therefore be said that the amplitude cross-spectrum of two processes $[X_t]$ and $[Y_t]$ defines the expected values of the product of the amplitudes with which each frequency ω affects $[X_t]$ and $[Y_t]$, and that the phase cross-spectrum defines the expected phase difference with which each frequency is involved in the two processes.

Spectral analysis, whose theoretical basis has thus been described briefly, is a logical extension of our work on outliers, non-stationarity tests in macroeconomic time series and that on long memory.[19] It is a particularly suitable mathematical tool for the development of our research programme and should give good results on condition that the statistical data series used are suitable for it. These series are examined below.

Data and the results of spectral analysis

3. Statistical data

The aim of our research is the comparison of the behaviour of the per capita GDP in 15 OECD countries. For this I use the now well-known database drawn up by Maddison [1995], expressed in 1990 US dollars for the period 1870-1994, and extended (until 2000) by EUROSTAT indicators.

Checking theoretical hypotheses on economic growth requires always new statistical sets.[20] The method of quantitative history launched in the 1960s by S. Kuznets, J. Marczewski and F. Perroux, is essential for reaching this aim. It consists of assembling historical facts in homogenous, comparable time units in order to measure changes in intervals of time (generally annually). The advantage of this method is that the moment of operation of the observer's choice is shifted. Instead of acting while observing the reality to be described, he operates during the construction of the reference system serving in the recording of facts rendered conceptually homogeneous. This methodology should allow for an empirical verification or the rejection of initial hypotheses hinged on the pattern of theoretical interpretation. However, a map is not the area it plots, and care must be

19. See especially Darné and Diebolt [2004, 2005], Diebolt [2005], Diebolt and Doliger [2008], Diebolt, Guiraud and Monteils [2003].

20. Interested readers should see, in particular Battilossi, Escario & Foreman-Peck [2013], Beach, Norman & Wills [2013], Becker, Cinnirella & Woessmann [2012], Bhaskar, Gupta [2012], Borowiecki [2013], Bugni [2012], Carson [2012], Clément [2012], Craig & Hammond [2013], Dupont & Weiss [2013], Edvinsson [2013], Felice [2012], Galor [2012], Greasley & Madsen [2013], Haupert & Murray [2012], Ho, Lai & Gau [2013], Holmlund [2013], James, McAndrews& Weiman [2013], Klemp [2012], Komlos & Küchenhoff [2012], Lampe & Sharp [2013], Nason & Vahey [2012], Parent [2012], Prentice [2012], Rei [2013], Sella & Marchionatti [2012], Sharp & Weisdorf [2012], Tirado, Pons, Paluzie & Martinez-Galarraga [2013], Zehetmayer [2013].

taken not to confuse reality and its description. The approach is not applicable to isolated historical events. It is used to describe the *history of the masses*, but is not sensitive to the *history of the heroes*. It is only an image of reality and does not draw all of reality's contours. Quantitative history does not aim at replacing traditional descriptive history. On the contrary, the two forms of historical investigation are strictly complementary and hence indispensable for a better knowledge of the past. The application of quantitative methods can nevertheless profoundly renew the terms that have progressively become legitimate. The great merit of statistical formalism is that it allows for the examination of the logical and quantitative consequences of historical proposals, which could not be obtained by a discussion based on literary documents and the like.

The proposed method has two advantages. Firstly, it is of immediate practical interest as it is an original reconstruction of the process of growth. It is also of theoretical interest as it provides better knowledge of the mechanisms governing the long development of the economic system. We are nevertheless aware that the statistical work provides only the quantitative aspect of changes in structure. Although it is important, it is not sufficient to provide the complete picture of the sequence of facts.

The decisive role of deductive theories in empirical research must therefore be stressed. Starting with a general idea, they attempt at identifying symptoms in reality by means of a chronological series of statistics. Like the *Frankfurter Gesellschaft für Konjunkturforschung* (founded in 1926 by E. Altschul), we recommend an economic semiology that would implement the results of statistical research and deductive reasoning of the theory. There is no conflict or compartmentalisation between empirical research and deductive theory; on the contrary, these disciplines are only truly valuable individually if they draw on each other's results. The validity of the theoretical hypotheses thus depends both on their external coherence, i.e. on their conformity with real facts, and their internal coherence, i.e. their ability to provide one or more solutions to the raised questions. The general equilibrium theory is extremely significant in this respect. It has given rise to much work concerning the validity of its bases and of the teachings drawn from it. In contrast, research on the existence of a solution has been carried out by only a handful of specialists.

Here, it is still possible to discuss the coherence of a theoretical hypothesis, but it is more important to submit it to empirical verification.

3.1. The scope of quantitative history

Quantitative history aims at drawing up a general macroscopic synthesis by constructing models integrated at the national level with the prospect of possible links between several national models. This requires a succession of research operations, the most important of which is the creation of chronological data series covering the whole of the period under consideration.

The initial work consists of sorting dozens or even hundreds of volumes of old statistics. The figures are transcribed and reclassified using a pre-established model (e.g. using national budget items). This meticulous research is a question of doing rather than learning and is carried out in the silence of archives and libraries. The classifications used in statistical documents change according to the year and the recording administration. It is necessary at all times to exert some judgment to decide on the matching of the original item and the item under which the figure is to be transcribed.

3.2. The quantitative history method

The quantitative history method applies when a large number of causes and their complexity and intermingling make the use of experimental methods impossible. The moment at which the observer's choice intervenes is shifted. Instead of being set during observation of the reality to be described, it applies during the elaboration of the system of reference used to count facts thus rendered conceptually homogeneous.

The definition just given essentially consists of three main phases:

- collection of documents;
- analysis of the data collected;
- interpretation of the results.

The first phase is mainly descriptive in order to prepare the real work of the researcher by co-ordinating the collected information. It is a preliminary task required for a serious analysis. All the documents related to the field of study are assembled. The data from archived documents must not be merely recorded, but have to be subjected to intelligent, perspicacious criticism. Some are discarded when considered unreliable; others must be corrected when their interpretation reveals sources of error. Finally, estimates may be required to fill gaps. The final results are assembled in a statistical table.

Having arrived at this mass of numerical information, the researcher must then put the figures in a logical order and classify them according to a previously established nomenclature. The data are reduced, substituted by a small number of representative series drawn by calculation from the ordered mass of numerical data.

The third and final interpretation phase consists of drawing conclusions from the analysis. It is a decisive stage as here an attempt is made to explain the observations. There is a vast scope of interpretative possibilities, ranging from merely checking hypotheses to forecasting future developments.

One has to be aware that the conclusions drawn from the analysis of the statistical sets contain a degree of uncertainty. Also the degree of the validity of the general observations has to be considered. Quantitative history is a long, slow process that is never free from difficulties. There are hesitations to overcome and problems to solve at every stage, as each new research operation is a new beginning and there are decisions that can only be taken alone.

4. Cliometrics

As mentioned above, the series are decomposed additively into a trend, a cycle and a random component (in which the cyclical and irregular components respect the statistical property of stationarity) to reveal the different cyclicity in the series studied. In other words, I plot the trajectory of per capita GDP between long trends and conjunctural cycles.

The approach common to most of these methods consists of firstly removing the trend from the series under study then isolating the cycle. Here we have left out the issue of seasonality. There are three main methods to remove the trend:

1) estimating a linear and deterministic trend and then deducting it from the series,

2) differentiating the series to eliminate the stochastic trend,

3) applying the Hodrick-Prescott [1997] filter.

The first two methods which, following D. DeJong [2007], we call respectively detrending and differencing, are based on the implicit assumption that the series under study, y_t grows at an approximately constant rate. If we take the logarithm of the series in question, the temporal variations of $\ln y_t$ are equivalent to the growth rate of y_t. Indeed $(\partial \ln y_t)/\partial t = (\partial y_t)/\partial t)/y_t = g_y$.

The "detrending" process supposes that the series has a *deterministic* trend, thus obeying a process which generates data in the form of:

$$y_t = y_0(1 + g_t)^t e^{u_t}$$

where u_t is a second-order stationary stochastic process. In logarithms, (1) becomes:

$$\text{ln} y_t = \text{ln} y_0 + t\text{ln}\left(1 + g_y\right) + u_t = \text{ln} y_0 + g_t t + u_t \qquad (2)$$

as $\ln\left(1 + g_y\right)$ can be approximated by g_y It is easy to estimate g_y in (2) by ordinary least squares, then simply subtracting this trend from $\text{ln}y_t$. The series is then said to be trend stationary.

In comparison, the differentiation method supposes that y_t has a stochastic trend and that the process generating y_t is given by:

$$\begin{aligned} y_t &= y_0 e^{\varepsilon_t} \\ \varepsilon_t &= \delta + \varepsilon_{t-1} + u_t \end{aligned} \qquad (3)$$

where u_t is once again a second-order stationary stochastic process. By taking the logarithms, (3) becomes

$$\ln y_t = \ln y_0 + \varepsilon_t. \quad (4)$$

The first difference of $\ln y_t$ in (4), taking into account (3), is given by:

$$\ln y_t - \ln y_{t-1} = \varepsilon_t - \varepsilon_{t-1} = \delta + u_t \quad (5)$$

As we have already mentioned, the $\ln y_t$ series is then said to be *difference stationary*. The δ estimator is equal to the average of $\ln y_t - \ln y_{t-1}$, which you then simply need to subtract from (5).

The choice between these two procedures occurs exclusively according to the decision whether the generating process is given by (2) or by (4). It is a difficult choice to make, since, as we have seen, the controversy initiated by C. Nelson and C. Plosser [1982] on the existence of a unit root is not quite conclusive.

The third approach to remove the trend of a series is Hodrick-Prescott's. It starts with the decomposition of $\ln y_t$ in the form:

$$\ln y_t = g_t + c_t, \quad (6)$$

where g_t is the growth component in $\ln y_t$ and c_t its cyclic component. The following step consists to estimate the values of c_t and g_t in minimising:

$$\textstyle\sum_{t=1}^{T} c_t^2 + \lambda \sum_{t=1}^{T} (g_t - 2g_{t-1} + g_{t-2})^2 \quad (7)$$

λ being a given parameter (generally taken as equal to 1,600 for quarterly series). Suppressing the trend leads in the end to:

$$\ln y_t - \hat{g}_t = \hat{c}_t. \quad (8)$$

In addition to these three techniques, there are filters called "band-pass filters" which do not require to remove first the trend of a series in order to extract the cyclical component; the general principle of these filters – Baxter-King [1999] and Christiano-Fitzgerald [2003] – is to eliminate all the cycles located outside a defined frequency spectrum (between 6 and 40 semesters). By proceeding in such a way, one would obtain an "optimal" filter; however in practice one can only get an approximation.

In the end there are as many different cycles as there are filters and even more, if one varies the specific parameters of each of these filters. This is the main criticism which can be addressed to this type of approach. One could add that it leads to fallacious fluctuations: see on that point Cogley [2006]. Furthermore, when the aim is to identify the cycle, one always comes back to Burns and Mitchell's definition. In this paper, I performed therefore a Hodrick-Prescott filtering.

Figure 1: LOGGDPt[21] series

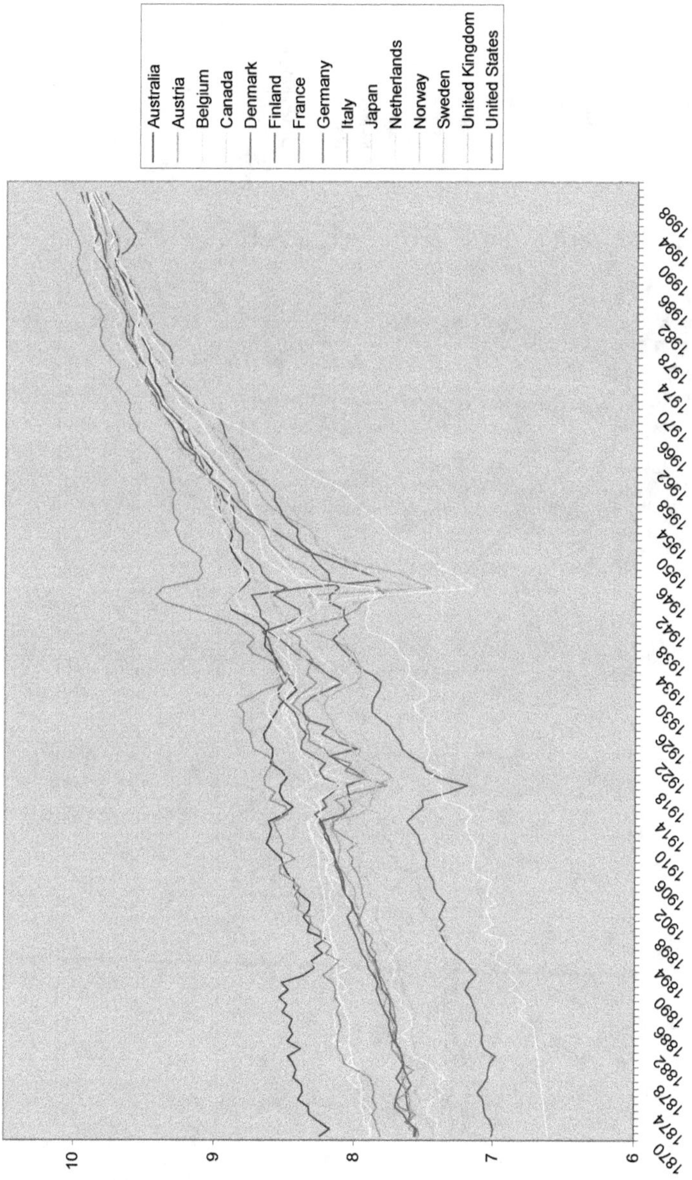

21. All the series are log-transformed.

Figure 2: Growth trends

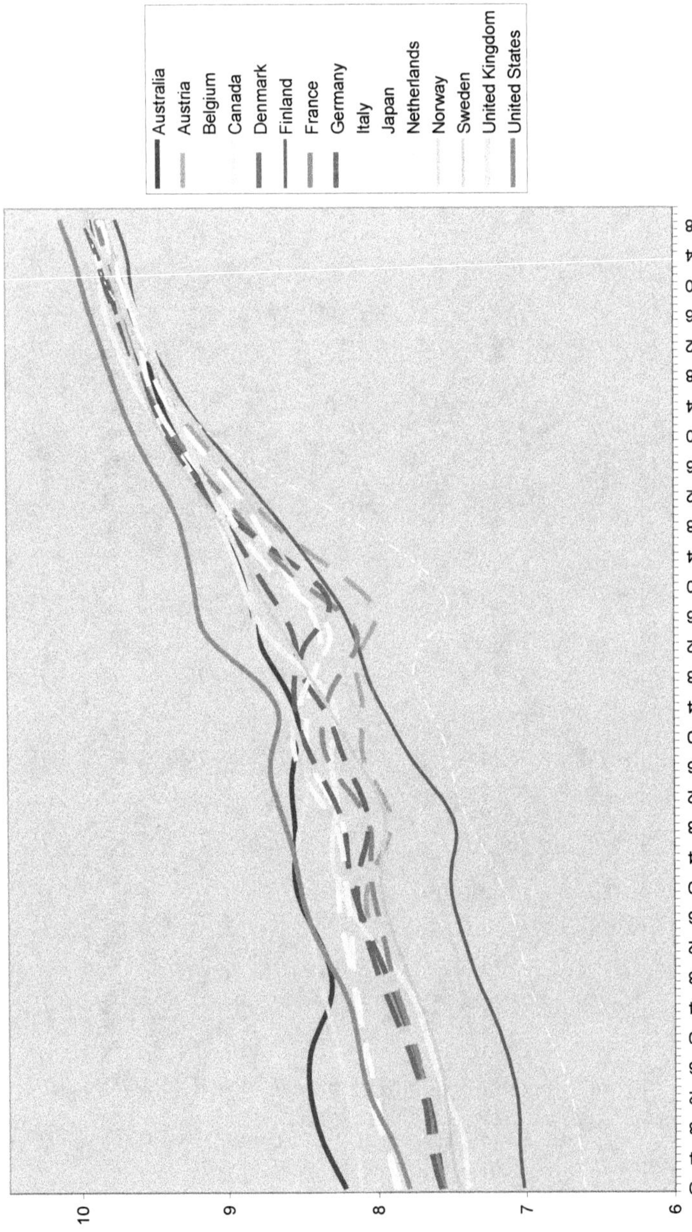

Prior comparison of the trend movements of per capita GDP (Figure 2) shows overall that until 1970 growth in English-speaking countries (United States, United Kingdom, Australia and Canada) was greater than growth in the countries of continental Europe (France, Germany, Denmark, Belgium, Austria and the Netherlands), which was in turn greater than that in Nordic countries (Finland, Norway and Sweden) and in Japan, which trailed at the back of all the OECD countries.[22] However, the growth trend has displayed convergence since the 1970 break. This would seem to be a sign of a catching up phenomenon as described by Barro and Sala-í-Martin [1992].

To test this, I develop a cointegration study using Johansen's test [1988] to find out whether there was a long-term stationary relation between the different series in order to confirm or invalidate our graphic observations. To set up the test, I used λ[23] calculated from the values, λ_i, of matrix A defining the long-term relations of the model:

$$\Delta Y_t = A_0 + AY_{t-p} + A_1\Delta Y_{t-1} + A_2\Delta Y_{t-2} + \cdots + A_{p-1}\Delta Y_{t-p-1} + \varepsilon_t.$$

The calculation is as follows: $\lambda = -n\sum_{i=r+1}^{k}\ln(1-\lambda_i)$. It obeys a probability law (similar to a chi-square) tabulated using the Johansen and Joselius simulation. The test operates by the exclusion of alternative hypotheses concerning the number of cointegration relations r. First, the null hypothesis H_0: $r = 0$ is tested against the alternative hypothesis $r > 0$. If H_0 cannot be rejected, the test procedure stops as there are no cointegration relations. If not, the next stage is performed consisting of $r = 1$ against $r > 1$. The pattern is repeated as long as H_0 is rejected. If H_0 is rejected in the test $r = k$ against $r > k$, this means that the variables are not cointegrated.

22. Italy is an exception here. It is at the level of the Scandinavian countries.

23. The λ used here is different from that used in the Hodrick-Prescott filter.

Table 1: Johansen's cointegration test

No. of CE(s)	Eigenvalue	Statistic	5 Percent	1 Percent
None	0.997166	4911.993	NA	NA
At most 1	0.992898	4161.153	NA	NA
At most 2	0.989859	3527.883	NA	NA
At most 3	0.982107	2940.208	NA	NA
At most 4 **	0.979245	2425.217	277.71	293.44
At most 5 **	0.958402	1929.224	233.13	247.18
At most 6 **	0.923238	1522.221	192.89	204.95
At most 7 **	0.900955	1193.640	156.00	168.36
At most 8 **	0.885827	897.6809	124.24	133.57
At most 9 **	0.828015	619.9159	94.15	103.18
At most 10 **	0.675564	394.5912	68.52	76.07
At most 11 **	0.598799	250.5057	47.21	54.46
At most 12 **	0.502727	133.6043	29.68	35.65
At most 13 **	0.291853	44.18128	15.41	20.04
At most 14	6.30E-05	0.008061	3.76	6.65

Our tests show clearly that the trend of per capita GDP series, that is to say national growth trends, are cointegrated. This does not mean that these trends are identical but that they are linked by linear relations, that is to say that they have common factors.

This analysis is therefore continued with on the one had a study of the national cyclical features of the 15 OECD countries and on the other a search for common factors in these cycles.

4.1. Analysis of spectra

The characteristics of the national cycles are first analysed individually.

Indeed, the aim is to find out whether all the countries display the same propensity for cyclical fluctuations and the same regularity in these fluctuations. It must be possible to determine whether a country typology can be shown according to the cyclical properties as the impetus and propagation of fluctuations at the international scale can only be fully understood if this national heterogeneity is taken into account [Fayolle and Micolet, 1997]. This is addressed by first analysing the graphic representations of the cyclical component and then the spectral density.

Graphic analysis of the fluctuations establishes in a general manner that the different countries are characterised by relative cyclical regularity but that the features of this cyclicity are unevenly distributed at the international level. It can be seen in particular that the cycles in Nordic countries (Norway, Finland and Sweden) have limited amplitude but are very regular, whereas the economic cycle is more marked and displays greater amplitude in all the other countries (except in Australia, where it is similar to that of the Scandinavian countries), especially between the wars.

However, these results should viewed in relative terms and subjected to spectral analysis as the cycle typology shows that duration and amplitude characteristics vary from one cycle to another and above all that cycles are similar to sets of Russian dolls and their influences can strengthen or oppose each other depending on whether the swings coincide or not or are in phase or not. Whence the advantage of spectral analysis for separating and analysing the different cycles integrated by per capita GDP and then putting forward a more perspicacious country typology in the relations of impetus and propagation of fluctuations at the international scale.

Application of the spectral density methodology described above showed an interaction between two types of cycles in each of the 15 countries analysed. Indeed, the spectral density functions (Figure 3) show that the cyclical movement can be decomposed into two distinct cyclical components. One is short and of the Kitchin type with a frequency of 3-5 years and relatively moderate amplitude and the other an intermediate phenomenon between the Juglar business cycle and a long Kondratieff type of cycle. The latter, a Kuznets type cycle with a frequency of 15-20 years and comparatively large amplitude, underlies GDP conjuncture.

Figure 3: Spectral Density GDPT

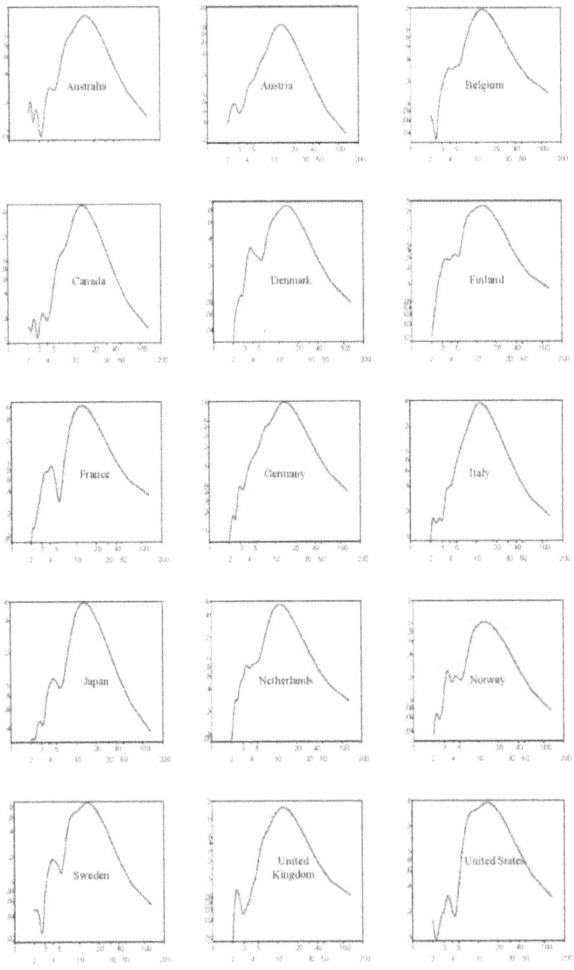

It should be noted that although the swing of short cycle is smaller than that of the intermediate cycle, it nevertheless has sufficient amplitude and volatility to inflect the overall movement of the cycle that may account for the differences observed in the graphic analyses at cycle aggregate level and thus invalidate the statistical characteristics generally used in the analysis of cycles. This justifies the use of spectral analysis and hence the analysis of cyclical international relations between fluctuations in the same categories.

With this double cyclical movement of per capita GDP combining short oscillations and slow intermediate movements, I consider that national economic fluctuations are first of all governed by storage behaviour. Here, the minor cycles reflect essentially storage and release phenomena by businesses and above all large investments involving large amounts of capital such as those for the construction industry or for transport and seen as a response to population factors as Kuznets type intermediate cycles basically govern conjuncture. The economic situation is therefore governed essentially by a 15-20-year frequency and not by short cycles of the Kitchin or Juglar type or by long movements of the Kondratieff type. I consider that the driving force underlying this frequency can be compared to the mechanisms proposed by Kuznets, that is to say an economic reaction to demographic mechanisms, for example via the movement of large investments or the labour market. Indeed, the links between the functioning of the labour market and demographic movements may be an explanation, in particular through three essential mechanisms linked to demographic factors.[24] These are first of all a cycle linking work and employment (the productivity cycle), then an effect linking unemployment and wages (the Phillips effect) and finally a link between demand and income (the consumption function). These three mechanisms also play greater or lesser roles according to the period and the country; they can increase or reduce the cycles and hence account for the international disparities observed.

This preliminary study of the characteristics of national cycles that shows agreement between the cycles characterising the different countries is followed by a study of the impetus and propagation relations at the international scale through cross-spectral analysis.

24. Easterlin [1968].

4.2. Analysis of cross-spectra

The search for international relations between the main economic cycles is the other fundamental component of this analysis.[25] I therefore incorporate the cycle approach in addressing the entire international economy through the multivariate spectral approach (i.e. cross-spectral analysis). This makes it possible to examine the similarities and synchronisation of the different national cycles. Here, I first analyse the *coherence*[26] between the different cycles using coherence of 0.7 or more as the criterion of significance. This is followed by study of the *phases*[27] of the cyclical processes whose coherence is significant. The results of the two methods can be represented schematically as follows to make it easier to examine and interpret the results:

25. This section has the ambition, with an alternative methodology, to be an original contribution to previous research with similar scientific orientations, but not necessarily similar aggregates and/or results. See especially A'Hearn & Woitek [2001], Backus & Kehoe [1992], Karadimitropoulou & Leon-Ledesma [2013], Kose, Otrok & Whiteman [2003], and Uebele [2011].

26. Coherence makes it possible to measure the degree of linear correlation between components of the same frequency in two processes. The closer it is to 1 for a given frequency, the more the two processes move in a similar manner for this frequency or periodicity.

27. The phase makes it possible to measure the time shift of a process in relation to another. A positive phase shows that the second series is ahead of the first and the opposite if it is negative. Interpretation of the phase is then strongly linked with coherence as the analysis of a lag between two processes is only meaningful if the processes are related, that is to say if their coherence is high.

Figure 4: Relation between intermediate cycles of the Kuznets type

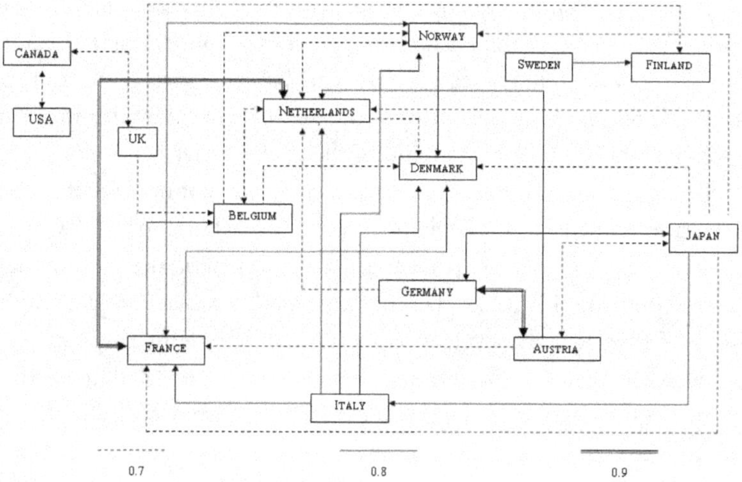

Coherence is represented by lines (dotted, unbroken or double unbroken) indicating their degree of importance (0.7, 0.8 and 0.9 respectively), while the phases are shown by the direction of the coherence relation with the beginning of an arrow showing the process that is ahead with regard to the process at its extremity (a double arrow means that there is no lag between the processes—they are synchronous).

It is seen in a general manner that the impetus and forces governing national intermediate cycles are not independent between countries and there is thus strong interconnection between national cyclicity. This can be shown in more detail by a grouping in three geographic zones and linked to notions of similar, common cycles. Indeed, a distinction should be drawn between a similar cycle and a common cycle. A cycle is referred to as being similar when the cyclical component that drives the movement of each series is founded on the same propagation mechanism but engendered by a specific impulse series so that the cyclical components can be markedly different and desynchronised. This similar cycle can be called common when the impulse series applied to it are perfectly correlated, that is to say the cyclical components are perfectly synchronised and differ only in their amplitude [Bentoglio, Fayolle and Lemoine, 2001].

Using this, a first parallel can be made between the English-speaking countries (United States, Canada and the United Kingdom) that are linked in a joint cycle through their common historical, political and geographic context. A second, much wider parallel can be set between the European countries in the broad sense (the countries of continental Europe and Scandinavia) where the characteristic of the cycle is that it is largely similar in all the countries of this zone and sometimes common with certain neighbouring countries (e.g. Belgium and the Netherlands and Germany and Austria), explained in particular by a flexibility of the labour market and geographic mobility of labour are made easier by geographical proximity. However, the cycle in the United Kingdom displays greater similarity with that of the United States and Canada than with the European countries. Finally, Japan seems to form a zone all by itself with a cycle similar to that of all the European countries.

In a general manner, a regime of growth and international fluctuations is defined by a combination of properties characterising the international area. The cyclicity of the economy at the international level is not independent of the hinging and compatibility of trend growths which, as has been seen above, indicates a phenomenon of catching up over a long period. This catching up is only possible through the efficiency and profitability of productive resources, whence conditioning with regard to constraints of external equilibrium and the cyclical interdependence found in all the countries studied [Fayolle and Micolet, 1997].

Conclusion

This analysis of national fluctuations and cyclical interconnections between countries with the same degree of development makes it possible to enrich our understanding of the cyclical mechanisms between nations. It gives a major, entirely new result for the understanding of economic dynamics in the nineteenth and twentieth centuries, that is to say the existence of a single intermediate cycle with a frequency of 15 to 20 years that calls into question or even contradicts (at least partially) previous work on economic cycles. This understanding of cyclical mechanisms is all the more essential today as it will make it possible to put forward more concerted and more cooperative economic policies aimed at parallel development of activities. Indeed, although growth cycles leave real but comparatively small room for intervention by the authorities on the determinants of growth, macroeconomic policies can nevertheless slow, shift, accelerate or dampen cyclical phenomena, whence the advantages of better understanding national cyclical features and their interaction at the international level.

References

A'Hearn B. & Woitek U. [2001]. More international evidence on the historical properties of business cycles. *Journal of Monetary Economics* 47(2): 321–46.

Abramovitz M. [1961]. The nature and significance of Kuznets cycles. *Economic Development and Cultural Change* 9(3): 225–48.

Adelman I. [1965]. Long cycles – Fact or artifact? *American Economic Review* 55(3): 444–63.

Backus D. & Kehoe P. [1992]. International evidence on the historical properties of business cycles. *American Economic Review* 82(4): 864–888.

Barro R. & Sala-í-Martin, X. [1992]. Convergence. *Journal of Political Economy* 100(2): 223–51.

Battilossi S., Escario R. & Foreman-Peck J. [2013]. Fiscal policy response to cycles under two regimes: Spain 1950-1998. *Cliometrica* 7(3): 267–94.

Baxter M. & King R. [1999]. Measuring business cycles: approximate band-pass filters for economic time series. *Review of Economics and Statistics* 81(4): 575–93.

Beach B., Norman S. & Wills D. [2013]. Time or spot? A revaluation of Amsterdam market data prior to 1747. *Cliometrica* 7(1): 61–85.

Becker S.O., Cinnirella F. & Woessmann L. [2012]. The effect of investment in children's education on fertility in 1816 Prussia. *Cliometrica* 6(1): 29–44.

Bentoglio G., Fayolle J. & Lemoine M. [2001]. Unité et pluralité du cycle européen. *Revue de l'OFCE* 78: 9–74.

Bhaskar V., Gupta B. [2012]. Parental altruism and child labor: examining the historical evidence from the United States. *Cliometrica* 6(3): 249–66.

Borowiecki K.J. [2013]. Conflict-induced migration of composers: an individual-level study. *Cliometrica* 7(1): 237–66.

Bouthevillain C. [1996]. Les cycles des grands pays industrialisés. *Économie et Statistique* 298: 71–90.

— [2002]. Filtre Hodrick Prescott et choix de la valeur du paramètre λ. In Banque de France *Notes d'études et de recherches: PIB potentiel et écart de PIB, quelques évaluations pour la France* 89: 10–21.

Bugni F.A. [2012]. Child labor legislation: effective, benign, both, or neither? *Cliometrica* 6(3): 223–48.

Carson S.A. [2012]. A quantile approach to the demographic, residential, and socioeconomic effects on 19th-century African-American body mass index values. *Cliometrica* 6(2): 193-209.

Charles A., Darné O., Diebolt C. & Ferrara L. [in press]. A new monthly chronology of the US industrial cycles in the prewar economy. *Journal of Financial Stability.*

Christiano L. & Fitzgerald T. [2003]. The band pass filter. *International Economic Review* 44(2): 435–65.

Ciriacy-Wantrup S. von [1936]. *Agrarkrisen und Stockungsspannen. Zur Frage der langen „Welle" in der wirtschaftlichen Entwicklung.* Berlin: P. Parey.

Clément M. [2012]. Food availability, food entitlements, and radicalism during the Chinese great leap forward famine: an econometric panel data analysis. *Cliometrica* 6(1): 89–114.

Cogley T. [2006]. Data filters. *New Palgrave Dictionary in Economics.* 2nd Ed. 10 p.

Craig L.A., Hammond, R.G. [2013]. Nutrition and signaling in slave markets: a new look at a puzzle within the antebellum puzzle. *Cliometrica* 7(2): 189–206.

Darné O., Diebolt C. [2004]. Unit roots and infrequent large shocks: new international evidence on output. *Journal of Monetary Economics* 51(7): 1449–65.

—, —[2005]. Nonstationarity tests in macroeconomic time series. In C. Diebolt & C. Kyrtsou in collaboration with O. Darné (Eds.) *New Trends in Macroeconomics.* Berlin: Springer: 719–37.

DeJong D., Dave C. [2011]. *Structural Macroeconometrics.* Princeton: Princeton University Press.

Diebolt C. [2004]. Die Behandlung des Trends bei Simon Kuznets. *Historical Social Research. An International Journal for the Application of Formal Methods to History* 29(1): 271–6.

— [2005]. Long cycles revisited. An essay in econometric history. *Économies et Sociétés*, Série AF : Histoire économique quantitative 32: 23–47.

— [2012]. Cliometrics of economic cycles in France. In L. Grinin, T.C. Devezas and A. Korotayev (Eds) *Kondratieff Waves. Dimensions and Prospects at the Dawn of the 21st Century. Journal of Globalization Studies* 3(2): 120–37.

—, Doliger C. [2008]. New international evidence on the cyclical behaviour of output: Kuznets swings reconsidered. *Quality & Quantity. International Journal of Methodology* 42(6): 719–37.

—, Guiraud V. & Monteils M. [2003]. *Education, Knowledge and Economic Growth. France and Germany in the Nineteenth and Twentieth Centuries.* Frankfurt am Main: Peter Lang.

Dupont B. & Weiss T. [2013]. Variability in overseas travel by Americans, 1820-2000. *Cliometrica*, 7(3): 319-339.

Dupriez L.H. [1935]. Einwirkungen der langen Wellen auf die Entwicklung der Wirtschaft seit 1800. *Weltwirtschaftliches Archiv* 42: 1–12.

Easterlin R.A. [1968]. *Population, Labor Force and Long Swings in Economic Growth. The American Experience.* New York: NBER.

Edvinsson R.B. [2013]. Swedish GDP 1620-1880: stagnation or growth? *Cliometrica* 7(1): 37–60.

Engle R. & Granger C. [1991]. *Long-Run Economic Relationships. Readings in Cointegration.* Oxford: Oxford University Press.

Eurostat [2000]. *Les chiffres clés de l'éducation en Europe 1999-2000.* Brussels : Commission européenne.

— [2000]. *L'Europe des quinze: chiffres clés.* Brussels: Commission européenne.

— [2002]. *Annuaire statistique.* Brussels: Commission européenne.

Fayolle J. & Micolet P.E. [1997]. Cycles internationaux: éléments pour une problématique appliquée. *Revue de l'OFCE* 62: 109–49.

Felice E. [2012]. Regional convergence in Italy, 1891-2001: testing human and social capital. *Cliometrica*, 6(3): 267–306.

Freeman C. Ed [1996]. *Long Wave Theory.* Cheltenham: Edward Elgar.

—, Louça F. [2001]. *As Time Goes By. From the Industrial Revolutions to the Information Revolution.* Oxford: Oxford University Press.

Galor O. [2012]. The demographic transition: causes and consequences. *Cliometrica* 6(1): 1–28.

Garvy G. [1943]. Kondratieff's theory of long cycles. *Review of Economic Statistics* 25(4): 203–20.

Gerster H.-J. [1988]. *Lange Wellen wirtschaftlicher Entwicklung. Empirische Analyse langfristiger Zyklen für die USA, Grossbritannien und weitere vierzehn Industrieländer von 1800 bis 1980.* Frankfurt am Main: Peter Lang.

Goldstein J.S. [1988]. *Long Cycles. Prosperity and War in the Modern Age.* New Haven: Yale University Press.

Granger C. [1969]. Investigating causal relations by econometric models and cross-spectral methods. *Econometrica* 37(3): 426–38.

—, Newbold P. [1974]. Spurious regressions in econometrics. *Journal of Econometrics* 2(2): 111–20.

Greasley D. & Madsen J.B. [2013]. The housing slump and the great depression in the USA. *Cliometrica* 7(1): 15–35.

Hamilton J. [1994]. *Time Series Analysis.* Princeton, NJ: Princeton University Press.

Haupert M. & Murray J. [2012]. Regime switching and wages in major league baseball under the reserve clause. *Cliometrica* 6(2): 143–62.

Ho T., Lai C. & Gau J.J. [2013]. Equilibrium and adjustment of exchange rates in the Chinese silver standard economy, 1928-1935. *Cliometrica* 7(1): 87–98.

Hodrick R. & Prescott E. [1997]. Post-War US business cycles: an empirical investigation. *Journal of Money, Credit and Banking* 29(1): 1–16.

Holmlund B. [2013]. Wage and employment determination in volatile times: Sweden 1913-1939. *Cliometrica* 7(2): 131–59.

Imbert G. [1959]. *Des mouvements de longue durée Kondratieff.* Aix-en-Provence: La Pensée universitaire.

James J.A., McAndrews J. & Weiman D.F. [2013]. Wall Street and Main Street: the macroeconomic consequences of New York bank suspensions 1866–1914. *Cliometrica* 7(2): 99–130.

Johansen S. [1988]. Statistical analysis of cointegration vectors. *Journal of Economic Dynamics and Control* 12(2–3): 231–54.

— [1992]. Determination of cointegration rank in the presence of a linear trend. *Oxford Bulletin of Economics and Statistics* 54(3): 383–97.

Juglar C. [1889]. *Des crises commerciales et de leur retour périodique en France, en Angleterre et aux États-Unis.* Paris: Guillaumin et Cie.

Karadimitropoulou A. & Leon-Ledesma M. [2013]. World, country, and sector factors in international business cycles. *Journal of Economic Dynamics and Control* 37(12): 2913–27.

Kitchin J. [1923]. Cycles and trends in economic factors. *Review of Economic Statistics* 5(1): 10–6.

Kleinknecht A. [1987]. *Innovation Patterns in Crisis and Prosperity. Schumpeter's Long Cycle Reconsidered.* London: The Macmillan Press Ltd.

Klemp M.P.B. [2012]. Prices, wages and fertility in pre-industrial England. *Cliometrica* 6(1): 63–77.

Komlos J. & Küchenhoff H. [2012]. The diminution of the physical stature of the English male population in the eighteenth century. *Cliometrica* 6(1): 45–62.

Kondratieff N.D. [1926]. Die langen Wellen der Konjunktur. *Archiv für Sozialwissenschaft und Sozialpolitik* 56: 573–609.

Kose A., Otrok C. & Whiteman H. [2003]. International business cycles: world, region, and country-specific factors. *American Economic Review* 93(4): 1216–39.

Kuznets S. [1930]. *Secular Movements in Production and Prices. Their Nature and their Bearing upon Cyclical Fluctuations.* Boston: Houghton Mifflin Co.

Lampe M. & Sharp P. [2013]. Tariffs and income: a time series analysis for 24 countries. *Cliometrica* 7(3): 207–35.

Lösch A. [1936]. *Bevölkerungswellen und Wechsellagen*. Jena: G.Fischer.

Maddision A. [1995]. *L'économie mondiale 1820-1992. Analyse et statistiques* Paris: OCDE.

Mensch G. [1977]. *Das technologische Patt. Innovationen überwinden die Depression*. Frankfurt am Main: Fischer Taschenbuch Verlag.

Metz R. [2002]. *Trend, Zyklus und Zufall. Bestimmungsgründe und Verlaufsformen langfristiger Wachstumsschwankungen*. Stuttgart: Franz Steiner Verlag.

— [2008]. *Auf der Suche nach den Langen Wellen der Konjunktur*. Stuttgart: Franz Steiner Verlag.

— [2011]. Do Kondratieff waves exist? How time series techniques can help to solve the problem. *Cliometrica* 5(3): 205–38.

Mitchell W.C. [1931]. *Der Konjunkturzyklus. Problem und Problemstellung*. Leipzig: H. Buske.

Nason J. & Vahey S. [2012]. UK World War I and interwar data for business cycle and growth analysis. *Cliometrica* 6(2): 115–42.

Nelson C. & Plosser C. [1982]. Trends and random walks in macroeconomic time series. *Journal of Monetary Economics* 10(2): 139–62.

Oparin D.I. [1930]. Das theoretische Schema der gleichmässig fortschreitenden Wirtschaft als Grundlage einer Analyse ökonomischer Entwicklungsprozesse. *Weltwirtschaftliches Archiv* 32: 105–34 and 406–45.

Parent A. [2012]. A critical note on 'This time is different'. *Cliometrica* 6(2): 211–9.

Petzina D. & Van Roon G. (Eds) [1981]. *Konjunktur, Krise, Gesellschaft. Wirtschaftliche Wechsellagen und soziale Entwicklung im 19. und 20. Jahrhundert*. Stuttgart: Klett-Cotta.

Prentice D. [2012]. The rise of the US Portland cement industry and the role of public science. *Cliometrica* 6(2): 163–92.

Priestley M. [1981]. *Spectral Analysis and Time Series*. New York: Academic Press.

Rei C. [2013]. Incentives in merchant empires: Portuguese and Dutch compensation schemes. *Cliometrica*, 7(1): 1–13.

Reijnders J. [1988]. *The Enigma of Long Waves*, Ph.D. thesis. Utrecht: Drukkerij Elinkwijk BV.

Schumpeter J.A. [1939]. *Business Cycles. A Theoretical, Historical and Statistical Analysis of the Capitalist Process*. London: McGraw-Hill Book Co.

Sella L. & Marchionatti R. [2012]. On the cyclical variability of economic growth in Italy, 1881-1913: a critical note. *Cliometrica* 6(3): 307–28.

Sharp P.R. & Weisdorf J.L. [2012]. French revolution or industrial revolution? A note on the contrasting experiences of England and France up to 1800. *Cliometrica* 6(1): 79–88.

Silverberg G. & Verspagen B. [2003]. Long memory and economic growth in the world economy since the 19th century. In G. Rangarajan & M. Ding (Eds.) *Processes with Long Range Correlations: Theory and Applications*. Berlin: Springer: 270–85.

Solomou S. [1987]. *Phases of Economic Growth, 1850-1973. Kondratieff Waves and Kuznets Swings*. Cambridge: Cambridge University Press.

Sombart W. [1928]. *Der moderne Kapitalismus. Historisch-systematische Darstellung des gesamteuropäischen Wirtschaftlebens von seinen Anfängen bis zur Gegenwart*. Leipzig: Duncker & Humblot.

Spiethoff A. [1902]. Vorbemerkungen zu einer Theorie der Überproduktion. Vortrag, gehalten am 17. Dezember 1901 in der Staatswissenschaftlichen Vereinigung zu Berlin. *Jahrbuch für Gesetzgebung, Verwaltung und Volkswirtschaft im Deutschen Reich* 26: 721–59.

— [1955]. *Die wirtschaftlichen Wechsellagen. Aufschwung, Krise, Stockung*. Tübingen: J.C.B. Mohr.

Spree R. [1991]. *Lange Wellen wirtschaftlicher Entwicklung in der Neuzeit. Historische Befunde, Erklärungen und Untersuchungsmethoden*, Special Issue of *Historical Social Research. An International Journal for the Application of Formal Methods to History* 4.

Tirado D.A. et al. [2013]. Trade policy and wage gradients: evidence from a protectionist turn. *Cliometrica* 7(3): 295–318.

Tugan-Baranowsky M. von [1901]. *Studien zur Theorie und Geschichte der Handelskrisen in England.* Jena: G. Fischer.

Uebele M. [2011]. Die Identifikation internationaler Konjunkturzyklen in disaggregierten Daten: Deutschland, Frankreich und Großbritannien, 1862-1912. *Economic History Yearbook (Jahrbuch für Wirtschaftsgeschichte)* 1: 19–44.

Van Ewijk C. [1984]. A spectral analysis of the Kondratieff-cycle. *Kyklos* 35(3): 468–99.

Vogel E.H. [1928]. Die Theorie des volkswirtschaftlichen Entwicklungsprozesses und ihre Fortbildung durch eine evolutionäre Konjunkturtheorie. *Jahrbücher für Nationalökonomie und Statistik* 128: 321–87, 481–518, and 663–705.

Wagemann E. [1928]. *Konjunkturlehre. Eine Grundlegung zur Lehre vom Rhythmus der Wirtschaft.* Berlin: R. Hobbing.

Wagemann E. [1931]. *Struktur und Rhythmus der Weltwirtschaft. Grundlagen einer weltwirtschaftlichen Konjunkturlehre.* Hamburg: Hanseatische Verlagsanstalt.

Wagenführ R. [1929]. *Die Konjunkturtheorie in Russland.* Jena: G. Fischer.

Weinstock U. [1964]. *Das Problem der Kondratieff-Zyklen. Ein Beitrag zur Entwicklung einer Theorie der „langen Wellen" und ihrer Bedeutung.* Berlin: Duncker & Humblot.

Woytinsky W. [1931]. Das Rätsel der langen Wellen. *Schmollers Jahrbuch für Gesetzgebung, Verwaltung und Volkswirtschaft im Deutschen Reich* 55: 1–42.

Zehetmayer M. [2013]. Health, market integration and the urban height penalty in the US, 1847–1894. *Cliometrica* 7(2): 161–187.

CIRCULATION DU CAPITAL ET EXPLICATION DU CHANGEMENT ÉCONOMIQUE CHEZ MARSCHAK, FRISCH ET LEONTIEF

Amanar Akhabbar[1]

Nous analysons une série de modèles macroéconométriques développés dans les années de haute théorie par Marschak, par Frisch et par Leontief. Ces modèles ont en commun de fonder l'explication de la croissance, des cycles et des fluctuations (le « changement économique ») sur l'analyse de la circulation des biens de capital entre les producteurs. Cette approche désagrège la fonction de production macroéconomique en introduisant plusieurs producteurs et plusieurs biens de capital. Nous montrons que ces modèles offrent deux explications du changement économique : l'une par la diffusion du changement technique à travers le réseau d'échanges entre producteurs ; l'autre par les problèmes de coordination dans la circulation du capital.

Capital circulation and the explanation of economic change by Marschak, Frisch and Leontief

We analyze a series of macroeconometric models developed in the years of high theory by Marschak, Frisch and Leontief. These models share an explanation of growth, cycles and fluctuations ("economic change"), based on the analysis of the circulation of capital goods among producers. They disaggregate the macroeconomic production function so as to introduce multiple producers and capital goods. We show that these models offer two main explanations of economic change: one is based on the spread of technological change through the producers' exchanges network; the other is based on the coordination problems between producers in the capital circulation process.

Mots clefs : Changement économique, capital, fonction de production macroéconomique, changement technique, incertitude, coordination.

Keywords: Economic change, capital, macroeconomic production function, technological change, uncertainty, coordination.

JEL classification: B22, B23, B24, B25

---

1. ESSCA School of Management, amanar.akhabbar@essca.fr.
Cet article s'inspire du chapitre 1 (partie 1) de ma thèse de doctorat (2008). Une version préliminaire de ce travail a été présentée à la session « Cycle et Croissance » du colloque de l'Association Charles Gide pour l'étude de la pensée économique organisé par le Gredeg à l'université de Nice Sophia-Antipolis, en juin 2012. Une version plus avancée a été présentée à l'occasion du Workshop on the History and Analysis of Business Cycles Theory organisé par Pascal Bridel et Muriel Dal-Pont au Centre Walras-Pareto de l'université de Lausanne le 25 octobre 2013. Les remarques, critiques et suggestions des participants présents lors de ces sessions m'ont été particulièrement utiles et je remercie tout particulièrement Richard Arena, Michael Assous, Alain Béraud, Pascal Bridel, Muriel Dal-Pont, Rodolphe Dos Santos Ferreira, Marion Gaspard, Harald Hagemann et Alain Raybaut. Je remercie également Olav Bjerkholt pour ses remarques. Je suis également redevable à deux rapporteurs anonymes qui ont permis d'améliorer significativement ce travail. Je demeure seul responsable des éventuelles erreurs et omissions.

Cet article est une contribution à l'histoire de la macroéconométrie du changement économique. La série de modèles que nous analysons étudie, ensemble ou séparément, la croissance, les cycles et les fluctuations économiques – phénomènes que nous appellerons « changement économique »[2]. Qu'ils expliquent la croissance, les cycles et/ou les fluctuations économiques, ces modèles relèvent d'une analyse macroéconomique de court terme. Produits par Jacob Marschak[3], Ragnar Frisch et Wassily Leontief, ces modèles sont développés à la même période, dans les « années de haute théorie » (1926-1939), et dans un registre qui deviendra, dans l'après-guerre, celui de la macroéconométrie. Il s'agit d'une époque où émergent la macroéconomie, l'économétrie et la comptabilité nationale, mais les économistes ne pensent pas encore systématiquement leur démarche en ces termes[4]. Nos trois auteurs articulent des dispositifs de modélisation mathématique, de mesure des agrégats des flux et des stocks nationaux, et ils établissent des correspondances entre mesure statistique et modèle mathématique : ce sont les débuts de la macroéconométrie. Dans ce qui suit, nous nous concentrerons sur l'explication théorique contenue dans les modèles.

Soulignons que ces trois auteurs se connaissent à plusieurs titres. En dépit de quelques différences, ils partagent une méthodologie commune combinant théorie, modélisation, économétrie et comptabilité nationale[5].

2. Par souci de simplicité nous suivons ici Leontief [1928] et son expression « *wirtschaftliche Veränderung* » [p. 594] pour désigner à la fois la tendance (croissance ou déclin), les fluctuations (régulières ou irrégulières) et les cycles. Tous les modèles que nous examinons offrent essentiellement des analyses de court terme.

3. Nous orthographions systématiquement le prénom de Marschak selon son orthographe anglaise (qu'il adopte à partir de 1933), *Jacob*, plutôt que l'orthographe allemande, *Jakob* (que l'on trouve dans ses premières publications).

4. Sur l'émergence de ces catégories et la transformation épistémologique de la science économique durant cette période voir Morgan [1990], Bodkin, Klein and Marwah [1991], Le Gall [1994], Dupont-Kieffer [2001 ; 2003], Vanoli [2002], Bjerkholt et Dupont-Kieffer [2010b], et Akhabbar [2010].

5. Dans la sélection des modèles que nous étudions, notre condition d'une articulation entre théorie, modélisation, économétrie et comptabilité nationale, a pour but d'examiner des modèles appartenant à un même registre scientifique, ce qui réduit notre champ d'analyse aux modèles sélectionnés. Pour cette raison nous excluons notamment les travaux de John von Neumann, ainsi que ceux de Friedrich Hayek, Fritz Burchardt, et Ragnar Nurske ou encore ceux d'Alfred Kähler, de Robert Remak, de l'abbé Potron et de Bernard Chait, qui présentent toutefois des affinités analytiques fortes avec les modèles de Marschak, de Frisch et de Leontief sélectionnés.

Notons que Marschak[6] et Leontief[7], tous deux d'origine russe, ont émigré en Allemagne où ils se trouvent (indépendamment) proches de Ladislaus von Bortkiewicz puis sont passés par le même institut de recherche à la fin des années 1920, le Kiel Weltwirtschaftsinstitut[8], alors dirigé par Adolph Löwe[9]. À cette époque ils travaillent notamment sur l'économétrie de l'offre et de la demande comme explication des phénomènes cycliques. Ils se situent dans la lignée de travaux tels que ceux de Henry Ludwell Moore, Henry Schultz ou encore Frisch. Cette démarche vise, notamment, à expliquer les variations des quantités et des prix des biens échangés par les mouvements des courbes d'offre et de demande et, par conséquent, d'identifier ces courbes et leurs déplacements. Dans ce registre, dans les années 1933-1934, Frisch, à l'Institut d'économie d'Oslo, et Leontief, à Harvard, s'opposent dans une vive controverse sur la construction économétrique des courbes d'offre et de demande. Au cours de cette controverse il est demandé à Marschak, alors à l'université d'Oxford, d'intervenir comme modérateur entre les deux économètres (voir Morgan [1990]).

Dans le même temps, nos trois auteurs examinent des explications du changement économique autres que celles fondées sur l'équilibre marchand entre offres et demandes. Leur nouveau point de départ est le tableau économique et le circuit économique : ce n'est plus la coordination par les prix qui importe mais la circulation des flux de marchandises dans le circuit économique. C'est cette dernière approche que nous étudions ici. Les trois auteurs l'explorent essentiellement dans cinq articles parus entre 1928 et 1937 : pour Marschak, dans *Annual Survey of Statistical Information: the Branches of National Spending* [1933], puis dans *Econometric Parameters in a Stationary Society with Monetary Circulation* [1934a] ; pour Frisch, dans

6. Pour des informations biographiques sur Marschak voir notamment Hagemann [1997 ; 2006 ; 2011] et Cherrier [2010].

7. Pour des informations biographiques sur Leontief voir notamment Rosier [1986].

8. Marschak est à Kiel entre 1928 et 1930, tandis que Leontief s'y trouve en 1927-1928 puis, après un séjour en Chine, entre 1930 et 1932, date à laquelle il quitte l'Europe pour les États-Unis où il est embauché à Harvard en 1932. Marschak quitte l'Allemagne en 1933 et s'installe à Oxford jusqu'en 1939, date à laquelle il émigre aux États-Unis. Sur ces événements, voir notamment Beckmann [2000], Hagemann [1997 ; 2006 ; 2009 ; 2011] et Rosier [1986].

9. Sur le lien entre les travaux de Leontief et ceux du 'groupe de Kiel', Hagemann [2009] souligne que la thèse de Leontief [1928] s'inscrit dans les travaux du groupe sur la croissance cyclique.

la première partie de *Circulation Planning: Proposal for a National Organization of a Commodity and Service Exchange* ; enfin, pour Leontief, dans son *Die Wirtschaft als Kreislauf* [1928], puis dans "Interrelations of Prices, Output, Savings, and Investment" [1937].

En dépit de la célébrité ultérieure de ces auteurs, les économistes n'ont que très peu fait référence aux travaux que nous avons sélectionnés. En effet, en mobilisant un argument bibliométrique, dont chacun connaît les limites, une recherche sur Jstor dans les catégories « Business » et « Economics » de 1926 à nos jours ne permet de trouver que 9 articles citant Frisch [1934] alors que la référence à Frisch [1933], c'est-à-dire à son célèbre système d'impulsion-propagation, apparaît 63 fois ; nous trouvons 2 articles (dont un de Marschak lui-même) se référant à Marschak [1934a] ; en revanche, nous trouvons 83 références à Leontief [1937], mais rarement à propos de l'explication du changement économique que l'article contient et, généralement, en référence à son système de comptabilité nationale intersectoriel et/ou à son modèle interindustriel comme précurseurs de l'analyse input-output. Pour comparaison avec une approche qui prend le contre-pied des modèles que nous présentons ici, c'est-à-dire des modèles macroéconométriques désagrégés, l'article de Solow [1957] « Technical change and the aggregate production function », qui repose sur un modèle macroéconométrique agrégé, compte près de 1 200 références.

Les modèles sélectionnés n'ont été, par ailleurs, que peu étudiés par les historiens de la pensée économique. Pour ce qui est de Frisch, la littérature se concentre sur son modèle d'impulsion-propagation de 1933 qui est agrégé, et donc hors de notre champ d'analyse[10]. En outre, quand son modèle de 1934 est évoqué c'est le plus souvent à propos de la solution normative que Frisch propose, sa théorie de la planification, la « circulation planning » [11], en réponse au problème économique de la Grande Dépression tel qu'il l'analyse d'un point de vue positif : nous n'examinons pas ici sa théorie de la planification mais son explication positive du

10. Pour des études détaillées du modèle de Frisch de 1933 et de son analyse des cycles, et sans prétendre à l'exhaustivité, voir Andvig [1978 ; 1981], Bjerkholt [2000 ; 2007a ; 2007b], Bjerkholt et Dupont-Kieffer [2010a ; 2010b], Blatt [1980], Boianovsky et Trautwein [2007], Dupont-Kieffer [2001 ; 2003 ; 2012a ; 2012b ; 2012c], Le Gall [1993 ; 1994], et Zambelli [2007].

11. Voir notamment Akhabbar [2011], Bjerkholt et Knell [2006], Dupont-Kieffer [2003] et [2012c].

changement économique[12]. Pour ce qui est de Marschak, c'est un auteur encore très largement sous-étudié eu regard à l'importance de sa contribution (voir Hagemann [1997 ; 2006 ; 2011] ; et aussi Mehrling [2010]). Récemment, Béatrice Cherrier [2010] a étudié le travail de Marschak sur l'incertitude en mobilisant des informations biographiques pour éclairer sa contribution, mais elle concentre son analyse sur ses travaux des années 1940 et 1950, autrement dit après notre période, et ne fait pas référence aux principaux travaux de Marschak que nous examinons ici [1932 ; 1933b ; 1934a ; 1934b]. Enfin, pour ce qui est de Leontief, la référence des historiens à ses travaux sur l'interdépendance input-output se concentre sur leur contribution à la comptabilité nationale ou à la planification ou encore à la théorie de la valeur[13] mais non sur l'explication du changement économique qu'ils contiennent. Notre article examine les explications du changement économique présentées dans ces travaux encore méconnus.

Dans chacun des modèles sélectionnés, l'explication du changement économique se fonde sur la circulation des biens entre les producteurs de l'économie. Il s'agit d'une démarche désagrégée où la fonction de production macroéconomique comprend plusieurs types de biens de capital : chaque producteur produit un bien qui lui est propre. Dans ces modèles, par souci de simplification, les biens de capital se réduisent au capital circulant et il n'y a pas de capital fixe et donc pas d'accumulation du stock de capital fixe: ce sont des modèles de flux. Notons que l'absence de capital fixe n'est pas importante pour notre argument, ce dernier reposant sur la circulation du capital (fixe ou circulant) entre les producteurs dans une perspective où la fonction de production est désagrégée (du côté du capital, pas du travail)[14].

12. Voir, néanmoins, Andvig [1978, p. 151-153], Bjerkholt et Knell [2006], et Dupont-Kieffer [2012c, p. 285-287] sur l'explication du changement économique contenue dans Frisch [1934].

13. Voir par exemple Akhabbar [2008], Baumol [2000], Baumol et ten Raa [2009], Kurz et Salvadori [2006], et Vanoli [2002].

14. Rappelons que ces modélisations macroéconométriques interviennent à une époque de grands débats dans la sphère de la « haute théorie », en particulier au sujet de la théorie de la production. C'est le cas aussi bien de la question des rendements – soulevée entre autres par Sraffa – que de l'assaut, alors fatal, contre la théorie autrichienne de la production. Sur ces sujets il existe une abondante littérature, aussi le lecteur se référera utilement, entre autres, à Cohen [1989 ; 2003 ; 2010], Keppler et Lallement [2006], et Repapis [2011].

Ouvrons ici une parenthèse car, pour le lecteur de ce début du XXIe siècle, ces modèles désagrégés où le capital est exclusivement du capital circulant peuvent avoir un caractère exotique au regard des modèles macroéconomiques standard contemporains. Ces derniers ont très largement recours à la fonction de production macroéconomique avec capital agrégé et, lorsqu'il y a désagrégation, c'est le plus souvent pour introduire différents types de biens de capital fixe et (rarement) des biens de capital circulant[15]. Comme le soulignait Marc Blaug, « c'est une des ironies de l'histoire de la pensée économique [...] que la théorie du capital, de Turgot à Wicksell, a toujours considéré le capital circulant et non le capital fixe comme le 'capital' par excellence » [Blaug, 1987, p. 427] et que, passé le pluralisme des années de haute théorie, depuis l'après-guerre c'est le capital fixe qui est le capital par excellence. Une explication de cela serait que la primauté donnée aux biens de capital fixe dans la fonction de production macroéconomique est directement liée au processus d'agrégation et au choix du revenu national comme indice du produit national. En effet, dans la définition courante du produit national d'une économie comme son revenu national, noté *Y*, l'économiste soustrait de la production totale, notée *Q*, les flux de biens et services qui ont été dépensés pour la production, notés *B*, c'est-à-dire le capital circulant[16]. Dans la série de modèles que nous étudions ici, ce n'est pas seulement *Y* qui est expliqué mais aussi *B* et *Q*[17].

Nous refermons là cette parenthèse sur la place du capital circulant dans l'analyse économique, car l'argument développé dans les modèles

15. Autrement dit, un modèle macroéconomique peut contenir une fonction de production désagrégée avec différents biens de capital fixe et être multisectoriel (chaque secteur produit un bien qui peut être soit consommé soit accumulé comme stock de capital fixe) sans introduire de capital circulant.

16. Soient les agrégats suivants dans une économie fermée sans État : *C* la consommation des ménages, *I* l'investissement, *K* le stock de capital fixe, *L* le travail employé. Avec $F(-)$ la fonction de production macroéconomique, nous obtenons : $Y = (Q - B) = (C + I) = F(K, L)$. Avec cette fonction de production, seul l'agrégat *Y* est expliqué et pas l'agrégat *B* ni l'agrégat *Q*.

17. Supposons que le volume des biens et services de capital circulant soit mesuré par la catégorie comptable des « consommations intermédiaires », même si cette catégorie n'appartient pas au même registre disciplinaire ni ne se recoupe parfaitement avec le capital circulant. Il apparaît alors que dans les pays industrialisés avancés, la part des consommations intermédiaires représente près de la moitié de la production totale et donc autant que le revenu national [ONU, 2009]. Cette part augmente dans les pays en cours d'industrialisation rapide comme la Chine. Autrement dit, les biens de capital circulant représentent un volume considérable de marchandises dont on perd la trace dans les modèles macroéconomiques agrégés.

sélectionnés de Marschak, de Frisch et de Leontief ne repose pas sur la nature du capital mais sur la circulation des biens de capital entre les producteurs. Dans cet article nous insisterons moins sur les différences théoriques, certes profondes comme nous le verrons plus loin[18] entre les approches de ces trois auteurs, que sur leur manière commune d'expliquer le changement économique à travers le processus de circulation du capital entre producteurs.

Le processus productif est réalisé à travers les échanges de biens entre les producteurs, chacun pouvant employer les biens d'autres producteurs comme facteurs de production pour la production de son propre bien. Comme l'écrit Leontief, ces relations d'achat-vente entre producteurs font du système économique le « *réseau* hautement complexe des interrelations mutuelles » entre les unités productives [Leontief, 1937, p. 110][19], (nous soulignons). Pour représenter la circulation du capital entre les producteurs, chacun des trois auteurs se réfère au *Tableau économique* de François Quesnay en le reformulant comme un tableau entrées-sorties[20]. Ce tableau entrées-sorties représente les flux des échanges entre les producteurs de l'économie. Marschak [1933a] semble être le premier des trois auteurs à exposer le principe du tableau économique comme tableau entrées-sorties (Tableau 1) et, à notre connaissance, cette formulation par Marschak du tableau économique comme tableau entrées-sorties n'avait pas encore été relevée par les historiens de la pensée économique[21].

18. Ces différences théoriques ont des effets importants sur les réponses aux questions touchant à la répartition du revenu, à l'analyse de la valeur et au statut de l'emploi. Autant de questions que nous laissons de côté dans notre article pour nous concentrer sur les variations des volumes et/ou des prix des productions sectorielles.

19. Notre traduction. Leontief emploie le mot *network* pour réseau [1937, p. 110]. Ce terme est déjà présent dans sa thèse de doctorat en allemand où il parle de *Netzwerk* [p. 588] et de *Netz* [*ibid.*].

20. Sur la référence commune de Marschak, Frisch et Leontief au tableau économique, voir Akhabbar [2008, partie I, chapitre 2 ; 2011].

21. Voir aussi Akhabbar [2008 ; 2011].

Vendu par / Acheté par	a	b	c	—
a	aa	ab	ac	—
b	ba	bb	bc	—
c	ca	cb	cc	—
—	—	—	—	—

Tableau 1. Le tableau économique de Marschak [1933a, p. 374]

Ce tableau économique représente les échanges entre les unités économiques *a*, *b* et *c*. Marschak note *ba* le montant en valeur des biens vendus par *a* à *b*. Ce tableau permet de visualiser par un dispositif graphique simple l'interdépendance générale entre les unités économiques : cette interdépendance est, dans les modèles explicatifs, à la base de l'explication du changement économique. L'interdépendance entre les unités économiques se fait à travers la circulation des biens de capital que les producteurs s'échangent entre eux.

Il s'agit ensuite pour chaque auteur d'offrir une explication du système économique ainsi représenté. Marschak [1933a] souligne que ce tableau économique donne lieu à une pluralité d'interprétations théoriques selon le sens donné aux unités économiques, *a*, *b*, *c*, etc. D'une part, selon Marschak [*ibid.*, p. 375], si les unités économiques (*a*, *b*, *c*) étaient l'agriculture, l'industrie et l'État respectivement, nous retrouverions le principe du tableau économique de Quesnay. D'autre part, si ces unités économiques sont les branches produisant respectivement les biens de production, les biens de consommation des travailleurs, et les biens de consommation des capitalistes, nous retrouverions le cadre analytique marxiste des schémas de la reproduction. Enfin, relève Marschak, en introduisant le temps, chaque unité économique (*a*, *b*, *c*) réalisant successivement l'une des étapes de transformation des « facteurs originaux » (travail et terre) en « biens intermédiaires » vers la production des biens de consommation finale, le tableau économique s'interpréterait à partir du cadre analytique autrichien[22]. Soulignons que, chez Marschak, le terme de

22. Par exemple le groupe de producteurs *a* transforme les facteurs orignaux en produits semi-finis, aussi appelés dans le vocable autrichien – notamment chez Hayek – « biens intermédiaires », qu'il vend

« bien intermédiaire » est à situer dans le cadre particulier de la théorie autrichienne de la production. En suivant Hayek, les biens intermédiaires sont les « biens de production qui ne sont pas des facteurs originaux [non produits, comme le travail et la terre] mais qui se situent entre ces facteurs originaux et les biens de consommation » [Hayek, 1931, p. 37][23]. C'est ce cadre autrichien que Marschak [1934a] emploie pour son étude du changement économique.

S'il se réfère au tableau économique comme tableau entrées-sorties comme celui de Marschak, chacun des trois auteurs que nous étudions construit un modèle mathématique à partir d'un cadre théorique différent. C'est ainsi que le modèle de Marschak relève de la théorie autrichienne, celui de Frisch, difficilement classable, se rapproche d'une théorie walrassienne de l'équilibre général à prix fixes[24], et, enfin, celui de Leontief, d'une analyse post-classique du flux circulaire[25]. Du point de vue de la représentation de la production, l'approche de Marschak repose sur une représentation verticale de la structure de production, où le processus productif est un processus temporel qui va des facteurs originaux vers les biens de consommation finale. Les modèles de Frisch et ceux de Leontief adoptent une représentation horizontale, c'est-à-dire intersectorielle de la structure de la production.

Une autre distinction importante entre les modèles étudiés relève de l'introduction ou non de paramètres subjectifs dans l'analyse du comportement des unités productives. Tout en prenant en considération des caractéristiques objectives réelles de l'économie (la technique notamment), Marschak [1934a] et Frisch [1934] font largement reposer l'explication économique sur des éléments relevant de la subjectivité des individus comme les anticipations, le moral des producteurs, le désir, le

au groupe *b* qui les transforme en d'autres biens intermédiaires, et ainsi de suite jusqu'au dernier groupe de producteurs qui transforme les produits semi-finis achetés en produits de consommation finale.

23. Sur la conception du capital de Hayek dans les années 1930, voir notamment Cohen [2003] qui insiste sur la nature désagrégée du capital et le caractère hétérogène des biens de capital chez Hayek, en continuité avec la notion du capital chez Böhm-Bawerk.

24. Pour l'approche de Frisch, voir notamment Andvig [1978 ; 1981], Bjerkholt [2000 ; 2007a ; 2007b], Bjerkholt et Dupont-Kieffer [2010a ; 2010b], Blatt [1980], Boianovsky et Trautwein [2007], Dupont-Kieffer [2001 ; 2003 ; 2012a ; 2012b ; 2012c], Le Gall [1993 ; 1994], et Zambelli [2007].

25. Pour une analyse du cadre classique des modèles de Leontief, voir Kurz et Salvadori [2006].

courage, ou encore leur attitude subjective face à l'incertitude. L'approche de Leontief [1928, 1937], en revanche, exclut les caractéristiques subjectives des agents et ne prend en considération que les éléments objectifs du système économique, à commencer par la technologie[26].

En dépit de ces différences il existe de profondes affinités analytiques et méthodologiques entre ces travaux. En effet, à notre connaissance, sur la période considérée, seules ces contributions réunissent les caractéristiques suivantes : d'une part, constituer un projet à la fois théorique et statistique d'analyse macroéconométrique du changement économique qui s'appuie explicitement sur un appareil de comptabilité nationale et un tableau économique entrées-sorties et, d'autre part, proposer un modèle mathématique d'analyse des interdépendances input-output basée sur la circulation des biens de capital[27]. Notre article portant sur l'explication théorique, cette seconde caractéristique commune est fondamentale : ces trois auteurs expliquent le changement économique à partir de l'analyse de la circulation du capital entre les producteurs.

Marschak, Frisch et Leontief expliquent le changement économique à partir de cette représentation de l'économie comme un système productif où les biens de capital circulent d'un producteur à un autre. La question à laquelle nous répondrons est la suivante : quelles sont les explications particulières du changement économique développées par les auteurs à partir de ce système de circulation du capital ? Nous montrons que deux grandes explications émergent de la série de modèles sélectionnés : une explication provenant du changement technique agissant sur la structure réelle de l'économie, et une autre explication provenant de la coordination dans la sphère des échanges entre les producteurs. Dans le cadre macroéconomique désagrégé décrit, ce sont les modèles construits par Leontief qui explorent l'explication réelle du changement économique, et les modèles de Marschak et ceux de Frisch qui examinent l'explication par

26. Cette distinction renvoie à celle, en économie, entre objectivisme et subjectivisme (pour une synthèse récente, voir Yagi et Ikeda [2012]). On la retrouve notamment dans la littérature post-classique influencée par la pensée marxiste (voir par exemple Bortkiewicz [1921]). Dans l'après Seconde Guerre mondiale, la pertinence de cette distinction pour les sciences sociales est discutée et remise en question (voir par exemple Bourdieu [1980]).

27. Et, dans le cas de Frisch [1934] et de Leontief [1937], la représentation des échanges et des flux par des matrices mathématiques entrées-sorties.

la coordination[28]. La première partie de notre article est consacrée à l'explication du changement économique par le changement technique et la seconde partie à l'explication par les problèmes de coordination.

1. Changement technique et changement économique

Commençons par examiner comment l'explication du changement économique de court terme par le changement technique s'exprime dans une approche par la circulation du capital entre producteurs. Parce que les modèles examinés dans cette première partie sont sans monnaie et font entièrement reposer l'explication du changement économique sur le changement technique, nous pouvons parler de théorie des cycles réels. La contribution d'une telle approche désagrégée est essentiellement d'affiner la représentation de la technologie en désagrégeant les *inputs* et le système de production : ceci permet de localiser le point où le changement a lieu et d'en suivre la diffusion et les effets à travers le réseau d'interdépendances entre les producteurs. Pour reprendre le vocabulaire de Frisch [1933], vocabulaire que l'on retrouve chez Leontief [1937], l'impulsion trouve son origine dans un choc[29] technologique mais, au lieu d'en suivre la propagation d'un agrégat à un autre comme chez Frisch [1933], un modèle désagrégé permet de la suivre d'un producteur à un autre. Il devient possible, d'une part, de localiser l'origine du changement par producteur ainsi que d'identifier sur quels facteurs spécifiques les changements et les chocs interviennent et, d'autre part, d'examiner la diffusion d'une impulsion locale dans le reste de l'économie. Le modèle d'impulsion-propagation de Frisch de 1933 étant agrégé nous ne l'examinons pas ici. Dans les modèles de Frisch de 1934 et celui de Marschak [1934a] la technologie est donnée et demeure inchangée. C'est Leontief qui entreprend le projet d'une modélisation désagrégée de la technologie dans une perspective macroéconométrique. Nous examinons comment ses

28. Rappelons que Frisch [1933] avait dans un premier temps fait reposer l'explication du changement économique sur le changement technique. Dans son modèle de1934, il ne reprend pas cette explication et explore les problèmes de coordination entre les producteurs. Frisch souligne que ces deux explications se complètent [1934, p. 271-272].

29. Sur une histoire des chocs et de leur observabilité dans la macroéconomie, voir Duarte et Hoover [2012]. Néanmoins, ceux-ci ne font pas référence aux modèles de Leontief que nous examinons dans cette première partie ni au modèle de Frisch de 1934 que nous examinons dans la partie suivante et qui a recours au concept de choc.

modèles parviennent à expliquer la croissance (1-1), les cycles (1-2) et enfin le changement dans la structure de la production (1-3).

1.1. Productivité et croissance

Leontief [1928] utilise un même modèle pour expliquer à la fois la croissance et les cycles. Il s'agit d'un modèle inspiré de la théorie classique du flux circulaire où *n* marchandises servent à produire *n* marchandises. Dans ce qui suit, nous suivons les notations et le formalisme de Leontief. Bien que Leontief parle de « modèle »[30], il n'y a pas à proprement parler de modèle mathématique mais plutôt un schéma théorique s'appuyant sur des formalismes mathématiques.

Prenons l'un des exemples donnés par Leontief, celui d'une économie à deux biens, A et B. Pour produire chacun des deux biens, il faut utiliser ces deux biens comme inputs : $A \oplus B \rightarrow A \oplus B$. Nous notons A_t et B_t les quantités de bien A et celles de bien B produites à la période t. Soit a la proportion de A_t qui est utilisée pour la production du bien A, et $(1 - a)$ celle utilisée pour produire du bien B. De la même manière, b est la proportion de B_t qui est utilisée pour produire du bien A, et $(1 - b)$ celle pour produire du bien B. Leontief appelle les coefficients a, b, $(1 - a)$, $(1 - b)$, les « coefficients de distribution ». On suppose que la rémunération du travail et de la propriété des moyens de production est incluse dans les coefficients de distribution.

Leontief montre que, dans cette économie, une reproduction[31] avec croissance est possible si et seulement si un gain de productivité intervient de manière permanente. Aussi, considérons le système productif suivant[32] :

$$aA_t \oplus bB_t \rightarrow A_{t+1} = \alpha A_t \text{ et } (1 - a)A_t \oplus (1 - b)\, B_t \rightarrow B_{t+1} = \alpha B_t$$

$$aA_{t+1} \oplus bB_{t+1} \rightarrow A_{t+2} = \alpha A_{t+1} = \alpha^2 A_t \text{ et } (1 - a)A_{t+1} \oplus (1 - b)\, B_{t+1} \rightarrow B_{t+2} = \alpha B_{t+1} = \alpha^2 B_t, \text{ etc.}$$

30. Leontief écrit : "*ein Modell des wirtschaftlichen Kreislaufs*" [1928, p. 603].

31. Leontief emploie explicitement le terme « reproduction » (*Reproduktion*) pour désigner le processus économique.

32. Nos notations.

Le coefficient α permet d'introduire des changements dans la productivité du système productif. Selon Leontief, dans une économie en reproduction simple[33], le coefficient α est égal à 1. Pour qu'une reproduction élargie intervienne, il faut dégager un surplus ce qui suppose ici qu'un gain de productivité se produise, c'est-à-dire une augmentation du coefficient α. Par ailleurs, il faut que cette augmentation de la productivité soit permanente et non provisoire sans quoi l'économie retourne à un système de reproduction simple. Ainsi, *in fine*, si $\alpha = 1$ alors le système fonctionne sous le régime de la reproduction simple. En revanche, si $\alpha > 1$ le système croît, il connaît « un changement progressif », tandis que si $\alpha < 1$, il connaît un « changement régressif » de contraction [Leontief, 1928 (1991), p. 191]. Ainsi, et sans référence explicite à la théorie marxienne, ce modèle de Leontief reprend le principe de la reproduction simple et élargie de Marx, mais en faisant reposer la croissance non pas sur le mode d'utilisation du surplus entre consommation et accumulation mais sur le changement technique.

1.2. Productivité et cycles

Avec ce même modèle, Leontief offre une explication des phénomènes cycliques comme résultats de chocs structurels exogènes : oscillations, fluctuations, et mouvements pendulaires sont au cœur de la thèse de Leontief [1928]. En outre, Leontief emploie le terme générique de « changement économique » (*wirtschaftliche Veränderung*) pour désigner l'ensemble de ces phénomènes.

Prenons l'un des exemples donnés par Leontief, celui d'une économie à trois biens, A, B et C. La combinaison de deux biens permet de produire le troisième bien : il n'y a donc pas de production jointe, les trois biens sont reproductibles (pas de facteur primaire), et aucun bien n'apparaît comme entrant dans tous les processus productifs ni n'apparaît comme produit sans être employé dans un processus comme entrant. La combinaison de bien A et B permet de produire du bien C ; la combinaison de bien A et C permet de produire du bien B ; et la combinaison de bien B et C permet de produire du bien A.

33. Littéralement : « *die einfache Reproduktion* » [Leontief, 1928, p. 590].

L'économie est initialement dans un état de reproduction simple, où à chaque période une seule unité de chaque bien est produite : soit (A, B, C) = (1, 1, 1) le vecteur des productions initiales de l'économie. Les coefficients de distribution sont donnés et mesurent la quantité de la production totale d'un bien *i* qui est consacrée à la production d'un bien *j*. Ici tous ces coefficients sont égaux à ½, ce qui est compatible avec l'hypothèse de reproduction simple.

À l'instant $t = 0$, Leontief introduit un choc de productivité non persistant[34] dans le secteur produisant du bien *A*. Ce choc génère une augmentation de 10 % de la production de *A*, soit une quantité de *A* de 1,1 au lieu de 1. Les autres secteurs n'ont pas connu de choc de productivité : il s'agit donc d'un choc local, c'est-à-dire sectoriel ou à l'échelle d'un producteur. Ce choc se répercute ensuite sur le reste de l'économie à travers le système d'interdépendance acheteur-vendeur entre les producteurs. Partant des données numériques calculées par Leontief [*ibid.*, p. 593], il apparaît qu'un tel choc génère des fluctuations dans l'ensemble de l'économie qui prennent la forme d'oscillations explosives. Ainsi, un choc local peut générer des fluctuations dans toute l'économie et l'explication des fluctuations est une explication technologique des cycles.

À partir de ce modèle très simple, Leontief étudie l'effet de changements, permanents ou temporaires, de différents coefficients du modèle, de manière à faire apparaître plusieurs types de phénomènes cycliques et de fluctuations. Aussi, c'est le même modèle qui est employé pour expliquer à la fois la croissance et les cycles : une théorie des cycles réels fondée sur l'analyse technologique. Leontief approfondit cette approche dans son modèle input-output matriciel (section suivante).

1.3. Productivité et changement structurel

Pour représenter le changement technique, Leontief introduit dans son modèle matriciel [1937, p. 111] un « coefficient de productivité » pour chacun des secteurs de l'économie[35]. Leontief note A_i l'indice de

34. Leontief [1928] considère que c'est le changement technique qui explique le changement de productivité.

35. Dans sa thèse, Leontief [1928] avait déjà introduit des « coefficients de productivité » (*Produktivitätskoeffizienten*).

productivité sectoriel qui est associé aux coefficients techniques de chacun des secteurs, ici le secteur i : soit le secteur i, qui produit un unique bien homogène i, dont la technologie est caractérisée par le vecteur des coefficients techniques[36] $(a_{1i}, a_{2i}, \ldots\ a_{ni})$, où le coefficient a_{ji} mesure la quantité physique de bien j nécessaire à la production d'une unité de bien i. Pour introduire les changements de productivité, on multiplie ces coefficients techniques par le scalaire $(1/A_i)$. La valeur initiale de A_i est de 1 pour tous les secteurs. La fonction de production de chaque secteur de l'économie est donc caractérisée par le vecteur des coefficients techniques suivant : $(1/A_i)\ (a_{1i}, a_{2i}, \ldots\ a_{ni})$.

Ce faisant, il est possible d'examiner l'effet d'un changement du coefficient de productivité d'un secteur sur ce même secteur et sur le reste de l'économie. Pour caractériser ce changement local et sa diffusion, Leontief [1937] reprend le terme de Frisch [1933] d'« impulsion » [Leontief, p. 110, 127, 129] auquel il adjoint les termes de « transmission » [*transmission*, p. 110] ou de « diffusion » (*spread*, p. 129). D'une part, Leontief montre que la réaction de l'économie dans son ensemble dépend du point initial de l'impulsion et, comme d'une période à une autre les secteurs dominants ou stratégiques changent, le comportement cyclique de l'économie change aussi : « La localisation de la cause première responsable des fluctuations économiques périodiques peut changer d'une période à une autre. Tandis que le rôle de l'industrie "stratégique", par exemple, peut passer d'une branche de production à une autre, le mouvement cyclique de toutes les autres industries doit nécessairement en être modifié. » [Leontief, 1935, p. 27] D'autre part, la réaction de l'économie à une impulsion dépend de la structure spécifique et détaillée et des techniques mises en œuvre dans chacun des secteurs et donc, en somme, de la structure capitalistique de l'économie, représentée par la matrice des coefficients techniques.

Selon Leontief, c'est la capacité à modéliser la diffusion de ces impulsions locales qui fait l'intérêt d'une théorie de l'interdépendance générale entre les unités productives car, en effet, le « mérite principal [de cette théorie] repose dans le fait qu'elle nous permet de tenir compte du

36. Cette relation est celle des fonctions de production dites de Leontief (ou Walras-Leontief), c'est-à-dire à rendements constants et facteurs de production complémentaires.

réseau hautement complexe des interrelations mutuelles qui transmettent les impulsions de n'importe quel changement local dans les recoins les plus reculés du système économique actuel » [*ibid.*, p. 110].

De sa théorie de l'interdépendance générale, Leontief ne cherche pas à déduire des théorèmes généraux sur les effets d'impulsions (changements locaux de productivité), mais il explore comment l'économie américaine concrète réagirait à de telles impulsions. Leontief utilise les données qu'il a collectées dans un tableau entrées-sorties consolidé à 10 secteurs, dont les ménages[37], pour l'économie américaine en 1919. De là, il évalue l'effet de la variation du coefficient de productivité de chacun des secteurs sur le produit et les prix des autres secteurs. Il en ressort que, pour ce qui est des magnitudes du changement des produits, dans chacun des cas, un changement de productivité locale a des effets toujours plus forts dans le secteur même d'où l'impulsion initiale est partie que dans les autres secteurs : le réseau des interrelations input-output semble ici agir comme un amortisseur. Par ailleurs, le sens de l'effet d'impulsion, à savoir positif ou négatif, n'est pas toujours le même que le sens du choc de productivité : par exemple, un choc positif de productivité dans le secteur agricole a un effet négatif sur le produit de tous les autres secteurs de l'économie, tandis qu'un choc positif dans le secteur de l'énergie, ou dans le secteur des métaux et produits métalliques, a un effet positif sur la production de tous les autres secteurs sauf celui du textile et sur les ménages.

Ces résultats, de nature empirique, montrent ainsi des différences de réaction des secteurs au même type de stimuli, autant en *ampleur* que dans la *direction* des changements : ce sont autant d'informations qui ne seraient plus accessibles dans un modèle macroéconométrique agrégé. En outre, le changement d'un coefficient de productivité n'a pas toujours les mêmes effets sur tous les secteurs et sur l'économie. Enfin, d'une économie à l'autre, d'un pays à l'autre, et d'une période à une autre, les effets d'un choc technique changent en fonction de la structure capitalistique spécifique de l'économie considérée.

37. Dans ce modèle les ménages sont un secteur comme les autres : la consommation finale est leur input, et les « services des ménages » (travail et services entrepreneuriaux notamment) sont leur output.

Pour conclure cette partie consacrée au rôle de la technologie dans l'explication du changement économique, il apparaît que l'approche macroéconomique désagrégée où est représentée la circulation du capital entre les producteurs permet d'affiner l'analyse du changement technique en examinant (i) des chocs locaux, ici par le coefficient A_i, (ii) des chocs macroéconomiques, comme ici par le coefficient α, et (iii) leur diffusion par un processus d'impulsion-diffusion (*primary impulse - spread*) à travers le réseau des interrelations entre producteurs. Un choc de productivité peut avoir des conséquences très différentes sur les autres secteurs de l'économie selon le secteur où il a lieu et selon la structure de l'économie : par conséquent, la localisation des chocs et la structure de l'économie importent pour expliquer l'effet de chocs technologiques. Désagréger le capital et la technologie c'est comprendre où les chocs ont lieu, comment ils se diffusent et quels effets ils ont sur le reste de l'économie.

2. Problèmes de coordination entre producteurs et changement économique

La deuxième explication du changement économique provient des problèmes de coordination entre les producteurs lors du processus de circulation du capital. Comme le note Frisch dans le contexte de la Grande Dépression, le changement économique ainsi que la crise et la dépression économiques trouvent leurs sources non seulement dans des causes réelles, comme le changement technique, mais aussi dans la forme prise par le processus d'échange et de circulation des marchandises entre producteurs : la crise « est d'une manière ou d'une autre liée à la forme actuelle de l'organisation de l'industrie et du commerce » [Frisch, 1934, p. 259]. Pour Frisch, le problème de cette organisation se situe dans l'absence de coordinateur central et donc dans la décentralisation des décisions puisque « la vie économique moderne est divisée entre de nombreux groupes ou régions » (*ibid.*) : la circulation du capital entre des unités productives différentes soulève des problèmes de coordination qui contribuent à expliquer le changement économique[38]. C'est que, pour Frisch [*ibid.*][39] les

38. Soulignons que la distinction entre des unités productives différentes disparaît dans une fonction macroéconomique agrégée où le capital est agrégé.

39. Rappelons que le modèle de Frisch [1934] que nous étudions est présenté par celui-ci au début de la première partie de son article « Circulation planning » : il s'agit d'une analyse économique *positive* du

agents prennent leurs décisions d'achat et de vente dans un environnement informationnel imparfait où leurs décisions reposent sur des anticipations quant aux comportements des autres producteurs. L'état du moral des producteurs joue alors un rôle décisif dans la dynamique économique. Marschak [1934a][40] accorde également une importance fondamentale aux « attitudes » et aux « comportements » des agents dans un environnement informationnel imparfait. Dans un monde marqué par des chocs erratiques et une connaissance imparfaite des états futurs du monde, les agents modélisés par Frisch et par Marschak forment des anticipations qui conduisent parfois à des choix sous-optimaux (Frisch) et, dans tous les cas, engendrent des fluctuations réelles ou nominales. Nous montrons d'abord comment ces comportements servent à expliquer la tendance économique, croissante ou décroissante (2-1), puis les cycles et les oscillations des productions sectorielles (2-2) et, enfin, les fluctuations de la demande de liquidité et de l'encaisse réelle (2-3).

2.1. Expliquer la tendance économique : anticipations, humeur et moral des agents

Frisch [1934] met en avant le rôle des anticipations dans les interactions entre producteurs dans une économie monétaire. Frisch construit un modèle dynamique à plusieurs agents dans le cadre d'une économie libre de marché à prix fixes[41].

Le cas le plus simple est celui d'une économie à deux agents. Soit l'économie présentée par Frisch [*ibid.*, p. 261-272] composée d'un fermier, noté a, et d'un cordonnier, noté b. Frisch s'interroge sur ce qui détermine le montant de biens échangés par les deux agents. Le montant de la

changement économique, et notamment des crises, qui précède la solution *normative* exposée par Frisch, à savoir son système de « circulation planning ». Ce dernier est étudié notamment par Bjerkholt et Knell [2006], Akhabbar [2011] et Dupont-Kieffer [2012c]. Ici, nous ne sommes concerné que par la partie positive de l'article de Frisch et nous ne nous référons pas à sa solution normative.

40. Le modèle de Marschak [1934a] que nous examinons constitue la suite de ses précédents travaux macroéconomiques [1932 ; 1933b]. Il est complémentaire d'autres travaux contemporains de Marschak [1933a ; 1934b ; 1936] et il annonce ses travaux microéconomiques ultérieurs (pour notre période [1937, 1938] et Makower et Marschak [1938]).

41. Frisch n'offre pas de fondements microéconomiques au postulat de fixité des prix, mais elle est compatible avec notre interprétation de ces modèles comme des modèles d'analyse de court terme. Voir Dupont-Kieffer [2012c].

consommation de bien *b* par le producteur *a* à la période t, a_t, dépend de la quantité de son bien qu'il a vendu à l'autre agent à la période précédente (b_{t-1}), et d'un certain « coefficient d'optimisme » (*Ibid.*, 262), α, qui exprime l'état du « moral » (*mood*) du producteur a : $a_t = \alpha b_{t-1}$. Et réciproquement pour l'autre agent, *b*, pour qui le montant de bien qu'il achète à *a* est tel que $b_t = \beta a_{t-1}$. Les coefficients α et β sont des coefficients d'optimisme : si le coefficient est égal à un, on est dans une situation de statu quo et l'agent anticipe que le futur sera comme le passé ; si le coefficient est supérieur à un, l'agent est optimiste car il anticipe que les commandes de marchandises vont augmenter en comparaison à la période précédente ; si le coefficient est inférieur à un, l'agent est pessimiste et anticipe une baisse des commandes comparé à la période précédente.

Dans la mesure où le montant (a_t, b_t) des transactions à la période t est déterminé par les conditions économiques de la période précédente (a_{t-1}, b_{t-1}) et les coefficients d'optimisme (α, β), nous avons là un processus formellement proche de celui des anticipations adaptatives. Toutefois, à la différence du principe des anticipations adaptatives, ici, l'agent économique ne prend pas explicitement en considération son erreur d'anticipation à la période précédente [42] : l'anticipation repose sur seulement deux éléments, à savoir les conditions économiques à la période précédente et son moral, mais pas explicitement sur l'erreur d'anticipation.

Dans le modèle, les données sont les coefficients d'optimisme et les quantités initiales a_0 et b_0. Les montants de biens échangés à chaque instant, (a_t, b_t) sont les inconnues à déterminer. Le système obtenu est le suivant :

$$\begin{cases} a_t = \alpha b_{t-1} \\ b_t = \beta a_{t-1} \end{cases} ; \qquad \text{soit : } \begin{cases} a_t = a_0 \gamma^t \\ b_t = b_0 \gamma^t \end{cases} \quad \text{avec } \gamma = \sqrt{\alpha\beta}\,.$$

42. Le texte de Frisch prête toutefois à interprétation puisque les coefficients d'optimisme « expriment comment les ventes à la période précédente influencent la politique de chacun à la période suivante » [1934, p. 262] : remarquons seulement que Frisch ne dit pas que les coefficients d'optimisme reflètent le moral des producteurs à un moment donné, mais qu'ils établissent le lien entre conditions économiques passées et présentes. Par conséquent, il n'est pas exclu qu'une déception sur les ventes passées conduise à un coefficient d'optimisme inférieur à un, reflétant un moral pessimiste. Dans ce cas, les coefficients d'optimisme refléteraient un processus adaptatif.

La production (a_t, b_t) suit une trajectoire générée par le système d'équations dynamiques dont la tendance dépend de γ. Ce dernier coefficient est un indice agrégé du moral des agents de cette économie. Il est calculé comme la moyenne non-linéaire de α et β : par conséquent, le bon moral d'un agent peut compenser l'effet sur la tendance du mauvais moral d'un autre.

Ce système génère deux mouvements : un mouvement tendanciel, de croissance si $\gamma > 1$, ou de décroissance si $\gamma < 1$, ainsi qu'un mouvement cyclique de deux périodes le long du *trend*. Les oscillations autour du *trend* expriment le décalage entre les conditions initiales et l'état du moral des agents. Dès lors, il est possible de montrer qu'une humeur dépensière *spending mood*, [*ibid.*, p. 263] conduit à un chemin d'expansion alors qu'une humeur économe, *saving mood* [*ibid.*] ou 'déflationniste', *deflationary mood* [*ibid.*, p. 269] génère un processus de contraction où « le système entier décline progressivement jusqu'à être réduit à néant » [*ibid.*, p. 263]. Ce phénomène de déclin est, selon Frisch, celui rencontré dans les économies industrialisées au moment où il écrit. En effet, sous les conditions indiquées, le comportement d'une partie des agents a pour effet de saper les débouchés d'autres agents ce qui, en retour, aggrave la situation de tous : « Ce cercle vicieux insensé, est ce que j'entends par le phénomène d'*incapsulating.* » [*Ibid.*, p. 259] À cet égard, Frisch parle aussi de « stagnation de la circulation » nationale et internationale[43].

2.2. Les cycles : *In the mood for cycles*

Frisch [1934] introduit ensuite un système de crédit. Il s'agit d'une forme particulière de crédit de type inter-producteurs, sans système bancaire. Les agents peuvent acheter des marchandises à crédit auprès d'autres agents et ainsi les créances des uns constituent les dettes des autres[44]. L'interdépendance entre les agents en est renforcée. Frisch considère que son modèle précédent (sans endettement) n'est pas « réaliste » car il autorise des trajectoires de croissance à l'infini [1934,

43. Son système de planification par une agence centrale, le « circulation planning » vise justement à mettre un terme à la « stagnation de la circulation » du capital et des échanges entre les agents.

44. En introduisant le système d'endettement et de crédit dans son modèle, Frisch renvoie explicitement à l'ouvrage de 1933 d'Irving Fisher, *Booms and Depressions.*

p. 265]. De fait, même si son modèle avec endettement peut engendrer des trajectoires exponentielles, Frisch n'explore que le cas de trajectoires « cycliques » où le cycle est amorti (*damped*) et l'économie converge vers un état stable [*ibid.*, p. 267-268]. Le système de crédit force alors les agents à converger quelques soient les écarts d'humeur ou de moral entre eux et de manière à faire apparaître des trajectoires stables[45].

Frisch introduit dans chacune des équations le montant que l'agent doit à l'autre agent comme la différence entre les achats de a (à b) et de b (à a), noté G_t . Avec $\alpha, \lambda, \beta, \mu$ des constantes non négatives et $G_t = (a_0 + a_1 + \ldots + a_t) - (b_0 + b_1 + \ldots + \ldots + b_t)$, nous obtenons le système suivant :

$$\begin{cases} a_t = \alpha b_{t-1} - \lambda G_{t-1} \\ b_t = \beta a_{t-1} + \mu G_{t-1} \end{cases}$$

Ce système de crédit implique en particulier que la croissance des dépenses d'un agent ne peut se faire indéfiniment sans que l'autre agent ne suive cette tendance et rattrape l'autre agent. Si le moral d'un agent peut compenser celui d'un autre, il n'en va pas de même avec le système de crédit, où l'interdépendance est différente. De plus, dans ce cas, la coordination entre les agents à travers le système de crédit génère un type nouveau de fluctuations qui ont une ampleur plus forte que les oscillations régulières le long du *trend*, et dont l'amplitude décroît avec le temps puisque le système de crédit pousse les agents à converger vers un équilibre : ce sont des oscillations amorties. Pour que ce dernier type de fluctuations présente une dynamique cyclique permanente, il faut ajouter un élément exogène d'entretien des cycles (*maintained oscillations*), à savoir les chocs aléatoires : Frisch [*ibid.*, p. 271] parle d'*erratic impulses, shocks, erratic shocks, accidental disturbances.* Dès lors, en soumettant en permanence le système d'échange à des chocs exogènes erratiques, Frisch fait apparaître des oscillations irrégulières qui sont maintenues dans le

45. Frisch considère que son modèle précédent (sans endettement) n'est pas « réaliste » car il autorise des trajectoires de croissance à l'infini [1934, p. 265]. De fait, même si son modèle avec endettement peut générer des trajectoires exponentielles, Frisch n'explore que le cas de trajectoires « cycliques » où le cycle est amorti (*damped*) et l'économie converge vers un état stable [*ibid.*, p. 267-268].

temps[46]. Ces cycles générés par les chocs erratiques et ne provenant pas des caractéristiques réelles de la production (la technique), mais provenant du système d'échange et de crédit entre les agents, Frisch les appelle *pure circulation-cycles* [*ibid.*].

En somme, les problèmes de coordination entre les agents suffisent à expliquer la dynamique économique et ses trois composantes que sont le *trend*, des fluctuations triviales autour du *trend*, et des fluctuations de coordination dans le système de crédit. Avec ce modèle, Frisch attire l'attention sur le moral des agents, les anticipations et le système d'échange et d'endettement.

2.3. Organisation industrielle, incertitude et fluctuations de l'encaisse réelle

Pour Marschak, comme pour Frisch, les problèmes de coordination dans la circulation du capital entre les producteurs jouent un rôle central dans l'explication du changement économique. Marschak explore ce problème par un exercice paradoxal consistant à modéliser une économie monétaire à l'état stationnaire où le stock de monnaie, m, et le revenu national, r_0, sont constants[47]. La perspective particulière adoptée par Marschak s'explique par son objectif qui ne consiste pas en premier lieu à modéliser le cycle des affaires mais d'abord à réfuter la théorie selon laquelle la vitesse de circulation de la monnaie n'est pas un facteur important pour comprendre la détermination du niveau des prix. Rappelons que pour les tenants de l'explication monétaire des cycles, comme par exemple Ralph G. Hawtrey, d'une part « les facteurs perturbateurs [de l'équilibre économique] agissent à travers des changements dans le niveau des prix » [Haberler, 1932, p. 46] et que c'est par la régulation du niveau des prix que passe celle du cycle économique, et, d'autre part, dans cette perspective, toute variation de la vitesse de la circulation de la monnaie est neutralisée et n'a donc pas d'effet sur le niveau des prix en raison d'une compensation du côté des

46. Frisch [1934, p. 271] utilise les chiffres de la loterie nationale norvégienne pour soumettre son système à des chocs aléatoires.

47. À la différence des modèles de Leontief, l'analyse de Marschak se situe dans le cadre d'une économie monétaire et, à la différence de Frisch, il traite d'une économie avec un système bancaire et financier.

transactions, conceptualisée par la « vitesse de circulation des biens » [Haberler, 1932, p. 29 ; Marget, 1932a ; 1932b]. Marschak examine la nature de la vitesse de circulation de la monnaie de manière à montrer que cette « neutralité » n'est qu'un cas limite. Autrement dit, pour ce qui concerne notre objet, à savoir l'explication du changement économique par les problèmes de coordination dans la circulation du capital entre producteurs, la contribution de Marschak ne vise pas directement à établir une théorie générale des cycles expliquant le mouvement des prix et/ou des quantités, mais à examiner une pièce particulière du mécanisme général de l'explication des prix, à savoir la thèse de la neutralité de la vitesse de la circulation de la monnaie dans l'explication du cycle économique. C'est dans cette perspective que nous retenons la contribution de Marschak[48].

Dans le modèle que nous examinerons, Marschak [1934a] n'explique pas, mais postule l'existence de fluctuations irrégulières et de fluctuations saisonnières *dans le cours* du processus de production, touchant la valeur des biens intermédiaires produits, tout en considérant que dans l'ensemble, sur la période considérée, le revenu réel demeure inchangé quelles que soient les fluctuations qui ont eu lieu. L'économie dans son ensemble est considérée comme stationnaire avec un revenu réel constant, noté r_0[49]. Marschak construit son modèle à partir de « l'équation des échanges », $m.v = t.p$, avec m, la masse monétaire, p, le niveau des prix des facteurs productifs[50], t, la valeur réelle des transactions par unité de temps, v, la vitesse de circulation de la monnaie. Partant de ce cadre, Marschak examine les comportements des producteurs dans la sphère monétaire, et notamment la détermination de leur « encaisse désirée » [Marschak, 1938, p. 311], pensée comme l'encaisse réelle, notée μ, telle que $\mu = m/p$ et, par conséquent, $v = t/\mu$. L'encaisse réelle se décompose en deux : l'encaisse

48. Pour faciliter la lecture et nous concentrer sur l'essentiel de son message, nous ne présentons dans le corps du texte que peu d'éléments du modèle de Marschak. Les notes de bas de page donneront plus de détails au lecteur intéressé.

49. Comme le souligne le titre de son article, « Econometric parameters in a stationary society with monetary circulation », l'économie est à l'état stationnaire. Le modèle vise à expliquer uniquement les fluctuations dans l'encaisse réelle et les prix nominaux.

50. On compte deux facteurs de production, le travail et le capital. L'économie étant à l'état stationnaire, Marschak postule que les prix relatifs de ces facteurs sont constants et il n'est donc pas nécessaire ici de distinguer entre les prix de chacun de ces facteurs. Le revenu national, r_0 est la somme des rémunérations des facteurs productifs versées au cours du processus de production.

réelle pour la mise en œuvre du processus productif, notée k, et l'encaisse réelle de réserve, l, telle que $\mu = k + l$. Nous ne traitons pas de l'encaisse k car Marschak la suppose constante et ne la soumet pas à l'incertitude à laquelle sont soumis les échanges. Dans une note de bas de page, Marschak relève qu'il serait possible d'intégrer l'incertitude à k, comme le lui aurait suggéré Karl Schlesinger, sans néanmoins donner de suite à cette suggestion. L'analyse de la demande de monnaie et de l'encaisse réelle est l'une des pièces maîtresse de la théorie monétaire du cycle des affaires, notamment dans l'établissement de la relation entre la masse monétaire et les prix. Nous étudierons comment Marschak introduit, comme Frisch, les problèmes de coordination comme facteur explicatif du changement économique. De fait, dans ce contexte, les variations de p et μ s'expliquent par celles de l à partir des problèmes de coordination dans le processus de circulation du capital entre les producteurs dans un environnement informationnel imparfait.

Partant de la distinction de Frank Knight dans *Risk Uncertainty and Profit*[51], Marschak distingue entre trois termes : le risque, le degré d'ignorance et l'incertitude. Marschak interprète le risque comme « la dispersion de la distribution de la fréquence d'événements alternatifs futurs » [Makower et Marschak, 1938, p. 271], tandis que le *degré d'ignorance* est défini comme l'incertitude au sujet de cette distribution (*frequency distribution*) [*ibid.*]. En effet, pour Marschak, parler d'incertitude ne suppose pas une ignorance totale des probabilités des états du monde, mais implique un certain degré d'ignorance quant à la fréquence des événements : « Dans la salle d'un jeu de roulette nous n'ignorons pas les probabilités qui sont assignées aux différents événements alternatifs ; et néanmoins, même là, il demeure une incertitude attachée au moindre événement. » [*Ibid.*] Chez Marschak [1934a ; 1938 ; Makower et Marschak, 1938], l'incertitude n'exclut pas l'existence d'informations quantitatives et de probabilités au sujet des événements futurs [Cherrier, 2010 ; Mehrling, 2010]. Dès lors, c'est parce que les producteurs doivent prendre des décisions dans un environnement incertain qu'ils constituent une encaisse de réserve (l). Et c'est la combinaison de cette incertitude et

51. Marschak fait aussi référence au *Treatise on Probability* de Keynes, 1921.

de la structure de l'organisation industrielle qui permet d'expliquer les fluctuations de l'encaisse de réserve.

Dans cette économie à l'état stationnaire, la technologie est donnée et supposée invariante[52], mais, d'une part, des fluctuations saisonnières et des fluctuations irrégulières affectent la valeur des biens intermédiaires au cours du processus de production et, d'autre part, l'organisation de la production entre les différents producteurs est susceptible de changer au cours de la période. Le processus productif peut être plus ou moins intégré et Marschak imagine une économie où le degré de différenciation de l'économie s'accroît de manière continue au cours de la période [1934a, p. 102]. L'intégration porte sur la division des étapes de production entre producteurs : moins le processus est intégré, plus les producteurs échangent entre eux et donc plus le volume des transactions transitant par le marché est élevé[53]. Les transactions entre producteurs s'effectuent dans un monde incertain au regard des conditions d'achat et de vente. Ainsi, plus les producteurs ont à échanger entre eux, plus ils sont exposés à l'incertitude : par conséquent, plus le système productif est désintégré, plus le volume des transactions est élevé et donc, plus les échanges entre producteurs et les problèmes de coordination sont importants, ce qui alimente l'encaisse réelle de réserve des producteurs[54].

52. Ce qui suit dans cette note n'est pas nécessaire pour suivre le reste du développement mais détaille certains aspects du modèle de Marschak. La technologie est représentée par la « fonction de manufacture », notée $r(x)$, qui indique la valeur réelle du produit à la période x. L'indice x indique la distance à l'acte de consommation finale, qui a lieu en $x = 0$. Le processus de transformation des facteurs productifs étant intertemporel, cette valeur augmente au fur et à mesure (pour une représentation graphique, Marschak [1934b] ; pour une analyse mathématique, voir Marschak [1934a]. On en déduit que le stock K de biens intermédiaires produits et consommés dans le processus productif est l'intégrale de zéro à l'infini de la fonction de manufacture, tel que $K = \int_0^\infty r(x)dx$. Marschak [1934a, p. 93] définit alors la « période moyenne de production » de Böhm-Bawerk comme $(1/F)$ avec $F = r_0/K$. La vitesse de circulation des biens est notée $V = t/K$.

53. Au moment où Marschak écrit, l'intégration, désignée par le « degré de différenciation » est un argument souvent cité dans l'explication macroéconomique et macroéconométrique des phénomènes monétaires et, comme le note Jan Tinbergen, « par 'degré de différenciation' est entendu le nombre moyen de changements de mains auquel les marchandises sont soumises avant de parvenir au marché final, c'est-à-dire le marché sur lequel les consommateurs les acquièrent » [Tinbergen, 1934, p. 26]. Voir aussi Haberler [1937, p. 61-63].

54. Rappelons qu'avec m la masse monétaire, p le niveau des prix des facteurs productifs, t la valeur réelle des transactions par unité de temps, v la vitesse de circulation de la monnaie, nous retrouvons l'équation de l'échange $mv = pt$. Soit μ l'encaisse réelle des agents économiques, avec $\mu = m/p = k + l$, avec k une encaisse de transaction *constante* et l l'encaisse de réserve.

La seule information dont disposent les agents au sujet des fluctuations au cours du processus productif est l'écart type σ caractérisant la variation de la valeur réelle espérée du revenu $E(\Delta r_x)$ au moment x, x étant la distance temporelle d'un bien à l'acte de consommation finale. Dans l'explication de l'écart type σ, Marschak distingue deux composantes : une composante aléatoire exogène à effet positif sur σ, notée s, et le degré de différenciation du processus productif, noté δ, qui mesure l'intégration verticale des producteurs[55] et dont l'effet sera discuté plus bas, tels que $\sigma = \sigma(s, \delta)$.

On note L la demande de liquidité pour motif de précaution et L_1 la demande de monnaie qui est substituée par des services bancaires et d'assurance, avec $L - L_1 = l$, l'encaisse réelle de réserve. L'incertitude intervient dans l'explication des fluctuations de l'encaisse de réserve à deux niveaux, sur L_1 et sur L. Tout d'abord, selon Marschak, « la diminution [de l'encaisse réelle de réserve] par les opérations des banques et des institutions financières est d'autant plus grande que le degré de certitude avec lequel ces institutions peuvent réaliser des prévisions sur les fluctuations est élevé » [*ibid.*, p. 97]. Autrement dit, si l'incertitude est un facteur déterminant de la réserve de liquidité, plus les institutions financières et bancaires sont en mesure de prévoir les fluctuations dans le processus de production, moins les agents ont besoin de constituer d'encaisse réelle de réserve : le système bancaire et financier vient ici réduire l'incertitude des producteurs et donc leur encaisse réelle de réserve.

En outre, plus le processus productif est différencié, c'est-à-dire plus les différentes étapes successives de production sont mises en œuvre par des unités de décision différentes, plus les producteurs sont exposés à l'incertitude dans les échanges. Pour illustrer ce principe, supposons, par exemple, qu'un processus de production, à un moment donné, ne soit plus réalisé par un même producteur mais scindé entre deux producteurs. Par exemple, au lieu du seul producteur A, nous avons A_2 et A_1 de manière à ce

55. Le degré de différenciation de l'économie est défini comme suit par Marschak : $\delta = (t - r_0)/r_0$, de telle manière que si l'économie est entièrement intégrée, c'est-à-dire que la production des biens de consommation finale est réalisée par une seule unité de production intégrée, alors le volume des transactions passant par le marché se réduit à la rémunération des facteurs de production, r_0, et à la valeur des biens de consommation finale vendus aux consommateurs, égale à leur revenu, r_0, et donc $t = 2r_0$ et, par déduction, le degré de différenciation de l'économie est $\delta = 1$.

que le degré de différenciation verticale dans l'économie augmente. L'indice x dans A_x porte sur la distance à l'acte de consommation finale où $x = 0$ est l'acte de consommation finale, ce qui explique que, dans le processus de production, le producteur qui intervient le premier est A_2, puis vient A_1 qui transforme le bien semi-fini produit par A_2, et ainsi de suite jusqu'à la production d'un bien fini, c'est-à-dire prêt à la consommation finale par les consommateurs. Dans le cas d'un tel changement dans l'organisation industrielle, ce qui avait lieu à l'intérieur de la firme A transite maintenant en partie par le marché à travers l'échange entre A_2 et A_1. Autrement dit, cette augmentation de la différenciation conduit à une augmentation du volume des échanges dans l'économie tout en laissant la production de biens intermédiaires et le revenu réel inchangés. Par conséquent, une partie des opérations productives est dorénavant soumise à l'incertitude liée aux problèmes de coordination des producteurs, ce qui amène à la formation d'une encaisse de réserve supplémentaire. C'est en effet le cas, selon Marschak, « puisque A_2 prévoit maintenant avec moins de certitude les intentions d'achat de A_1, et que ce dernier est informé avec moins d'exactitude sur les conditions auxquelles A_2 a l'intention de lui vendre, que si ces affaires étaient réalisées sous la direction d'un management unique » [Marschak, 1934a, p. 99]. Ceci amène alors à introduire le degré de différenciation δ comme variable explicative de l'écart type σ qui justifie la formation d'une réserve de liquidité. Plus le degré de différenciation est élevé, plus l'encaisse réelle de réserve est élevée et comme l'économie connaît, par hypothèse, un processus continu de différenciation, l'encaisse de réserve s'accroît et est de plus en plus soumise au facteur incertitude.

En résumé, l, la réserve de liquidité, est affectée par des fluctuations dont l'écart type est σ. Comme cet écart type est expliqué d'une part par un élément exogène aléatoire s, et, d'autre part, par le degré de différenciation des producteurs δ, on obtient $\sigma = \xi(s, \delta)$ et $l = l(s, \delta)$. L'encaisse réelle de réserve est croissante avec l'écart type de l'élément aléatoire affectant les valeurs réelles espérées des revenus, et croissante également avec le degré de différenciation car moins le processus productif est intégré, plus les producteurs échangent entre eux et donc plus le volume de transactions soumis à l'incertitude augmente.

Cette analyse vient s'emboîter dans le mécanisme général de l'explication autrichienne du cycle des affaires avec, en particulier, le lien entre, d'une part, l'encaisse réelle ($\mu = k + l = k + l(s, \delta)$), qui est un déterminant de la vitesse de circulation de la monnaie puisque $v = t/\mu$, et, d'autre part, le mouvement des prix, p. La théorie de Marschak de l'encaisse réelle lui permet de ne pas faire de v un résidu ou une donnée qui viendrait soutenir la thèse de sa neutralité car, comme l'écrit Marschak à propos des théories monétaires des cycles, « nous ne voulons pas que la vitesse de circulation sauve la situation tel un *deus ex machina.* » [1938, p. 311]. Marschak montre alors que la proposition de la théorie quantitative de la monnaie selon laquelle v n'a pas d'effet sur p, en raison d'une neutralisation du changement de la vitesse de la circulation de la monnaie, n'est qu'un cas particulier et que dans la plupart des cas une variation de v implique une variation des prix [1934a, p. 104-107]. Nous n'examinons pas plus avant les liens entre vitesse de la circulation, encaisse réelle, et prix, car cela nous amènerait bien au-delà de notre objectif. Nous retiendrons que les problèmes de coordination entre les producteurs est, selon Marschak, l'une des pièces majeures du mécanisme explicatif du cycle des affaires.

En conclusion, si le modèle macroéconomique construit par Marschak est conçu de manière à pouvoir explorer les nombreux aspects des cycles économiques, y compris des effets du changement technique sur le revenu (r_x), Marschak concentre sa contribution sur les problèmes soulevés par la théorie monétaire alors en pleine effervescence. Il s'agit en particulier de repenser l'équation de l'échange sur laquelle repose la théorie quantitative de la monnaie. C'est dans ces circonstances que Marschak met en place le cadre analytique général que nous avons examiné : une analyse macroéconométrique fondée sur un modèle macroéconomique désagrégé de la production où les problèmes de coordination entre producteurs dans la circulation du capital sont un élément de l'explication du changement économique.

La circulation du capital est pensée à travers la représentation autrichienne de la production où les facteurs originaux sont transformés d'une étape à l'autre du processus productif jusqu'à passer de l'état de produits semi-finis (ou biens intermédiaires) en produits finis disponibles pour la consommation finale. Aussi, l'analyse ne se concentre pas en particulier sur le revenu national mais sur l'ensemble de la circulation du capital car, pour Marschak, certes « les mouvements de revenu total sont [...] l'élément principal à prendre en considération dans toute description du cycle économique [,] toutefois, les proportions du revenu associées aux différents groupes de producteurs ou aux différents départements [de l'économie...] ne sont pas moins importantes » [1933a, p. 375]. Autrement dit, le tableau économique ne doit pas être agrégé de manière à se concentrer sur l'explication du revenu national, mais il doit être pensé de manière à faire apparaître la circulation du capital entre les producteurs car c'est dans le cours de ce processus de production que se situe la véritable explication du changement économique. L'explication que Marschak met en avant dans ses travaux de 1933-1934 lui permet de clarifier les fondements de la théorie monétaire associée à la théorie autrichienne du cycle des affaires en montrant que, même dans une économie à l'état stationnaire où le revenu réel national est constant et la technologie donnée, les problèmes de coordination dans le cours de la circulation du capital entre les producteurs jouent un rôle important dans la théorie du cycle des affaires puisque ces problèmes permettent de réviser l'explication de la vitesse de la circulation de la monnaie et de la relation entre celle-ci, l'encaisse détenue par les producteurs, et les prix.

Retenons, pour ce qui concerne la question traitée dans cette seconde partie, qu'à la manière de Frisch à la même période, Marschak construit un modèle macroéconomique désagrégé car c'est cette approche qui est en mesure de rendre compte du phénomène fondamental que sont les problèmes de coordination entre les acteurs économiques. Si chez Frisch ces problèmes de coordination trouvent leur source dans des états d'humeur et d'anticipations différents entre les agents, chez Marschak, ils se situent dans les comportements rationnels des agents confrontés à l'incertitude dans l'échange marchand[56]. Dans un cas comme dans l'autre, le modèle macroéconomique doit être désagrégé de manière à mettre en scène l'interdépendance entre les différents producteurs afin de rendre

56. Dans les années qui suivront ces publications, Marschak « allégera » son analyse du cadre macroéconomique de ses articles de 1933 et 1934 pour approfondir l'analyse des comportements individuels des acteurs économiques. Il cherchera à donner des fondements microéconomiques plus rigoureux à la demande de liquidité dans un cadre informationnel marqué par l'incertitude et le risque en la fondant sur la théorie du choix rationnel (pour notre période, voir Marschak [1937 ; 1938] ainsi que Marschak et Makower [1938]). Voir Cherrier [2010] et Mehrling [2010].

compte de l'explication du changement économique par les problèmes de coordination lors de la circulation du capital.

3. Conclusion

Dans cet article nous avons examiné une série d'articles publiés durant « les années de haute théorie » (1926-1939) et rarement étudiés, que ce soit ensemble ou séparément. Ces articles ne sont pas seulement très largement ignorés par les économistes en général mais aussi par les historiens de la pensée économique qui se sont concentrés sur d'autres parties des œuvres de ces auteurs, y compris lorsqu'il s'agit de l'explication du changement économique.

Si nous avons rassemblé ici ces articles, ce n'est pas seulement parce qu'ils appartiennent au même registre, alors naissant, de la macroéconométrie et qu'ils proposent, chacun explicitement, une reformulation du tableau économique de Quesnay en un tableau entrées-sorties, mais aussi parce qu'ils contiennent une forme commune d'explication du changement économique dans un horizon de court terme. À la manière du tableau économique, les modèles de Marschak [1933a ; 1934a], de Frisch [1934] et de Leontief [1928 ; 1937] offrent une représentation macroéconomique désagrégée présentant des biens de capital hétérogènes de manière à rendre apparente la circulation du capital entre les producteurs. À l'opposé, dans une fonction de production macroéconomique avec capital agrégé, la circulation du capital entre producteurs n'apparaît pas explicitement.

Cette approche offre deux grands types d'explications du changement économique : l'une par le changement technique, et l'autre par les problèmes de coordination entre les producteurs. Comparativement à l'analyse macroéconomique agrégée, elle permet de prendre en considération des phénomènes qui sont aplatis et écrasés lors de l'agrégation de la fonction de production : d'une part les phénomènes liés à l'interaction et à la circulation du capital (circulant ou fixe) entre les producteurs et, d'autre part, les problèmes de coordination entre producteurs. Avec cette macroéconomie désagrégée à plusieurs producteurs, il devient possible d'expliciter ces processus et phénomènes.

Par ailleurs, cette approche permet d'affiner l'analyse du changement technique en montrant comment ses différentes formes interviennent localement et se diffusent à travers le réseau d'interdépendances input-output dans le reste de l'économie. Elle permet aussi de distinguer entre, d'une part, des chocs locaux, touchant un seul ou un nombre restreint de producteurs afin de se diffuser, ou non, dans le reste de l'économie, et, d'autre part, des chocs macroéconomiques qui touchent uniformément tous les producteurs. Par la désagrégation, les chocs techniques perdent une part du mystère qui entoure ce que la macroéconomie consacrera comme la productivité générale des facteurs de production (TFP, *total factor productivity*) : c'est un pas vers un peu plus de lumière jetée sur les boîtes noires que sont la TFP et le résidu de Solow[57] car il devient possible d'identifier la source du choc ou du changement technique. C'est ainsi que Leontief introduit des coefficients de productivité pour chaque producteur ou secteur de manière à pouvoir évaluer l'effet d'une impulsion locale et sa diffusion dans le reste de l'économie. Par cette désagrégation, le modèle permet de s'approcher au plus près du point d'origine, voire de l'innovation, d'où provient le changement technique.

D'autre part, en identifiant la multitude des producteurs, cette approche désagrégée permet d'expliciter les problèmes de coordination entre les producteurs en présence d'incertitude, de risque ou de différence d'humeur entre les producteurs. Ajoutés à des chocs irréguliers sur le système d'échanges, à des modes de coordination entre ces agents économiques et, en particulier, au jeu des anticipations, émergent des fluctuations voire des crises. Marschak montre que la situation d'incertitude des agents d'une économie soumise à des chocs erratiques les amène à constituer des encaisses réelles de réserve qui sont sensibles au processus d'intégration verticale dans l'économie, remettant en question certains fondamentaux de la théorie monétaire des cycles à propos de la relation entre vitesse de circulation de la monnaie et prix. Frisch quant à lui montre que les différences de moral et d'humeur entre les producteurs suffisent à expliquer la tendance économique ainsi que certaines formes de cycles. Il propose un indice agrégé du moral des agents. Pour Frisch comme pour Marschak, c'est dans la séparation et la décentralisation des unités de décisions productives que se situe une partie de l'explication du changement

57. Sur le résidu de Solow comme une « boîte noire », voir Mata et Louçã [2009].

économique car celles-ci apportent avec elles les problèmes de coordination entre producteurs.

Après les « années de haute théorie », l'approche macroéconomique désagrégée, la représentation de la circulation du capital entre les unités productives, et la prise en compte du capital circulant se fait plus rare. Dans les années 1950 il est mis un terme au statut du capital circulant comme « capital par excellence » (déjà cité). Depuis lors, les précautions de l'ancien étudiant puis assistant de recherche de Leontief à Harvard, rapidement émancipé de la tutelle de son professeur, Robert Solow, en avançant sa fonction de production macroéconomique avec capital agrégé ne sont plus de mise : « En ce temps d'études économétriques conçues rationnellement et de super-tableaux input-output, il faut plus que l'habituelle "suspension volontaire de l'incrédulité" [58] pour parler sérieusement de la fonction de production agrégée. » [1957, p. 312] Tirant un trait sur les approches désagrégées du capital développées par les approches autrichienne, paréto-walrasienne ainsi que post-classique, la fonction de production agrégée s'installe au cœur de la macroéconométrie du changement économique.

Pourtant, en dépit de la quasi-hégémonie de la fonction macroéconomique avec capital agrégé, l'approche désagrégée n'a pas perdu de sa force et de sa pertinence et elle semble même avoir donné récemment quelques signes nouveaux de vitalité. C'est ce que montre une série de travaux récents, depuis la révolution de la nouvelle économie classique, qui offrent une représentation désagrégée des biens de capital, y compris circulant, dans le cadre des deux grandes explications examinées dans notre article, à savoir par le changement technique[59] et par les problèmes de coordination[60].

58. De l'anglais *willing suspension of disbelief.*

59. Voir, par exemple, pour une sélection : Kydland et Presott [1982], Lilien [1982], Long et Plosser [1983], Cooper et Haltiwanger [1990 ; 1996], Durlauf, Romer et Sims [1989], Forni et Reichlin [1998], Shea [1998], Huang, Liu et Phaneuf [2004], Jaimovich et Rebelo [2009], Foerster, Sarte et Watson [2011]. Voir aussi Louçã [2004] et Duarte et Hoover [2012].

60. Voir Basu [1995], ainsi que Basu, Fernald et Kimball [2006]. Pour Backhouse et Laidler [2004], la domination dans l'après-guerre d'une macroéconomie agrégée, depuis le modèle IS-LM jusqu'aux modèles RBC à agent représentatif, a mis de côté des facteurs explicatifs fondamentaux au point que « *In a few years' time, then, we may look back on the late twentieth century with a sense of incredulity . . . we may wonder how economists could ever have thought that differences among agents would not matter for the workings of the economy, and how they could have failed to see that coordination failures are endemic in complex systems* » [p. 52].

Bibliographie

Akhabbar Amanar [2008]. *Wassily Leontief et l'analyse input-output. Essai d'histoire et d'épistémologie*, Thèse de doctorat, Université Paris 1 Panthéon-Sorbonne, juin 2008, Paris.

— [2010]. « L'étrange victoire. Wassily Leontief et la transformation de la science économique », *Revue Européenne des Sciences Sociales*, 1(XLVII), p. 33-62.

— [2011]. « Tableaux économiques et analyse des business cycles chez Marschak, Frisch et Leontief », *Working Paper : University Library of Munich*, MPRA papers 34556. Publié dans *Léon Walras : un siècle après (1910-2010)*, Arnaud Diemer et Jean-Pierre Potier (dir.) [2013], Bruxelles : Éditions Peter Lang, p. 191-226.

Andvig Jens-Christopher [1978]. « Wicksell's influence on Frisch's macroeconomics in the thirties », *Scandinavian Journal of Economics* 80(1), p. 148-167.

— [1981]. « Ragnar Frisch and business cycle research during the interwar years », *History of Political Economy* 13(4), p. 695-725.

Basu Susanto [1995]. « Intermediate goods and business cycles: implications for productivity and welfare », *The American Economic Review* 85(3), p. 512-531.

—, John G. Fernald et Miles S. Kimball [2006]. « Are technology improvements contractionary? », *The American Economic Review* 96(5), p. 1418-1448.

Baumol William [2000]. « Leontief's great leap forward: beyond Quesnay, Marx and Bortkiewicz », *Economic Systems Research* 12(2), p. 141-152.

— et Thijs ten Raa [2009]. « Wassily Leontief: in appreciation », *European Journal of the History of Economic Thought* 16(3), p. 511-522.

Beckmann Ulf [2000]. *Von Löwe bis Leontief: Pioniere der Konjunkturforschung am Kieler Institut für Weltwirtschaft*. Marbourg : Metropolis-Verlag.

Bjerkholt Olav [2000]. « A Turning Point in the Development of Norwegian Economics – the Establishment of the University Institute of Economics in

1932 », Memorandum, Department of Economics, University of Oslo, No 36/2000.

Bjerkholt Olav [2007a]. « Ragnar Frisch's contribution to business cycle analysis », Memorandum, Department of Economics, University of Oslo, n° 2007-08.

— [2007b]. « Ragnar Frisch's business cycle approach: the genesis of the propagation and impulse model », *The European Journal of the History of Economic Thought* 14(3), p. 449-486.

— et Mark Knell [2006]. « Did Ragnar Frisch discover input-output economics? », *Economic Systems Research* 18(4), p. 391-410.

— et Ariane Dupont-Kieffer [2010a]. « Ragnar Frisch and the probability approach », *History of Political Economy* 43(Annual Supplement), p. 109-139.

— et — [2010b]. « Ragnar Frisch's Conception of Econometrics », *History of Political Economy* 42(1), p. 21-74.

Blatt John M. [1980]. « On the Frisch model of business cycles », *Oxford Economic Papers* New Series, 32(3), p. 467-479.

Blaug Mark [1987]. « Circulating capital », *In* John Eatwell, Murray Milgate et Peter Newman (dir.) *The New Palgrave, A Dictionary of Economics* vol. 1, p. 426-427.

Bodkin Ronald G., Lawrence Klein et Kanta Marwah [1991]. *A History of Macroeconometric Model Building.* Londres: Edward Elgar Publishing.

Bortkiewicz Ladislaus von [1921]. « Objektivismus und Subjektivismus in der Werttheorie », *Ekonomisk Tidskrift* 23(12), p. 1-22.

Bourdieu Pierre [1980]. *Le sens pratique.* Paris : Les Éditions de Minuit.

Cohen Avi J. [1989]. « Prices, capital, and the one-commodity model in neoclassical and classical theories », *History of Political Economy* 21(2), p. 231-251.

Cohen Avi Jonathan [2003]. « The Hayek/Knight capital controversy: the irrelevance of roundaboutness, or purging processes in time? », *History of Political Economy* 35(3), p. 469-490.

— [2010]. « Capital controversy from Böhm-Bawerk to Bliss: badly posed or very deep questions? Or what "we" can learn from capital controversy even if you don't care who won », *Journal of the History of Economic Thought* 32(1), p. 1-21.

Cooper Russell et John Haltiwanger [1990]. « Inventories and the propagation of sectoral shocks », *The American Economic Review* 80(1), p. 170-190.

— et — [1996]. « Evidence on macroeconomic complementarities », *The Review of Economics and Statistics* 78(1), p. 78-93.

Cherrier Béatrice [2010]. « Rationalizing human organization in an uncertain world: Jacob Marschak, from Ukrainian prisons to behavioral science laboratories », *History of Political Economy* 42(3), p. 443-467.

Duarte Pedro Garcia et Kevin D. Hoover [2012]. « Observing shocks », *History of Political Economy*, 45(Annual Supplement), p. 226-249.

Dupont-Kieffer Ariane [2001]. « Deux approches de l'économie quantitative de l'entre-deux-guerres : l'économétrie de Ragnar Frisch face à l'empirisme de Wesley Clair Mitchell », *Revue économique*, 52(3), p. 605-615.

— [2003]. *Ragnar Frisch et l'économétrie : l'invention de modèles et d'instruments à des fins normatives*, Thèse de doctorat, Université Paris 1 Panthéon-Sorbonne, Paris.

— [2012a]. « The accelerator principle at the core of Frisch's 1933 rocking horse model. Tracing back the influences: American institutionalism and Norwegian investment cycles theories », *Journal of the History of Economic Theory* 34(4), p. 447-473.

— [2012b]. « Lindahl and Frisch: national accounting in the interwar years as the empirical interface of their macroeconomics », *Journal of Economic and Social Measurement* 37(1-2), p. 145-174.

— [2012c]. « Ragnar Frisch's "Circulation Planning": an attempt at modelling general equilibrium », *Œconomia* 2(3), p. 281-303.

Durlauf Steven N., David Romer et Christopher A. Sims [1989]. « Output persistence, economic structure, and the choice of stabilization policy », *Brookings Papers on Economic Activity* 2, p. 69-136.

Foerster Andrew T., Pierre-Daniel G. Sarte, et Mark W. Watson [2011]. « Sectoral versus aggregate shocks: a structural factor analysis of industrial production », *Journal of Political Economy* 119(1), p. 1-38.

Forni Mario et Lucrezia Reichlin [1998]. « Let's get real : a factor analytical approach to disaggregated business cycle dynamics », *The Review of Economic Studies* 65(3), p. 453-473.

Frisch Ragnar [1933]. « Propagation problems and impulse problems in dynamic economics », In *Economic Essays in Honour of Gustav Cassel.* Londres : George Allen & Unwin Ltd, p. 171-205.

— [1934]. « Circulation planning: proposal for a national organization of a commodity and service exchange », *Econometrica* 2(3), p. 336-528; et, « Circulation planning Part III. Mathematical appendix », *Econometrica* 2(4), p. 422-435.

—, W. Keilhau et I. Wedervang [1936]. *Plan til en Økonomisk strukturundersØkelse for Norge.* (Plan for a structural survey of Norway). Oslo : Fabritius & Sonners Boktrykkeri.

Haberler Gottefried [1932]. « *Money and the business cycle* », *In* R. M. Ebeling (dir.) *The Austrian Theory of the Trade Cycle and Other Essays.* Ludwig von Mises Institute, Auburn, Alabama, [1996], p. 37-64.

— [1937]. *Prosperity and Depression. A Theoretical Analysis of Cyclical Movements.* Series of League of Nations Publications: Economic and Financial, Genève : the League of Nations, 1943.

Hagemann Harald [1997]. « *Jacob Marschak* », *In* R. Blomert, H.U. Esslinger, et N. Giovannini (dir.) *Heidelberger Sozial- und Staatswissenschaften: Das Institut für Sozial- und Staatswissenschaften zwischen 1918 und 1958.* Marbourg : Metropolis Verlag, p. 219-254.

— [2006]. « Jacob Marschak (1898–1977) », In R. Emmett (dir.) *The Biographical Dictionary of American Economists,* 2. Londres : Thoemmes, p. 596-603.

— [2009]. « Wassily Leontief and his German period », *13th Annual Conference of the European Society for the History of Economic Thought, Technical Change and Economic Analysis.* Thessalonique, Université de Macédoine, Grèce, 23-26 avril.

— [2011]. « European *Émigrés* and the 'Americanization' of economics », *European Journal of the History of Economic Thought* 18(5), p. 643-671.

Hayek Friedrich [1931]. *Prices and Production.* New York, NY : Augustus M. Kelly Publishers.

Keppler Jan Horst et Jérôme Lallement [2006]. « The origins of the U-shaped average cost curve: understanding the complexities of the modern theory of the firm », *History of Political Economy* 38(4), p. 733-774.

Huang Kevin X. D., Zheng Liu et Louis Phaneuf [2004]. « Why does the cyclical behavior of real wages change over time? », *The American Economic Review* 94(4), p. 836-856.

Jaimovich Nir et Sergio Rebelo [2009]. « Can news about the future drive the business cycle? », *The American Economic Review* 99(4), p. 1097-1118.

Kurz Heinz D. et Neri Salvadori [2006]. « Input-output analysis from a wider perspective: a comparison of the early works of Leontief and Sraffa », *Economic System Research* 18(4), p. 373-390.

Kydland Finn E. et Edward C. Presott [1982]. « Time to build and aggregate fluctuations », *Econometrica* 50(6), p. 1345-1370.

Le Gall Philippe [1993]. « Les contributions de Kalecki et Frisch à la macrodynamique du cycle et la naissance de l'économétrie », *Revue d'économie politique* 103, p. 551-578.

— [1994]. *Histoire de l'économétrie, 1914-1944. L'érosion du déterminisme*, Thèse de doctorat, Université Paris I Panthéon-Sorbonne, Paris.

Leontief Wassily [1928]. « Die Wirtschaft als Kreislauf », *Archiv für Sozialwissentschaft und Sozialpolitik* 60, p. 577-623. Traduction partielle en anglais [1991], « The economy as a circular flow », *Structural Change and Economic Dynamics* 2(1), p. 177-212.

— [1935]. « Price-quantity variations in business cycles », *The Review of Economic Statistics* 17(4), p. 21-27.

— [1936]. « Quantitative input and output relations in the economic systems of the United States », *The Review of Economic Statistics* 18(3), p. 105-125.

— [1937]. « Interrelations of prices, output, savings, and investment », *The Review of Economic Statistics* 19(3), p. 109-132.

Lilien David M. [1982]. « Sectoral shifts and cyclical unemployment », *Journal of Political Economy* 90(4), p. 777-793.

Long John B. et Charles I. Plosser [1983]. « Real business cycles », *Journal of Political Economy* 91(1), p. 39-69.

Louçã Francisco [2004]. « Swinging all the way: the education of Doctor Lucas and foes », *History of Political Economy* 36(4), p. 689-734.

Mata Tiago et Francisco Louçã [2009]. « The Solow residual as a black box: attempts at integrating business cycle and growth theories », *History of Political Economy* 41(annual supplement), p. 334-355.

Makower Helen et Jacob Marschak [1938]. « Assets, prices and monetary theory », *Economica* New Series, 5(19), p. 261-288.

Marget Arthur W. [1932a]. « The definition of the concept of a "velocity of circulation of goods". Part I », *Economica* 38, p. 431-456.

— [1932b]. « The relation between the velocity of circulation of money and the "velocity of circulation of goods". Part II », *Journal of Political Economy* 40(4), p. 477-512.

Marschak Jacob [1931]. *Elastizität der Nachfrage.* Tübingen : J.C.B. Mohr.

— [1932]. « Vélocité du capital et vélocité de la monnaie », Paper delivered at the meeting of the Econometric Society in Paris, Octobre, 1932.

— [1933a]. « Annual survey of statistical information: the branches of national spending », *Econometrica* 1(4), p. 373-386.

— [1933b]. « Volksvermögen und Kassenbedarf », *Archiv für Sozialwissenschaft und Sozialpolitik* 68(4), p. 385-419.

— [1934a]. « Econometric parameters in a stationary society with monetary circulation », *Econometrica* 2(1), p. 91-111.

— [1934b]. « A note on the period of production », *The Economic Journal* 44(173), p. 146-151.

— [1936]. « An empirical analysis of the laws of distribution », *Economica* 3(10), p. 221-226.

— [1937]. « Utilities and probabilities in human choice », In *Report of Third Annual Research Conference on Economics and Statistics.* Colorado Springs : Cowles Commission for Research in Economics, p. 79-82.

— [1938]. « Money and the theory of assets », *Econometrica* 6(4), p. 311-325.

Mehrling Perry [2010]. « A tale of two cities », *History of Political Economy* 42(2), p. 201-219.

Morgan Mary S. [1990]. *The History of Econometric Ideas.* Cambridge : Cambridge University Press.

ONU [2009]. *Système de comptabilité nationale 2008 (SCN 2008).* Travaux et publication sous l'égide de l'ONU, la Commission européenne, de l'OCDE, de la Banque Mondiale et du FMI. New York, NY : ONU.

Repapis Constantinos [2011]. « Hayek's business cycle theory during the 1930s: a critical account of its development », *History of Political Economy* 43(4), p. 699-742.

Rosier Bernard (dir.) [1986]. *Wassily Leontief : textes et itinéraire.* Paris : La Découverte.

Shea John [1998]. « What do technology shocks do? », *NBER Macroeconomics Annual* 13 (Annuel), p. 275-310.

Sraffa Piero [1960]. *Production of Commodities by Means of Commodities.* Cambridge : Cambridge University Press.

Solow Robert M. [1957]. « Technical change and the aggregate production function », *The Review of Economics and Statistics* 39(3), p. 312-320.

Tinbergen Jan [1934]. « Annual survey of significant developments in general economic theory », *Econometrica* 2(1), p. 13-36.

Vanoli André [2002]. *Histoire de la comptabilité nationale.* Paris : La Découverte.

Yagi Kiichiro et Yukihiro Ikeda (dir.) [2012]. *Subjectivism and Objectivism in the History of Economic Thought.* Londres : Routledge.

Zambelli Stefano [2007]. « A rocking horse that never rocked: Frisch's "propagation problems and impulse problems" », *History of Political Economy* 39(1), p. 145-166.

THE LAW OF DIMINISHING ELASTICITY OF DEMAND IN HARROD'S *TRADE CYCLE*

Michaël Assous[1], *Olivier Bruno*[2], *Muriel Dal-Pont Legrand*[3]

In *The Trade Cycle*, Roy Harrod [1936a] propounded the Law of Diminishing Elasticity of Demand. The present paper tries to clarify the precise role Harrod assigned to this law in his *The Trade Cycle Theory*. We discuss the micro and macro foundations of the Law of Diminishing Elasticity of Demand and argue that it explains one of the main mechanisms that stabilize the economy during the trade cycle. In addition, we highlight how the Law of Diminishing Elasticity of Demand allowed Harrod to micro-found a non-linear saving function that can give rise to an endogenous countercyclical value of the multiplier. The paper concludes by reviewing the main arguments related to the Law of Diminishing Elasticity of Demand proposed in the late 1930s.

La loi de l'élasticité de la demande décroissante dans le* Trade Cycle *(1936) de Harrod

Roy Harrod [1936a] introduit la loi de l'élasticité de la demande décroissante dans son ouvrage The Trade Cycle. *Dans cet article, nous nous proposons de clarifier le rôle que ce dernier assigne à cette loi dans son analyse du cycle économique. L'étude de ses fondements microéconomiques et macroéconomiques permet dans un premier temps de reconsidérer l'un des mécanismes "stabilisateurs" clés à l'œuvre au cours du cycle. Dans un second temps, l'analyse révèle la manière dont Harrod mobilise la loi de l'élasticité de la demande décroissante pour fonder microéconomiquement une fonction d'épargne non linéaire et ainsi, conclure au caractère contracyclique du multiplicateur de revenu. L'article fait finalement état des principaux commentaires dont la loi de l'élasticité de la demande a fait l'objet à la fin des années 1930.*

Keywords: Trade cycle, imperfect competition, law of diminishing elasticity of demand, Harrod.

Mots clefs : Cycles, concurrence imparfaite, loi de l'élasticité de la demande décroissante, Harrod.

JEL classification: B22, E32

1. Department of Economics, University of Paris I, Pantheon-Sorbonne, PHARE. E-mail: Michael.Assous@univ-paris1.fr

2. Université de Nice Sophia-Antipolis, GREDEG-CNRS, SKEMA Business School, OFCE DRIC. E-mail: Olivier.Bruno@gredeg.cnrs.fr

3. University of Lille 1 and Clersé CNRS. E-mail: muriel.dal-pont-legrand@univ-lille1.fr

1. Introduction

Harrod's reflections on imperfect competition are at the heart of his inquiry into the theory of business fluctuations [Besomi, 1998; Aspremont, Dos Santos Ferreira and Gérard-Varet, 2011; Assous, 2015]. Harrod formulated his view of cycle theory within a two-step process constituted by his 1934 paper on "Doctrines of imperfect competition" and his 1936 book, *The Trade Cycle*.

First, Harrod emphasized the importance for trade cycle theory of imperfect competition because of its compatibility with decreasing cost. "The key which the doctrines of imperfect competition provide for solving the mystery [concerning movements away from the general equilibrium of output] is that [...] industries may be subject to the law of decreasing costs (in the long and short periods)" [Harrod, 1934: 465]. His exploration of the implications of decreasing cost led him to conclude that imperfect competition provides an equilibrium approach to business cycles relying upon the existence of multiple long period equilibria. Instability then may result from alternative producers' (correct) expectations leading the economy to experience successive periods of high and low equilibria.

Second, during 1935, Harrod was gathering the analytical components – the accelerator and the multiplier – of *The Trade Cycle*, and devising a new mechanism to generate an equilibrium model of advance, which was at the same time sufficiently unstable as to promote cyclical growth (cf. Bruno and Del Pont Legrand [2014]). In resorting to imperfect competition, Harrod then explained that turning points could result from changes to the values of the coefficients of the multiplier and the accelerator. This provides the context for the Law of Diminishing Elasticity of Demand, which states that when people become more affluent, they pay less attention to price changes. By showing that changes in demand elasticity likely change income distribution shares, Harrod defines an explicit mechanism that describes how the economy adjusts during different phases of the economic cycle and its eventual stabilization. He killed two birds with one stone. In addition to the stability issue, without resorting to the Law of Diminishing Returns, he managed to explain the stylized fact that "the commodity price fluctuation has greater amplitude than that of (money) rewards to prime factors." [Harrod, 1936a: 84]

The first readers of *The Trade Cycle* were generally aware that the relevant coefficients determining the "line of steady-advance" were assumed not to be constant, and that their variation was central to Harrod's growth cycle analysis. Somewhat strangely, most mentioned only in passing, the importance of Harrod's Law of Diminishing Elasticity of Demand and its implication on the dynamics. Most comments were limited to the relevance of Harrod's law for explaining the behaviour of price along the business cycle.

We examine this episode in the history of macroeconomics in four steps. In Sections 2 and 3, we restate Harrod's 1936 basic model of imperfect competition and clarify the role of the Law of Diminishing Elasticity of Demand in Harrod's analysis of income distributive shares. Section 4 considers the possible different ways in which changes to demand elasticity are likely to stabilize the economy over the cycle. We argue that a reconsideration of this law has strong implications for Harrod's explanation of business cycle turning points. Section 5 provides a brief survey of the reviews of Harrod's trade cycle model published in the 1930s.

2. In quest of a new "stabilizer"

Harrod addressed the problem of instability at the micro and macro levels. At the micro level, three determinants of the capitalist producer's level of output are identified: (i) the rate at which factors are hired; (ii) the power of those factors to produce; and (iii) the rate at which producers can exchange their products. The "stabilizing forces" associated with each of these determinants are supposed to depend on "(i) Plasticity of Prime costs, (ii) the Law of Diminishing Return and (iii) – under imperfect competition only – the Law of demand" [Harrod, 1936b: 30]. Points (i) and (ii) determine how much the marginal product of each factor varies if an individual producer expands output, while (iii) states that marginal revenue is negatively related to output, with demand elasticity determining the slope of the marginal revenue curve. As long as the marginal cost curve is increasing and the marginal revenue curve is decreasing, Harrod concludes that there will be a stable equilibrium.

At the macro level, these three determinants are reconsidered. First, because of growing population, Plasticity of Prime cost is no longer a great stabilizing force: in a "modern world", total output may increase over a period of time without any pressure for a rise in the rate of pay for prime factors. Second, because of growing capital stock, the Law of Diminishing

Returns has a slight effect, particularly when output is low.[1] Harrod conceded that the only tendency towards diminishing returns, accounting for some part of the changes in prices, might result from the employment of progressively inferior quality labour, and growing carelessness on the part of management: "in the normal cycle the human factor is much more important. As output increases duds may be taken on . . . " [Harrod, 1936b: 53] However, this factor may not be so important. After a first weeding out of inefficient plants, Harrod seriously doubted there would be a marked increase in marginal returns. Thus, at the macro level, a large part of the stability process remains to be accounted for.

This was the point when Harrod introduced the Law of Diminishing Elasticity of Demand whose stabilizing force was considered critical: "This is a stabilizer and, in the writer's judgement, of greater importance than the other two" [Harrod, 1936b: 30], although Harrod admitted that its "very existence" was not "certainly established". Nonetheless, he "ventured to believe that it is the most important of the three" forces [Harrod, 1936b: 30]

To see the problem, consider the depiction in Figure 1, which shows a decreasing marginal revenue curve and an increasing marginal cost under monopolistic competition: the price on the vertical axis is a relative price (relative to the general price level). The horizontal axis shows the quantity of goods. As long as equilibrium is studied at the micro level, the marginal cost and marginal revenue curves are drawn on the assumption that all other prices and income (as well as everything else) remain constant. For example, let us say that at a given price p_0, an excess supply of goods appears. The standard adjustment mechanism is as follows: because marginal revenue is greater than marginal cost, entrepreneurs sustain losses and the quantity produced decreases. The process continues until the equilibrium price $p*$ and quantity $q*$, are reached.

What would happen at the macro level if, for some reason, an excess supply of goods were to appear? Now, what might bring about an

1. "Prime work costs are said to rise in the short period on the principle that increasing quantities of prime factors applied to a given quantity of fixed equipment must yield diminishing returns. But the period to which that dictum relates is too short for trade cycle analysis. It is well known that within the course of the boom, plant is rapidly extended, sometimes even beyond the limit of requirements at the peak." [Harrod, 1936a: 86] His approach conflicts with Keynes who, assuming that the quality of capital as well its stock can be considered given in the short-run, admitted that the Law of Diminishing Return is likely to operate in the short-run.

equilibrium between aggregate supply and aggregate demand if the three determinants exert no stabilizing or de-stabilizing influence over output?

> . . . as output falls there will be no change in rates of pay to prime factors, no change in their marginal productivity as output recedes, and no increasing elasticity of demand. Then, if a fall in prices occurs, the system will move irretrievably to the position of zero outputs. If it stops short of that it must be because some stabilizing forces have come into being – wages rates have fallen, or marginal productivity has increased as output receded, or demand has become more elastic and sufficiently so to offset the drop in prices. In absence of the first two stabilizers, this law established that as long as any excess supply of goods will appear, prices will drop output will fall and this will make individual demand curve more elastic. [Harrod, 1936b: 44]

Let us say that firms have produced huge excess. Now, let us say that a decrease in the quantity supplied lowers income. Then, because demand depends upon income as well as prices, as the quantity supplied falls, the marginal revenue curve shifts back to, say, MR_1. Then the income adjustment force comes into play alongside the price adjustment force. It can be seen that these forces push in opposite directions. The relative price effect (movement down along the marginal revenue curve) brings us closer to equilibrium, while the income effect shifts the marginal revenue curve to the left, moving us further from equilibrium. Without knowing the relative magnitudes of the shifts, we cannot say whether equilibrium will be achieved. It is for precisely this reason that Harrod concludes that the Law of Demand "does not apply to the community as whole" and highlighted the importance of the Law of Diminishing Demand Elasticity.

Figure 1

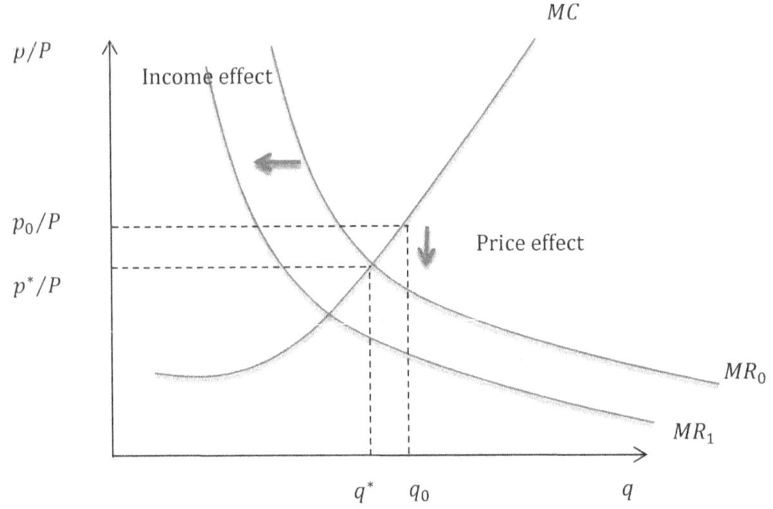

The Law of Diminishing Demand Elasticity is important because it determines precisely how much the marginal revenue curves will shift as quantity (global income) varies. By postulating this Law, Harrod was hence able to clarify the relationship between aggregate demand and aggregate supply. In the presence of an excess supply of goods, as income falls, demand elasticity increases, and a negative shift to profit occurs, followed by a decrease in the saving rate, which eventually comes with a rise in aggregate demand. Thus, as long as income keeps falling, the gap between aggregate supply and aggregate demand eventually vanishes.

In a nutshell, when money wages are fixed (no plasticity of primary factors) and the marginal product of labour remains unchanged (no decreasing returns), changes in income provide all the adjustment. The assumption that income distribution changes due to the change in demand elasticity allows to explain why income ceases to fall in the case that an excess supply of goods appears. As soon as the profit margin falls and a shift to profit takes place, aggregate demand increases and the excess supply of goods vanishes. We now need to look at how Harrod justified his law.

3. The law of decreasing demand elasticity and the shift to profit

In his 1936 trade cycle book, Harrod assumes that entrepreneurs can make marginal revenue equal to marginal cost. This is the condition for the maximization of profit in any given set of circumstances. In his view, this assumption was critical for an investigation of the economy's dynamics:

> The leading principle of the theory of imperfect competition is that entrepreneurs tend to equate marginal cost to marginal revenue. This is a tendency which should operate in the short period. Insufficient attention appears to have been paid to this in trade-cycle studies. The following considerations are based on the supposition that it is realized. [Harrod 1936a: 84]

Harrod was well aware that systematic mistakes were at the heart of the turning point in his business cycle analysis:

> for instance, it will be shown later why orders given for capital goods in the very last phase of the boom must inevitably prove unprofitable. But to suppose that in the short-period decisions how much current to produce there is systematic error in one direction enduring throughout the whole phase of the boom or the whole phase of the slump by all or most entrepreneurs seems to me altogether far-fetched. [Harrod 1936b: 76]

As soon as entrepreneurs are assumed to equate marginal revenue to marginal cost, two important conclusions can be drawn with regard to the observed movements in profits and prices. Maximum available profit per unit can only change if one or both of two things occur: (i) a change in the relation between the marginal and the average prime cost of production; (ii) a change in the relation between marginal revenue and price. Abstracting from fixed costs, we have:

$$\frac{\Pi}{Y} = \frac{pq - APCq}{pq} = 1 - \frac{APC}{p}$$

where APC is the variable average cost and Π is the gross profit (i.e. inclusive of depreciation and interest). This equation expresses the profit margin for the individual firm. For the whole economic system, where ε is the elasticity of demand, we have:

$$\frac{\Pi}{Y} = 1 - \frac{APC}{MC/\left(1 - \frac{1}{\varepsilon}\right)}$$

which allows us to conclude that the profit margin (i) increases with output, since with normal U cost curves the ratio APC/MC decreases along the relevant extent of marginal cost, (ii) decreases with elasticity of demand. Harrod's proposal of the Law of Diminishing Demand Elasticity emphasizes point (ii).

The Law of Diminishing Demand Elasticity results mainly from the psychological principle underlying consumers' and business establishments' habits. On the one hand, Harrod thought the expected value from searching for better opportunities among close substitutes was a decreasing function of their income. Rich people, unlike poor people, want to avoid the discommodity of searching for the cheapest market, and tend to "slip by imperceptible stages into careless habits" as their income expands.[2] On the other hand, for enterprises, in good times, "imaginative planning is . . . more remunerative than attention to rigid economy."[3]

The view that the shape of the marginal revenue curve may be an important factor in determining the income distributive share is easily illustrated. If the counter-cyclicality of demand elasticity is taken for granted, for a given marginal cost, the profit share will decrease/increase once the slump/recovery has set in.

> The greater the shift to profit, the smaller the increase of consumption entailed, in accordance with the multiplier, by the given increase of net

2. "With an expanding income, a man may slip by imperceptible stages into careless habits. A contraction recalls him to his senses. He is loath to relinquish enjoyments to which he has become accustomed and immediately begins to cast about for means of meeting adversity with the least inconvenience to himself. That same force of habit, which in times of improvement tends to make him an imperfect buyer reinforces his activity when it is a question of economizing. He seeks to economise with the smallest possible loss of substantial utility." [Harrod, 1936a: 87]

3. "The same force acts upon business establishments. The management will take greater pains to avoid a given reduction of dividends than to secure an increase of like amount when dividends are rising in any case. The prospect of bankruptcy may be still more stimulating. There is no reason to suppose that the professions, so often made by the management in the depression, that they are exerting special efforts to secure economy, are mere eye-wash. Economy is always profitable. But there are good psychological reasons why its benefits should be more vividly appreciated when depression sets in." [Harrod, 1936a: 87]
"Economists are too apt to think of the search for the cheapest market as a continuous and all-pervasive process. That is, in fact, only true of dealers in an organized market, of Ricardo in the money market. For others, whether consumers or producing firms, the search for cheapness entails special efforts made on special occasions. During te growing affluence of the boom habits become hardened, part of the extra means are taken out in the wastage due to not bothering too much. When incomes begin to fall people are forced to economize; cherished habits have to be abandoned willy-nilly. At this point they are shaken out of their lethargy; they begin to sit up and take notice. They resent and resist the curtailment of their wonted pleasures and become willing to take great pains to seek ways and means for mitigating their hardships. Their efforts to find cheapness become strenuous and eager. Nor are commercial firms exempt from this influence upon their purchase policy; they, too, have received a nasty jolt and must strain every nerve to reduce costs; there is no reason to suppose that these are empty. It is not unreasonable to suppose that entrepreneurs, faced with bankruptcy as they often are, devote quite unusual attention to this subject." [Harrod, 1936b: 86–7]

> investment, and the more likely is the existing rate of increase of capital goods to be found to be excessive. This is certainly a striking paradox, since high profit is usually supposed to be the signal for headlong advance. But the reasoning on which it is based seems to be irrefutable. It could only be disputed by a denial of the view that a larger proportion of high profit than of general income tends to be saved. Moreover, it accords with the observed fact that a spectacular accumulation of profit occurs only in the later phase of the boom, that is, shortly precedes a break in that boom. [Harrod 1936b: 92]

The importance of Harrod's cost analysis and Law of Diminishing Demand Elasticity for the dynamics of saving lies in the fact that it enhances the tendency of profits to rise relative to wages, as activity increases. A change in distribution favourable to profits, increases the propensity of the community to save. Thus, the Law of Diminishing Elasticity of Demand has a crucial influence in causing the value of the multiplier to fall as activity increases. It is worth considering in detail the implication of these variations on the dynamics of the economy.

4. Instability, the cycle and the law of diminishing elasticity of demand

The main idea proposed by Harrod is that "by a study of the interconnections between the multiplier and the Relation (the Acceleration Principle) the secret of the trade cycle may be revealed." [Harrod, 1936b: 70] More specifically, Harrod believed that changes in investment are transformed into changes in output as a result of the multiplier and, in turn, these changes in output, through the operation of the acceleration principle, induce further changes in investment, which then feed into further changes in output, and so on. According to Harrod, this cumulative mechanism is in line with Keynes's proposition in his *Treatise on Money*, that if investment exceeds saving, the system will be stimulated to expand, and vice versa. However, Keynes's argument relies on static equilibrium while Harrod assumes dynamic equilibrium. On the one hand, expansion in a static economy means a new level of income higher than the previous level. On the other hand, in a dynamic economy, expansion occurs as soon as there is a divergence between the "line of steady-advance" of the economy and the current rate of growth. Harrod defines the line of steady advance as:

> . . . one in which the ratio of the increment of output to the previous level is constant . . . the proportionate increase of net investment on the given day over net investment on the day preceding is equal to the

> proportionate addition to the stock of capital goods available for the use on a given day. The experience of the given day will be the primary test as to whether the advance is likely to remain steady. [Harrod, 1936b: 89]

Harrod defined three variables that would appear to be the main determinants of the equilibrium dynamics since they govern the value of the line of steady-advance of the economy: (i) the propensity to save among agents that receive an income; (ii) the change in profit share resulting from a change in output (shift to profit); and (iii) the desired capital-output ratio for new capital goods. According to Harrod, these determinants are dynamic because "they determine the rate of growth of output, whereas the static determinants relate to the level of output at a particular point of time." [Harrod, 1936b: 89–90]

These three variables comprise all the elements determining whether the existing rate of advance is to be increased, maintained or diminished. Note that, in this view, the definition of the line of steady-advance in *The Trade Cycle* differs from Harrod's 1939 definition of the "warranted growth rate". In his 1939 contribution, the "warranted growth rate" of the economy appears as an "equilibrium state of the economy" since it determines: "The level of output at which producers will feel in the upshot that they have done the right thing, and which will induce them to continue in the same line of advance. Stock in hand and equipment available will be exactly at the level they would wish to have them." [Harrod, 1939: 22]

In *The Trade Cycle*, the "line of steady-advance" of the economy is only a "state of the economy" that will be preserved if and only if the three dynamic factors remain constant over time. Also according to Harrod, along the line of steady-advance, there is no chance for variations in these three determinants to be offset, and the cycle is inevitable. However, Harrod immediately underlines that there are some stabilizing mechanisms that prevent the connection between the relation and the multiplier to be destabilizing for the whole economy. The first mechanism relies on interest rate changes during the cycle that may offset the cumulative effect of the accelerator (the relation):

> Drawing again from the field of observation, we find interest rates tending to be high in the boom and low in the slump. Thus, so far as the rate of interest is concerned, net investment is discouraged in the boom. And this is right and proper. The stimulus to net investment afforded by the Relation being so great, it is fortunate that we have the rate of interest to provide some counterweight. [Harrod, 1936b: 59]

conditions of obviously imperfect competition did not appear to encourage the raising of prices. Producers do not care about the risk to trade connections, upsetting advertising campaigns, losing good will and imperilling real business equity for transient advantages. The more imperfect the competition, the more these considerations appear to prevail. However, if demand tends to become less elastic in good times, and traders do not take advantage of this situation, then Harrod's law fails as an explanation for rising prices and profits.

It is interesting to note that, by resorting to monopolistic competition, Michał Kalecki [1938] comes very close to Harrod's theory of income distribution. However, his analysis, unlike Harrod's, was based on the determinants of the profit margin in both Robinson's argument related to changes in the degree of collusion, and the law of diminishing returns. First, Kalecki admits that more spectacular rises in profit margins are likely to occur in those industries where output fluctuates considerably, and where average (prime) costs are heavily influenced by output, for example, the mining, iron, steel and raw materials sectors. Second, (and this works in the opposite direction to profit margin), the threat of entry of new competitors is likely to be low when economic activity is low, and be less encouragement to reduce prices. In other words, firms already in the market may feel less worried about higher mark-ups on cost in periods of low activity, but periods of high economic activity are a good time to enter the market since customers may be finding it difficult to find suppliers. These two effects work in opposite directions and may perfectly cancel out each other. If they do so, the assumption that the profit margin is constant during the business cycle is sensitive. If businesses are highly sensitive to the threat of entry, and the law of diminishing returns operate slightly, then the profit margin may be countercyclical: the profit margin will be higher when activity is low than when activity is high. If businesses are only weakly sensitive to the threat of entry and the Law of Diminishing Returns operates slightly, then the profit margin will be procyclical.

According to Kalecki, the considerable stability of the profit share over the longer term is the result of simultaneous changes in the degree of imperfection of the market and of increasing real costs in raw materials sectors. In contrast to Harrod, Kalecki concludes that the propensity to save remains constant during all the business cycle. Kalecki implicitly dismisses Harrod's argument of business cycle turning points based on changes in the propensity to save. In other words, because distribution effects are assumed to be negligible, the only stabilizing effects must necessarily arise from changes in the acceleration coefficient.

Finally, several authors have questioned the practical importance of Harrod's Law of Diminishing Elasticity of Demand for the study of the economic cycle, on the grounds that it is irrelevant to assume that elasticity is perfectly known by entrepreneurs. Stafford [1937: 73] points out that:

> In reality new elements enter into the problem – of uncertainty, concerning demand and rivals policies, of cost, of the nature of producers' interest in their businesses, and finally, of the meaning of marginal revenue. M. Harrod places too great a stain upon the useful preparatory results obtained in the field of imperfect competition, without gaining anything substantial from it.

However, most authors are reluctant to admit that while Harrod assumes that investors might make systematic mistakes in certain phases of the cycle, producers can be assumed to have perfect expectations when deciding how much current output to produce.

References

Abramovitz M. [1938]. Monopolistic selling in a changing economy, *Quarterly Journal of Economics* 52(2): 191–214. *Not in text*

Aspremont C. d', R. Dos Santos Ferreira and L.-A. Gérard-Varet [2011]. Imperfect competition and the trade cycle: aborted guidelines from the late 1930s. *History of Political Economy* 43(3): 513–36.

Assous M. [2015]. Harrod. In G. Faccarello & H. Kurz (Eds) *Handbook of the History of Economic Analysis, Vol. 1. Great Economists since Petty and Boisguilbert.* Cheltenham: Edward Elgar.

Besomi D. [1998]. Failing to win consent: Harrod's dynamics in the eyes of his readers. In G. Rampa, L. Stella, and A.P. Thirlwall (eds) *Economic Dynamics, Trade and Growth. Essays on Harrodian Themes.* New York: Palgrave Macmillan: 38–88.

Bruno O., and Dal Pont Legrand M. [2014]. The instability principle revisited: an essay in Harrodian dynamics. *European Journal for the History of Economic Thought* 21(3): 467-84.

Dunlop J.T. [1938]. The movement of real and money wage rates, *Economic Journal* 48(191): 413–34.

Hansen A.H. [1937]. Harrod on the trade cycle. *The Quarterly Journal of Economics* 51(3): 509–31.

Harrod R.-F. [1934]. Doctrines of imperfect competition. *Quarterly Journal of Economics* 48(3):442–70.

— [1936a]. Imperfect competition and the trade cycle. *Review of Economics and Statistics* 18(2): 84–8.

— [1936b]. *The Trade Cycle. An Essay.* Oxford: Clarendon Press.

Kalecki M. [1938]. The determinants of distribution of the national income, *Econometrica* 6(2): 97–112.

Robinson J. [1936]. Review of R.F. Harrod, *The Trade Cycle. Economic Journal* 46(184): 691–3.

Stafford J. [1937]. 'The Trade Cycle'. *The Manchester School,* 8(1): 69–84.

GROWTH AS AN OBJECTIVE OF ECONOMIC POLICY IN THE EARLY 1960s: THE ROLE OF AGGREGATE DEMAND

Johannes A. Schwarzer[1]

This paper sheds light on economic policy discussions in the early 1960s about whether there is an optimal level of demand to maximise the rate of growth. This discussion was influenced by the Cold War, which urged policy makers particularly in the USA to achieve higher rates of growth than the Soviet Union. As it was assumed that good demand management can damp the business cycle, regulating and deciding upon the level of demand pressure in the economy was regarded as an important tool for economic policy. The main debate therefore evolved around the question whether or not the economy should be run at high demand pressure and inflation to foster growth or if some slack in the economy and deflationary tendencies are a prerequisite for a prosperous growth path.

La croissance, objectif de la politique économique au début des années 1960 : le rôle de la demande agrégée

Cet article traite des discussions du début des années 1960 concernant la détermination d'un niveau de demande optimal susceptible de maximiser le taux de croissance. Ce débat eut lieu dans le contexte de la guerre froide où les décideurs, notamment aux États-Unis, étaient tenus de réaliser des taux de croissance supérieurs à ceux de l'Union soviétique. Supposant qu'une maîtrise appropriée de la demande pouvait infléchir le cycle économique, la régulation et la décision du niveau de la pression de la demande étaient considérées comme un instrument majeur de la politique économique. Aussi, le débat a principalement consisté à déterminer si l'économie pouvait ou non fonctionner en présence de fortes pressions inflationnistes et des niveaux de demande élevés, favorables à la croissance, ou si un certain ralentissement de l'économie et des tendances déflationnistes constituaient une condition préalable à une trajectoire de croissance prospère.

Keywords: Economic policy, growth, aggregate demand, trade-off, Phillips curve.

Mots clefs : Politique économique, croissance, demande agrégée, compromis, courbe de Phillips.

JEL classification: B22, E61, O40

1. University of Hohenheim, Department of Economics (520h), 70593 Stuttgart, Germany.
E-mail: johannes.schwarzer@uni-hohenheim.de.
I thank John Black, Olivier Bruno, Harald Hagemann, Niels Geiger, Richard Lipsey, and two anonymous referees for most helpful comments and suggestions. All responsibility for the views expressed in this paper as well as for any remaining errors is of course mine alone.

1. Introduction

Today, policy discussions in the 1960s are usually associated with the idea of a long-run trade-off between inflation and unemployment given by a stable Phillips curve—a belief that was heavily countered by Phelps [1967] and Friedman [1968]. The debates in the 1960s, however, went farther than just arguing about the optimal combination between unemployment and inflation, that is, in today's terms, moving along a stable Phillips curve. There also was a lively discussion on the medium to long-run consequences of running the economy at different levels of demand pressure and hence at different combinations of unemployment and inflation. These debates focused on the impact of the rate of inflation on allocative efficiency, on the role of strong demand for capital formation and labour market dynamics, as well as on the overall impact of the state of demand on technical progress.

The discussion in the 1960s was based on three elements: First of all, growth became a most important policy objective due to the Cold War. Many contributions in the 1960s thus focused on the rate of growth from the point of view of economic policy and not necessarily from a founded theoretical analysis. Second, even though nearly all authors were aware that growth in the long run crucially depends particularly on technical progress, investment was nevertheless regarded as the driving force of the growth process taking place within the timespan important for economic policy. As investment was assumed to depend on the level of aggregate demand, regulating the demand pressure by fiscal and monetary policies seemed to be a promising approach to foster economic growth. In this view, stabilisation policies and active demand management did not only have a short-run influence but were also important for the medium to longer run. These two elements, that is, growth as an objective of economic policy and the important role of demand policies, will be discussed in Section 2.

The third element in this debate was the perceived trade-off between the rate of inflation and the rate of unemployment as given by the Phillips curve. Even though most contributions did not make reference to Phillips' [1958] seminal paper, the conflict between the two variables was at the heart of the discussion. This trade-off emerged due to various imperfections in the economy, most notably cost-push forces (for example, aggressive unions), causing inflationary pressures even in the case of excess unemployment. Regulating the level of aggregate demand in this debate thus not only meant to achieve the objective of high rates of growth, but also to balance the rate of inflation versus the rate of unemployment (see, for example, Fellner [1960: 94ff.]).

Hence, at least on theoretical grounds, inflation and unemployment were thought to be closely connected to the rate of growth even though three different lines of thought can be distinguished: On the one hand, many economists believed that a high-pressure economy would be beneficial for the rate of growth. Most arguments pointed at the stimulating environment for investment due to inflation lowering the real rate of interest and a high level of demand stabilizing sales perspectives. These arguments were based on a Keynesian understanding of growth theories, that is, the Harrod-Domar model [Harrod, 1939; 1948; Domar, 1946; 1947] in which investment plays an important role for the rate of growth. However, many arguments were not backed up by deeper analysis (see, for example, Scitovsky and Scitovsky [1964: 440]). On the other hand, in particular Paish [1958; 1962; 1968] pointed out the positive effects of strong competitive pressures brought about by some slack in the economy. Growth in this framework did not depend on accelerator-type investment dynamics, but on the consequences of strong competitive pressures on firm-level efficiency and the need for innovations in order to survive in an overall weak market. A third line of thought remained very skeptical about a strong influence of the overall level of demand pressure on the rate of growth. Many economists, in particular those focusing on Phillips curve analysis and related policy questions, stayed close to Keynesian growth arguments, but based their skeptical view on empirical evidence which seemed to show that the rate of inflation and unemployment have, if at all, only a small influence on the rate of growth. These three different views will be discussed in Section 3.

Section 4 will focus on a most interesting contribution by Black [1959] which disentangles these different views within the Phillips curve framework. The conclusion will outline what might be learned from the discussion in the 1960s and what might have been lost since Friedman's introduction of a "natural rate of unemployment" into the Phillips curve concept.

2. Growth as an Objective of Economic Policy and the Role of Stabilisation Policies

2.1. Growth as a Policy Objective in Times of the Cold War

The discussion about the role of the overall state of demand for the rate of growth started in the 1950s, but became particularly pronounced in the early 1960s due to the slow rate of growth in the USA compared to the Soviet Union, and in the UK compared to the rest of the industrialised world [Wilson, 1961: 4; Johnson, 1963a: 46]. The rate of growth hence became a first priority objective of policy [Tobin, 1964: 1] particularly in the USA due to the Cold War, which also made economists talk about the "Soviet challenge" [Baran, 1960: 119] or the "Russian threat" [Baumol, 1958: 57]. Whereas the USA only reached an average growth rate of 3.3 per cent in the 1950s, the USSR achieved 7.6 per cent [Klein and Bodkin, 1964: 410].[2] Furthermore, the Cold War made it necessary to discuss growth as a matter of national security in the USA [Newman, 1958: 245; Lewis, 1958: 377; Rostow, 1960: 110; Smith, 1960: 272; Commission on Money and Credit, 1961: 9; Johnson, 1963c: 280; Wilson, 1963: 604ff.; Klein and Bodkin, 1964: 369; Tobin, 1964: 5]. A high rate of growth was regarded to be of utmost importance, since "a major objective of economic growth is to provide an expanding base for actual or potential national security outlays" [Kendrick, 1964: 242].

Not only the rate of growth as such, but also technical progress was regarded as an essential factor in times of the Cold War. As both were assumed to be interrelated—"if technology helps growth, growth in turn helps technology, and on technology defence largely depends" [Wilson, 1963: 605]—the rate of growth became the dominant policy objective. This obsession with growth went so far that the rate of growth in many contributions was often treated "as an end in itself" [Alhadeff et al., 1964: 531]. Even the "Golden Rule of Accumulation" by Phelps [1961] as an important contemporary contribution to growth theory on how to achieve maximum consumption was either just ignored or bypassed by many authors. Furthermore, individual decisions on saving and investment as the ultimate benchmark for an optimal rate of

2. It is worth noting that some economists were less concerned with the apparently high growth rates of the Soviet Union. Particularly Nutter [1962] pointed at the possibility of inaccurate statistics which probably overstated Soviet growth rates and at special factors (for example "the expansion of territory and resources") which might have boosted growth rates of the Soviet Union in the short run.

growth [Tobin, 1964: 2; Kendrick, 1964: 244] were also discarded in most contributions. For example, Musgrave [1958: 609] was clearly aware that "the ultimate objective of economic activity is consumption" but at the same time remarked about the "optimal rate of growth in the economy" in light of the high Russian growth rates that "this may be answered more or less easily by reference to Russia: Whatever we do, the Russian rate of growth is likely to exceed ours, simply because they are at a much earlier stage of the game; therefore, if we want to maintain our relative advantage, we had better grow as fast as we can."

Due to this competition with the Soviet Union, Fellner [1960: 98] emphasised that policies aiming at a higher rate of saving in order to foster growth do not necessarily "violate the time-preference scales of the public" as positive external effects of a higher rate of growth (for example on defence) are not taken into account by private decisions. Thus, the optimal rate of growth was not regarded to be determined by individual preferences any longer, but became subject to economic policy. Denison [1962: 69] even went as far as to suggest "that the public be persuaded that acceleration of growth must be made an overriding national goal. Moreover, it must probably be persuaded of this for reasons other than the increase in individual welfare—probably reasons related to the external situation facing the country." In the same vein Anderson and Cornwall [1961: 174] emphasised that "[i]f we wish to maintain our market system and at the same time to avoid being outstripped by the Soviet Union, some way will have to be found to manipulate the market forces to achieve the desired growth goals." Time preferences, thrift, and individual decisions as such hence were accepted as indicating an optimal rate of growth in a fair-weather world, but given the threats of the Cold War even Tobin [1964: 6] was not reluctant to state that "[s]ome hazards are great enough to bias our choice to favor the future over the present" as "[a] high GNP might be the difference between victory and defeat rather than the difference between more or less consumption."

Growth as a policy objective hence involved strong interventions into the free market economy. This development was met with much scepticism. In particular Friedman [1959], who pointed at the importance of individual decisions so that "[w]hatever rate of change in the statistical aggregate [output] results from the effort of freemen to promote their own aspirations is the right rate," feared that the Cold War might create a difficult and dangerous environment for economic policy as "departures we must make to survive" may overcharge the corrective forces of a free society. Johnson [1963b: 139] even went as far as to remark that "the recent emphasis on the desirability of a high rate of growth seems to me to involve grafting on to a free enterprise system standards appropriate to a planned economy with military and political ambitions." Johnson [1963a: 47] therefore critically noted that "[t]he movement towards some form of economic planning for growth has gone farthest in the United Kingdom, with the establishment of the National Economic Development Council" of which also Richard Lipsey, a pioneer of Phillips curve analysis [Lipsey, 1960], was part of the staff [Lipsey, 1997: xxiv]. The National Economic Development Council [1963b: viii] explicitly had the aim "to increase the rate of sound growth." Such a rate of growth was set to be equal to 4 per cent of national output [National Economic Development Council, 1963b: iii]. In the USA, particularly the Joint Economic Committee [1958], and the Commission on Money and Credit [1961] published studies about the possibility of achieving a high rate of growth while maintaining price stability and full employment.

2.2. The Role of Demand Management and Stabilisation Policies

Growth not only became a most important objective of economic policy, it also was thought that economic policy has the appropriate tools to influence the rate of growth by managing the economy accordingly. This optimism is most visible in Samuelson's [1955: 337] statement that "[w]ith proper fiscal and monetary policies, our economy can have full employment and whatever rate of capital formation and growth it wants." This optimism about fine-tuning the economy is also very pronounced in Anderson and Cornwall [1961: 174] as they remarked that "[m]ost economists by now are accustomed to think of the government as an agency for damping fluctuations and at least edging the economy toward full employment." The economics profession in the 1960s hence was very optimistic about managing the economy and there was the belief that good demand management "ironed out the business cycle" [Harrod, 1967: 19]. In the same vein, Wilson [1961: 3] stated that "the trade cycle, if it has not been altogether conquered, has been much subdued". It is therefore not surprising that there was also an edited volume published on the possible obsolescence of the business cycle [Bronfenbrenner, 1969: v]. In sum, stabilisation policies had two short-term objectives: On the one hand, "to regulate the pressure of demand for labour" and on the other hand, "to keep the fluctuations of the unemployment percentage within fairly narrow limits" [Godley and Shepherd, 1964: 26]. Fine-tuning the economy with respect to choosing and regulating the pressure of aggregated demand hence seemed achievable by stabilisation policies so that "[i]t is for the Government to decide at what pressure it wishes to run the economy, and to try to keep it there" [Godley and Shepherd, 1964: 26]. This optimistic attitude towards managing the economy is described by Minsky [1968: 45] in retrospect about the early 1960s noting that it was believed that "business cycles as they had been known would be a thing of the past" and that "the perfected tools of economic policy would 'fine-tune' the economy so that, period by period, it would stay on a course of sustained growth."

Thus, "sustained growth" relied on successful stabilisation policies to damp the business cycle and to keep the economy at full capacity output (see, for example, Smith [1957: 53ff.]; Phillips [1961: 367f.]). This implied that economic policy needed to assure that the growing output of the economy will also be demanded [Musgrave, 1958: 607; Klein and Bodkin, 1964: 377]. In this sense, economic stability not only meant to keep the economy "at a happy mean", that is, to damp the ups and downs, but to assure "a level of activity very close to full employment" [Turner, 1958: 671]. Stabilisation policies thus had the difficult task to maintain ongoing full employment with minimal fluctuations, which required a sophisticated analysis of the interrelationships between economic variables and appropriate tools to analyse the impact of different policies. One of the first economists to incorporate such new methods regarding stabilisation policies was Phillips [1954; 1957], who applied tools from engineering to the issues of economic stability [Turnovsky, 2000: 296ff.]. Phillips [1962: 9f.] furthermore was convinced that confidence about economic policy is an important stabiliser itself. Phillips' intuition is that expectations about a sound policy, especially aggressive in fighting severe slumps, will stabilise investment and as such the whole economy because of the thereby created confidence that exactly such an enormous downturn will not be likely to last for a long time. Also Balogh [1958: 232] pointed at the necessity of stabilisation policies to create confidence as otherwise there might be "shocking consequences", that is, a strong economic downturn, so that "only foolish people will not let sleeping accelerators lie". Stabilisation policies hence were regarded as necessary to dull Harrod's "knife-edge" [Solow, 1956: 65]. Samuelson [1957: 569] thus emphasised that preventing the "excesses of the boom" but also "offsetting slumps" will be beneficial for economic growth (see also Kendrick [1964: 239]). Stabilisation policies to achieve a maximal rate of growth were also believed to be necessary in an otherwise neoclassical growth context. For example, Cornwall [1963: 1f.] remarked that the long-run growth rate will depend on supply-side factors if full employment can be achieved by a perfectly functioning price system. If, however, full employment cannot be assured by the market system itself, demand policies are a powerful and necessary tool to increase the rate of growth so that "the system moves toward a long-run equilibrium growth rate determined solely by supply factors, as in the neoclassical world" [Cornwall, 1963: 21]. Thus Cornwall [1963: 2] pointed out that demand policies actually make it possible that the maximum growth rate (restricted by conditions on the supply side) can be fully realised so that "growth can and should be looked upon as a problem of adequate demand as long as an economy is subject to periodic recessions" (see also Nelson [1966: 1186] for a comparable approach, and Johnson [1963a: 65f.] for a related and critical comment on economic policy in Canada).

However, not all economists at that time thought that damping cyclical fluctuations is a necessary condition to achieve high rates of growth. For example, Fishman and Fishman [1958: 65] pointed out that "[d]evoted followers of Schumpeter may . . . question whether it is possible to maintain growth without cyclical fluctuations, and whether any attempts to eliminate or even sharply reduce cyclical fluctuations may not result in economic stagnation" as "Schumpeter believed that there is an inherent causal relationship between economic growth and cyclical fluctuations, and that cyclical fluctuations are the mechanism through which growth occurs." Samuelson [1957: 566] hence speculated that "[p]erhaps the booms and the busts of the last century were the inevitable costs of progress, the necessary price we must pay for vital growth." In the same vein, Newman [1958: 246] pointed at the "surging and pulsating character" of a growing economy and hence at a possible "conflict between growth and employment as objectives of economic policy."

This conflict seemed to be most pronounced if restrictive demand policies were necessary to fight inflationary pressures arising due to cost-push forces, that is, for example, unions pushing up wages independently of the state of demand (see Bronfenbrenner and Holzman [1963: 600ff.] on the cost-push demand-pull debate in the 1950s and 1960s). This dilemma of fighting cost-push inflation by increasing the rate of unemployment made economists think about the long-run consequences of such a restrictive policy. For example, Rostow [1960: 111] asked: "Does control of inflation require in our democratic society a damping of the rate of growth?" In this respect Hoover [1960: 377] remarked about a study of the Joint Economic Committee [1959] that this contribution puts forward the "central thesis of the sacrifice of growth on the altar of price stabilization" (see also Wilson [1961: 3f.] and National Economic Development Council [1964: 8] regarding the stop-and-go policies in the UK). In this sense, the Phillips curve trade-off was augmented by a third dimension [Smithies, 1958: 611; Phillips, 1962: 11; Klein and Bodkin, 1964: 386; Scott and McKean, 1964: 2]. Scitovsky and

Scitovsky [1964: 429f.] hence pointed out that "[t]he most controversial question . . . is how inflation on the one hand and unemployment on the other affect the rate of growth of the economy." Also the Commission on Money and Credit [1961: 12] remarked that "the possibility of conflict among these goals is a very real one."

In sum, the discussion about an optimal level of demand pressure was influenced by the Cold War (which made the rate of growth a most important policy goal), the belief in stabilisation policies to overcome the business cycle and to keep the economy at a specific utilisation level (which made the level of demand an important policy tool), and the possible conflict between unemployment, inflation, and growth (which made the optimal level of demand a difficult policy choice). Three different views about this optimal level of demand will be distinguished in the next section.

3. Three Different Views

3.1. The Keynesian View

The view most prevalent in many contributions might be labelled Keynesian since the authors of these contributions particularly stress the role of demand-induced investment for the rate of growth. The rate of investment, as in Harrod's [1936; 1939] growth model, was at least implicitly assumed to depend on the (expected) growth of aggregate demand. For example, the National Economic Development Council [1963a: 44f.] remarked that "[t]he incentive to invest is also likely to be greater when demand is high than when there is a good deal of excess capacity." The National Economic Development Council [1964: 7] hence stated that "growth is encouraged by a high pressure of demand."

This high level of demand was assumed to generate inflation via the Phillips relation as employers compete for the last remaining factors of production. On a positive side, this higher rate of inflation was viewed to be beneficial for growth as profits may be higher if wages lag behind prices (see Klein and Bodkin [1964: 411]; for empirical falsification of this argument, see Bach [1958: 37], Kessel and Alchian [1960: 43ff.], and Reuber [1962: 220f.]). This effect might even increase labour supply if workers are trying to keep their standard of living by working more [Bach, 1958: 36]. Also, the real rate of interest might be lowered if the nominal rate does not adjust fully to the higher rate of inflation, so that the marginal efficiency of capital rises and therefore induces further investment [Kaldor, 1959: 289ff.; Scitovsky and Scitovsky, 1964: 463f.]. The rise in prices, it was argued, may create an "optimistic atmosphere" [Baumol, 1958: 51] or a "general spirit of optimism" [Smithies, 1958: 612f.]. This positive effect of inflation for the rate of growth, however, was doubted by many scholars since it implied some kind of money illusion. In particular Johnson [1963d: 64] opposed this line of thought as "[t]his argument assumes that the rate of interest at which entrepreneurs can borrow is unaffected by the expectation of inflation, implying that though borrowers are aware of inflation lenders are not" (see also Wilson [1961: 15]; Johnson [1966: 24]).

The beneficial influence of a strong demand pressure on investment, however, is only the most apparent one, and the proponents of maintaining excess demand emphasised additional advantages of such a policy since most authors were fully aware that long-run growth also depends on growth of the labour force and, even more importantly, on technical progress. The level of demand was assumed to influence the rate of technical progress due to various reasons: First of all, strong demand may cause shortages and bottlenecks, in particular on the labour market. On the one hand, these bottlenecks were viewed as obstacles to further expansion, but on the other hand it was thought that they would induce research and the application of new means of productions to overcome the shortages. This mechanism was, for example, emphasised by the National Economic Development Council [1963a: 45] stating that "labour shortage provides a strong incentive to invest in labour-saving equipment which will raise productivity." In the same vein, Scitovsky and Scitovsky [1964: 441] remark "that physical shortages of a productive factor are the most powerful inducements for developing and adopting new methods of production that economize that factor. A full-employment situation, therefore, by creating both a general shortage of labor and specific bottlenecks of specific skills and types of labor is especially favorable to labor-saving innovations and growth." As every such innovation involves risks and usually huge investments in new machinery, Scitovsky and Scitovsky [1964: 441] argue that the willingness to implement these innovations will be greater if there is high confidence that economic activity will remain on a high level (see also Turner [1958: 682]; Harrod [1967: 16f. 1969: 325]). Furthermore, Scitovsky and Scitovsky [1964: 434] point out that full employment will make unions and workers accept the introduction of such labour-saving technical progress in a cooperative way (see also Balogh [1958: 231]; National Economic Development Council [1963a: 45]). Based on the same arguments as outlined above, the Commission on Money and Credit [1961: 43] concluded that "measures to stimulate aggregate demand to attain low levels of unemployment are basic to an adequate rate of economic growth."

The Commission on Money and Credit [1961: 43] also remarked that the induced technical progress usually would lay off workers. Therefore, inter-sectoral or inter-industry movements of labour become necessary. This labour mobility was assumed to depend positively on demand pressure, so that "a strong demand for labour increases mobility and therefore the efficiency of resource allocation and indirectly the rate of growth" (Johnson [1963d: 64]; see also Samuelson and Solow [1960: 190]; National Economic Development Council [1963a: 27]). Thus, a high demand pressure (a low rate of unemployment), was regarded as beneficial for overall growth as structural adjustments might be easier and the overall dynamism of the economy could be higher. In this line of thought, Reuber [1962: 12] emphasised that "the problems of adjusting to changing economic conditions, whatever the source of these changes, is much more difficult when the economy has considerable excess capacity than when it is running at full steam" (see also Bach [1958: 38]). In sum, technical progress and the necessary structural adjustments were assumed to be facilitated by a high demand pressure. At least in theory, a high rate of investment met a high rate of technical progress so that the stock of machinery, which was regarded as the factual incorporation of this technical progress (see also Johansen [1959]; Solow [1960]) received frequent updates and improvements (see, for example, Fellner [1960: 94]). Furthermore, high mobility of labour was assumed to accompany this progressive economic setup.

This positive relation between growth and the level of demand made the Keynesian view prone to the Phillips curve trade-off. A high level of demand seemed necessary to assure high rates of economic growth, while inflation, at least at a certain point, was still regarded as an evil. This conflict was especially pronounced if an increase in the unemployment rate seemed necessary to achieve price stability, as then inflation had to be traded off against unemployment *and* a high rate of growth. This problem led Turner [1958: 684] to conclude that "growth cannot be reconciled with price stability" (see also Balogh [1958: 239], Fishman and Fishman [1958: 70f.]). Wilson [1961:9] furthermore pointed at the issue that an anti-inflation policy inflation might overshoot and therefore cause a loss in output and growth (see also Klein and Bodkin [1964: 425]). Chandler [1960: 214f.] therefore cautioned that policies which will "maximize the short-run rate of growth" may lead to such a high rise in prices that necessary restrictive policies will be accompanied by a "disappointment of widely held highly inflationary expectations" which "could be quite damaging to employment, output, and growth". The Keynesian view hence faced the dilemma that there seemed to be an inherent conflict between unemployment and the rate of growth on the one hand, and the rate of inflation on the other hand.

3.2. The Paishian View

In contrast to the Keynesian view, some economists proposed that an overall restrictive policy would be necessary to foster growth. This view was particularly held by the British economist Frank W. Paish, at that time professor at the London School of Economics. Paish [1962: 331f.] supposed that "the permanent maintenance of the small proportion of unused capacity suggested here would be more likely to increase than decrease the rate of growth of capacity." For Paish [1962: 94], especially very high levels of employment raise the problem of "bottle-necks" in the economy which were thought to be an obstacle for growth, as well as a cause of inflation and misallocation (see also Baumol [1958: 50ff.]; Wilson [1961: 17]; National Economic Development Council [1963a: 44]; Phillips [1968: 229]). Furthermore, Paish [1968, 22] argued that overall efficiency would be increased by a higher level of unemployment and slack of demand as there is "the need for firms to be efficient in order to survive". Those firms which were able to stay in the market due to high demand are now sorted out or forced to raise their efficiency as their "costs of production are above the average" [Paish, 1962: 94f.; see also Paish, 1958: 104f.]. Paish [1968: 22] therefore concluded that "[a] condition of excess demand . . . provides an ideal climate for keeping inefficient firms alive and thus for slowing down the improvement in the average efficiency of the system as a whole." Furthermore, the Commission on Money and Credit [1961: 42] remarked that it might also be possible that high demand renders the use of old machinery and less skilled labour necessary and profitable, with negative effects on average productivity. Moreover, full employment may cause higher demand for consumption goods but not for investment goods. Therefore, Bronfenbrenner [1963: 115f.] stated that "[i]nsofar as full employment is associated with high consumption while rapid growth requires high saving and investment, there is a trade-off here too." Klein and Bodkin [1964: 417] thus came to the conclusion with respect to the USA that "[t]his is the American problem in a nutshell—too much consumption and too little capital formation holding down the rate of economic expansion."

Also Long [1960: 152ff.] pointed at the positive effects of a higher rate of unemployment: From the late 1940s to the late 1950s in the USA, real GNP per worker rose faster at high levels of unemployment while at the same time inflationary pressures were weak [Long, 1960: 153]. This might be explained by the following three different effects of a higher rate of unemployment [Long, 1960: 156]. First of all, there is a "lubrication effect": A larger worker pool is advantageous for an economy in continuous development as emerging enterprises then have the possibility to acquire more workers than usually released by dying industries (see also Minsky [1961: 2]). This larger worker pool thus makes a high rate of growth compatible with price stability as otherwise rising industries would have to bid away resources from other sectors which would result in wage and price increases. Second, there is an "insecurity effect" in the sense that a high level of unemployment will discipline wage demands of workers and unions and will furthermore discourage unnecessary job hopping. Third, the "pencil-sharpening effect" will set in: Slack in the economy and thus increased competition will force employers to increase productivity and to resist high wage claims in order to keep costs down. In sum, all three effects of a higher unemployment rate might be considered beneficial for achieving both a high rate of growth and price stability.

Sumner [1968: 304ff.], however, criticised these arguments and conclusions. Particularly the effect of permanent slack in the economy on investment is in the focus of attention as there are good reasons to assume that permanently unused capacity will be detrimental for overall long-term expectations and therefore for investment and the rate of growth (see also Scitovsky and Scitovsky [1964: 442]). Also a study by Junankar [1970: 290] directly aimed at investigating Paish's hypothesis came to the conclusion that "[i]n all the models investigated spare capacity affected investment adversely. Thus the policy implications . . . are that in order to stimulate investment and through it growth, the economy should be run within the full capacity zone."

The advantage of Paish's view with regard to economic policy is that growth and price stability are not conflicting policy objectives as they are in the Keynesian case. To the contrary, the resulting price stability due to excess capacity was assumed to be an important prerequisite for growth. For example, Jacoby [1958: 645] points at the issue that inflation distorts investment decisions by making the distinction between real and nominal values more difficult (see also Eckstein [1958: 361]). Furthermore, inflation may lower the rate of saving [Jacoby, 1957: 20]. Price stability also was assumed to indirectly have positive effects on the rate of growth: a specific contemporary argument against running the economy at high levels of employment and in favour of price stability was the difficult task of maintaining a balance-of-payments equilibrium in a fixed exchange rate system like Bretton Woods—a particular issue at that time in the UK [Wilson, 1961: 17ff.]. Disequilibria in the balance of payments might especially arise in periods of high growth as imports also rise strongly (for example, to overcome bottlenecks; see National Economic Development Council [1963a: 44]), while exports may be hampered by the domestic rise in prices (see the empirical investigation by Ball et al. [1966]). Thus, there was a perceived trade-off between growth and keeping the balance of payments in equilibrium [National Economic Development Council, 1964: 6; Klein and Bodkin, 1964: 414f.]. This was also emphasised by Dow [1964: 399ff.]: Running the economy at a low demand pressure and thus at higher unemployment and in its wake greater price stability was regarded as a precondition for achieving a high rate of growth while keeping the balance of payments in equilibrium. Thus, some excess capacity and therefore "greater price stability seems desirable, partly for its own sake, but largely as a means of getting the growth of exports to pay for the imports needed for faster growth" [Dow, 1964: 403].

Harrod [1963: 89], however, remained critical regarding the suggested beneficial consequences of low inflation due to slack in the economy: If investment is forestalled as a reaction to excess capacity, the growth rate will be equally weak and inflationary pressures thus may arise regardless of high unemployment as "it is easier to prevent an inflationary rise of incomes if you are growing at a higher rate."

In sum, the Paishian view suggested some excess capacity to increase the rate of growth while keeping inflation in check. The trade-off in this line of thought hence was very different to that of the Keynesian view: Growth and low inflation on the one hand, a higher rate of unemployment on the other hand.

3.3. The Sceptical View and Empirical Evidence

Besides these two lines of thought, there were also economists who were very skeptical about any influence of the overall level of demand on economic growth. For example, Johnson [1963b: 141] stated that "there is no a priori reason why, other things equal, the rate of growth should vary with the average level of unemployment" and that "there is no a priori reason for expecting a higher normal level of employment, accompanied presumably by a higher rate of price increase, to produce a higher rate of growth." These economists remained skeptical not necessarily on pure theoretical grounds, that is, they not always based their arguments on the neoclassical growth model [Solow, 1956; 1957; Swan, 1956] in which the steady state rate of growth depends solely on the growth rate of the labour supply and technical progress.

Most notably, Phillips [1962: 13f.] stayed within the Keynesian growth model, but his calculations about the implications of a higher average unemployment rate and hence a smaller amount of investment led him to the conclusion that the effects of running the economy at a (slightly) higher rate of unemployment are "extremely small". Furthermore, the resulting "possible extra incentive or compulsion to invest in cost-reducing equipment" [Phillips, 1962: 14] might counter any negative effect of a higher rate of unemployment. Thus, for Phillips [1962: 14], the rate of growth depends on structural factors like "the willingness to save, and the more general influences of educational improvement, research, and so on". On all these structural determinants of the rate of growth "very small changes in aggregate demand and unemployment" would not have a big influence. In sum, Phillips [1968: 229] concluded that "[i]n my view the objective of . . . growth is almost independent of the objectives of short-term economic management".

Tobin [1964: 4ff.] also took the point of view that full employment and the rate of growth are not interrelated goals. An economy may profit if unemployment is removed, as this enables a generally higher consumption path without trading off consumption today against consumption tomorrow. However, in the long run, it is the growth of capacity and not fluctuations in its utilisation that determine the rate of growth. Furthermore, a too high demand pressure above the growth rate of capacity will be frustrated by inflation. Demand policy hence should be focused on the optimal combination between unemployment and inflation (as given by the Phillips curve) and not on influencing the rate of growth. In this sense, Tobin [1964: 4] concluded that "[f]ull employment is, therefore, not a reason for faster economic growth; each is an objective in its own right."

Most economists remaining sceptical based their position on empirical research and evidence. For example, Johnson [1963c: 279] remarked with respect to the bad growth performance of both the USA and the UK, while there was high unemployment in the USA and low unemployment in the UK, that growth and the rate of unemployment do not seem to be interrelated.

Most interestingly, the very first study which explicitly calculated gains and losses of lower unemployment and higher rates of inflation, Reuber [1962], did not further discuss the influence of different levels of unemployment and inflation on the rate of growth as Reuber [1962: 7] came to the conclusion "that there is no discernible relationship between the long-run rate of economic growth and either the stability of prices or the level of unemployment" (see also Reuber [1962: 87ff.]; Reuber [1964: 113f.]). Therefore, the Phillips curve only shows a trade-off between unemployment and inflation on which economic policy has to focus [Reuber, 1962: 10]. The rate of growth thus should be fostered "by other branches of government equipped with instruments that are better suited for influencing such factors as education and long-run capital accumulation, on which the long-run rate of growth seems mainly to depend" [Reuber, 1964: 115].

With respect to the role of inflation for the rate of growth it was found empirically that the influence of the rate of inflation was negligible in most cases [Bach, 1958: 34ff.; Eckstein, 1958: 373; Bhatia, 1960: 108ff.; Wilson, 1961: 6ff.; Allais, 1969: 378]. However, some exceptions are worth mentioning: even though mild inflation as such might even be beneficial for growth [Johnson, 1963b: 140f.; Johnson, 1963d: 61; Conard, 1964: 95f.], sudden and unanticipated changes, that is, a high variance in the rate of inflation, were found to be an obstacle for growth [Klein and Bodkin, 1964: 412]. Even deflation, if steady and predictable, may not conflict with rapid growth [Friedman, 1958; 251ff.; Johnson, 1963d: 64]. Dorrance [1966, 94] thus concluded that the rate of inflation becomes only important in times of strong increases or decreases as "rapid inflation seriously inhibits growth."

4. Growth and the Phillips Curve

To disentangle these different views about the factors responsible for growth, Black [1959] reviewed this debate in a Phillips curve framework. Actually, Black [1959: 146] chose an upward-sloping aggregate supply curve in employment-inflation space (see Figure 1). The relation hence is not exactly a Phillips curve, but is nevertheless much in line with the main idea of the Phillips curve that higher demand pressure causes wages and thus prices to rise. Moreover, the curve strongly resembles the one used by Phillips [1954:

307f.].[3] Additionally, the reason for the shape of the curve comes close to the bargaining power explanation given by Phillips [1954: 307f.] as Black [1959: 146] also points at the higher bargaining power of different groups in the economy the closer the economy is to full employment. Furthermore, an unequal distribution of demand across sectors (very much in line with Lipsey [1960, 17ff.]) and the emergence of bottlenecks are additional reasons why inflationary cost-push pressures arise in the economy before full employment is reached. In general, the stronger the market imperfections are, the more pronounced the conflict between inflation and unemployment becomes [Black, 1959: 149].

The location of the curve is assumed to depend on two forces: The curve as well as the level of full employment (which coincides with full capacity utilisation) F will be shifted horizontally to the right due to technical progress and population growth.[4] Moreover, it can be endogenously shifted to the right by induced investment which depends on the (previous) level of demand [Black, 1959: 149]. Vertical shifts arise due to adjusting inflation expectations, "as both buyers and sellers get attuned to regarding a given rate of increase of prices as normal".[5] In sum, both shifts are not independent of the level of aggregate demand and the thereby achieved rate of inflation and the level of employment (and output). However, horizontal and vertical shifts are opposing forces. Whereas horizontal shifts to the right allow a higher rate of aggregate demand at the same rate of inflation, upward shifts of the relation increase the conflict between inflation and unemployment. Therefore, given the three parameters of the relation, that is, the slope of the aggregate supply curve, the strength of induced investment, and the elasticity of inflation expectations, Black [1959: 150] points out that there might be an "optimum rate of growth of monetary demand, which will serve in the long run to maximise the rate of growth of actual output". This idea of an optimum level of aggregate demand is depicted in Figure 1.

3. Black [1959: 145, n. 1] also thanked Phillips for "comments and suggestions" so that it can be assumed that Phillips probably was not too opposed to Black's assumptions. However, John Black, in a letter to the author dated 2 February 2014, remarked that "I simply cannot recall what he said, on paper only as we never met." Therefore, one should not "infer any approval from Phillips."

4. Following Leeson [1997: 158f.], these horizontal shifts might be also in line with Phillips [1954: 307f.].

5. Lewis [1958: 379ff.] also discusses some of these shifts in a price-level output diagram.

FIG. 1. The Trade-Off Between Inflation, Employment, and Growth.

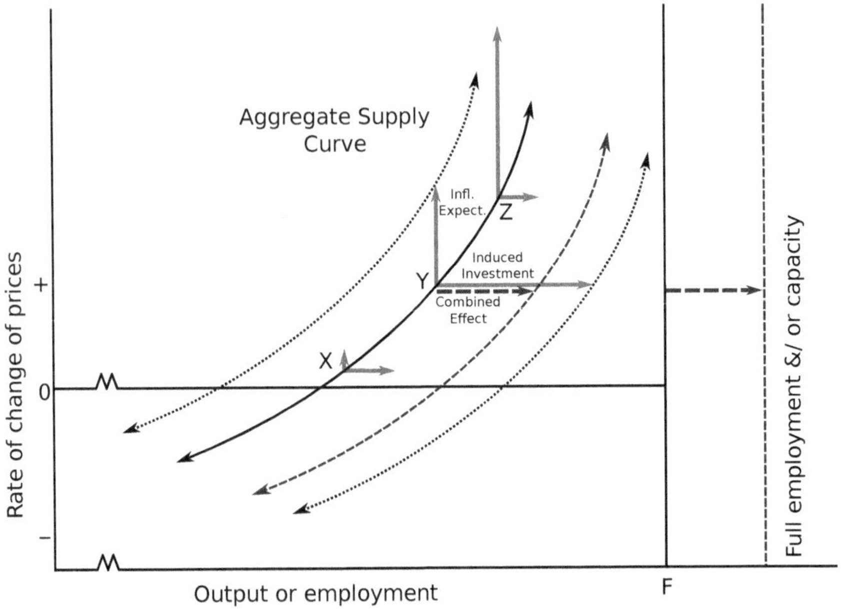

Source: Own illustration based on Black [1959: 149].
Modified and reproduced with permission by John Wiley & Sons.

At the aggregate demand level *Y*, the rightward shift of the curve due to induced investment and the upward shift due to adjusting inflation expectations (dotted supply curves) are such that the combined forces (dashed arrow) correspond to the maximal possible rightward shift of the schedule (dashed curve) and at the same time of the full capacity boundary (dashed vertical line). A higher level of aggregate demand such as *Z* does not induce the same capacity-expanding effect of investment[6] while at the same time inflation expectations are strongly elastic (in the figure this would even cause a combined upward shift of the relation). On the other hand, a lower level of demand *X*, while causing only a minor adjustment of inflation expectations, may fail to induce a strong rise in investment so that the combined rightward shift of the relation will be weaker than that in *Y*.

Black [1959: 152] hence concluded that with this model it becomes possible to disentangle different views about the interdependencies between

6. Black [1959: 150f.] referred to Hayek's business cycle theory [Hayek, 1931] and his emphasis on the misdirection of investments in times of the boom (see for a discussion Hagemann and Trautwein [1998: 299f.]). Hence, even though the absolute amount of investment might be higher in *Z* than in *Y*, the actual effect on enhancing productive capacity will not necessarily be greater.

unemployment, inflation, and growth. Believers in classical economic principles and of "a dynamic version of the quantity theory of money" would argue that there is no pronounced conflict between inflation and unemployment (so that the curve is more like a kinked supply curve) and that inflation expectations are strong. Investment decisions in this line of thought are not based on recent output levels, but on the long-run profitability of investment projects which depend on secular productivity developments and the interest rate. Thus, any increase in aggregate demand will not succeed in accelerating the rate of growth as the vertical forces are always stronger than the horizontal ones. Keynesians, however, build their proposal of increasing aggregate demand upon the assumption that inflation expectations are rather inelastic or at least that induced investment more than compensates any upward shift of the relation. An increase in aggregate demand hence is optimal even in the case of a conflict between inflation and unemployment as there is always a positive level of demand pressure to maximise the rate of growth.

5. Conclusion

The discussion has shown that there was a lively debate in the 1960s about the optimal demand pressure to maximise the rate of growth. Three elements of this debate stand out and are worth recalling: First of all, the Cold War made the rate of growth a most important policy objective. This overriding importance of the rate of the growth made it acceptable to discuss means to foster a growth rate higher than indicated by individual preferences. One of those instruments considered was—besides encouraging and promoting research, education, and technical progress—the level of demand pressure. The state of aggregate demand was considered important as demand-dependent investment was regarded as one of the driving forces of growth. The second element of this debate was the belief that it is indeed possible to choose the level of demand via fiscal and monetary policies. This element hence included an optimistic view regarding the power of stabilisation policies to damp cyclical fluctuations and to fine-tune the economy. Together, these two elements built the basis for the discussion about an optimal pressure of demand to maximise the rate of growth (see, for example, Anderson and Cornwall [1961: 163]). However, the choice of the aggregate demand pressure not only had implications for the rate of growth, but also for the level of unemployment and the rate of inflation. This third element in the debate, the Phillips curve, pointed at the possible conflict between all three goals as discussed by Black [1959].

Many economists believed that a high demand pressure will have the benefit of removing unemployment as well as fostering growth by creating an optimistic outlook and due to positive effects of a higher rate of inflation on investment. Bruno and Easterly [1996: 139] therefore summarise that "the traditional view that inflation was destructive [to growth] no longer seemed so compelling. It was the Golden Age of the Phillips Curve, in which inflation and growth were positively related" (see also Brown [2001: C32]). This Keynesian view can be called a "carrot theory" [Lipsey, 2010: 171] which relied on the idea that "the best way to get more investment is to have a rising demand for end-products and an assurance that this will continue. Look after the aggregate demand for end-products and investment will look after itself" [Harrod, 1967: 11]. However, the assumptions on which these arguments rested are questionable, in particular the non-adjustment of the nominal rate of interest to a higher rate of inflation.

Critiques of this approach, most notably Paish, did not target this assumption in particular. Rather the argument that technological change will proceed faster and investment will be higher in a buoyant economy was criticised by the Paishian view. This line of thought feared that a high demand pressure and the absence of the risk of failure will weaken market forces as it will free firms from the competitive pressure to innovate in order to survive. This view hence can be called a "stick theory" [Lipsey, 2010: 171] which was based on the assumption that "[f]or a high rate of growth of output per man-hour we need an economic climate in which all producers are under continual pressure to keep down their costs" [Paish, 1968: 22]. This view, however, can be criticised in the sense that a temporary crisis may indeed assure the survival of the fittest. But ongoing slack in the economy may sooner or later harm the willingness to invest and to take the risk usually associated with innovations.

Both approaches have in common that growth was considered as a variable that can be influenced in the short and medium run by appropriate demand polices. It is, however, striking to note that many contributions did not take fully into account the neoclassical proposition that in the long run the rate of growth solely depends on population growth and technical progress, so that, for example, a higher rate of saving and investment will only have transitional effects. Not only this issue, but also the fact that many contributions ignored important theoretical concepts like the "Golden Rule" might be best explained by the pressing issues of the Cold War, so that policy debates focused on the years immediately ahead. In this respect Tobin [1964: 9] emphasised that even if in the long run there is no choice about the rate of growth, but only about consumption levels, the transitional period might be very long so that practically and within the timespan of economic policy, society can choose among different rates of growth. Moreover, there was a theoretical gap (to be closed by Cass [1965] and Koopmans [1965], based on Ramsey [1928]) with regard to the choice of the optimal growth path in a transitional period to the "Golden Rule" consumption level. Johnson [1964: 24] critically remarked about this issue that "[i]t is of little help to know where one should be going, if one is not told when one ought to arrive." The definition of an optimal rate of growth as an objective of economic policy hence was regarded as more difficult than other goals of economic policy like full employment and price stability [Musgrave, 1958: 597; Commission on Money and Credit, 1961: 31; Reuber, 1962: 35f.; Johnson, 1963d: 65f.]. The Cold War furthermore might explain the general emphasis on the rate of growth of output, and not always the rate of growth of per-capita income: For example, Kendrick [1964: 249] remarked that although per-capita income is a better measure for the quality of growth (see also Klein and Bodkin [1964: 379]), growth of output as such (even in the case of declining per-capita income at the same time) is nevertheless "of significance from the military . . . viewpoint".

However, not all demand-oriented contributions regarded a high level of demand as the only necessary and sufficient condition for a rising output level. Technical progress, for example, was considered as a "key factor" by the National Economic Development Council [1963b: 29ff.] and the Commission on Money and Credit [1961: 34] emphasised the importance of education "to take full advantage of" technical developments. Nonetheless, even these long-run growth forces like technical progress and ongoing increases in general efficiency (for example improved labour market dynamics) were assumed to also depend partly on the level of aggregate demand. In particular, investment was regarded as an important way to incorporate technical progress into the economy.

A third group of economists doubted that the pressure of demand has a strong and remarkable influence on the rate of growth. These economists took the point of view that growth depends particularly on technical progress and that the temporary effects on output due to a rise in the utilisation level of available resources needs to be distinguished from the long-run growth of capacity. Also Phillips belonged to this group, even though he argued within the framework of Keynesian growth models. Nevertheless, Phillips believed that the driving forces of growth are research and education and not demand-induced investment. Empirical studies found only a small influence of the rate of unemployment or of the rate of inflation on economic growth—at least as long as the variance of inflation remained low.

The contribution by Black [1959] tried to disentangle these different views within the Phillips-curve framework and focused on the optimal demand pressure in order to maximise the rate of growth. The trade-off between inflation, unemployment, and growth hence took centre stage. This debate found its end in the late 1960s with the introduction of Friedman's "natural rate of unemployment" as the more the economy was regarded in the sense of Friedman [1968], the less did a discussion of these issues make sense—as the choice between inflation and unemployment vanished so did the thereby connected questions. Since then, monetary policy is assumed to be neutral (also with regard to the rate of growth) as pointed out by Friedman [1968: 11]. In the framework of Black [1959], this implied that now the economy was regarded as in the classical case, built upon the assumption of elastic price expectations and low induced investment (and without a structural conflict between inflation and unemployment).

However, some modern theoretical approaches, like evolutionary theory based on the assumption of endogenous and path-dependent technical change, still point at the likely case of an important role of the state of aggregate demand and the long-run consequences of monetary and fiscal policies. Factors like capacity utilisation, the level of unemployment, and the rate of inflation in such a framework can still cause long-run impacts in the economy [Lipsey and Scarth, 2011: xxxff.]. On these grounds Lipsey [2010, 167ff.] suggested that the concept of a unique natural rate of unemployment should be replaced by a non-accelerating inflation band of unemployment (see Figure 2).

FIG. 2. The Non-Accelerating Inflation Band of Unemployment.

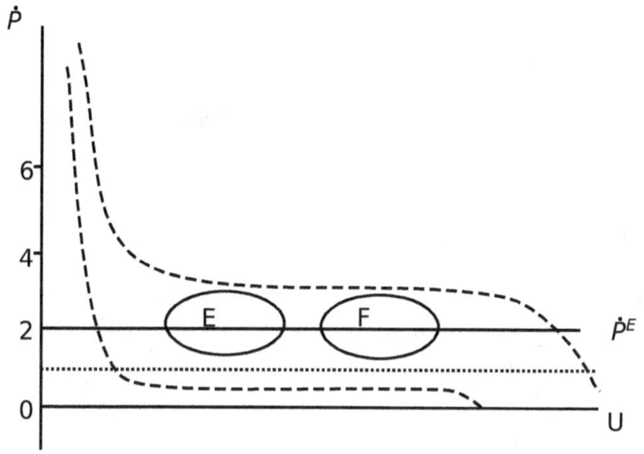

Source: Lipsey [2010: 168]. Redrawn by the author and reproduced with permission by ACCEDO Verlagsgesellschaft.

This implies that various combinations between inflation and unemployment can be possible since the system will not have a unique equilibrium (a natural rate of unemployment) any more, as different levels of unemployment can be compatible with the expected rate of inflation (credibly fixed by the central bank) around which the actual rate of inflation fluctuates. Therefore, the economy may end up, depending on the overall environment including endogenous technical change and economic policy, in the range of the ellipse *E* but also *F*, both solutions being compatible with an expected rate of the credible inflation target of the central bank (here: 2 per cent).[7]

In such a framework, some arguments of the debate in the 1960s, for example under which circumstances—in this discussion high demand as in the ellipse *E* or strong competitive pressure as in *F*—technical progress will be incorporated faster into the economy are probably worth to be considered even today.

7. The experience of the macro economies of many first world countries since the advent of successful inflation targeting conforms to this evolutionary view. See for a deeper discussion and empirical evidence Carlaw and Lipsey [2012].

Références

Alhadeff D.A. et al. [1964]. The Commission on Money and Credit's research studies: a collective review article. *The Journal of Finance* 19(3): 497–533.

Allais M. [1969]. Growth and inflation. *Journal of Money, Credit and Banking* 1(3): 355–426.

Anderson W.H.L. and J. Cornwall [1961]. Problems of growth policy. *The Review of Economics and Statistics* 43(2): 163–74.

Bach G.L. [1958]. How important is price stability in stable economic growth? In Joint Economic Committee (Ed.) *The Relationship of Prices to Economic Stability and Growth: Compendium of Papers Submitted by Panelists Appearing before the Joint Economic Committee.* Washington, D.C.: United States Government Printing Office: 33–47.

Ball R.J., J.R. Eaton, and M.D. Steuer [1966]. The relationship between United Kingdom export performance in manufactures and the internal pressure of demand. *The Economic Journal* 76(303): 501–18.

Balogh T. [1958]. Productivity and inflation. *Oxford Economic Papers* 10(2): 220–45.

Baran P.A. [1960]. Discussion. *The American Economic Review* 50(2): 119–23.

Baumol W.J. [1958]. Price behavior, stability, and growth. In Joint Economic Committee (Ed.) *The Relationship of Prices to Economic Stability and Growth: Compendium of Papers Submitted by Panelists Appearing before the Joint Economic Committee.* Washington, D.C.: United States Government Printing Office: 49–59.

Bhatia R.J. [1960]. Inflation, deflation, and economic development. *Staff Papers – International Monetary Fund* 8(1): 101–14.

Black J. [1959]. Inflation and long-run growth. *Economica* 26(102): 145–53.

Bronfenbrenner M. [1963]. A sample survey of the Commission on Money and Credit research papers. *The Review of Economics and Statistics* 45(1): 111–28.

— (Ed.) [1969]. *Is the Business Cycle Obsolete?* New York, London, Sydney, Toronto: Wiley Interscience.

— and F.D. Holzman [1963]. Survey of inflation theory. *The American Economic Review* 53(4): 593–661.

Brown G. [2001]. The conditions for high and stable growth and employment. *The Economic Journal* 111(471), C30–C44.

Bruno M. and W. Easterly [1996]. Inflation and growth: in search of a stable relationship. *Proceedings of the Federal Reserve Bank of St. Louis* (May): 139–46.

Carlaw K.I. and R.G. Lipsey [2012]. Does history matter? Empirical analysis of evolutionary versus stationary equilibrium views of the economy. *Journal of Evolutionary Economics* 22(4): 735–66.

Cass, D. [1965]. Optimum growth in an aggregative model of capital accumulation. *The Review of Economic Studies* 32(3): 233–40.

Chandler L.V. [1960]. Discussion. *The American Economic Review* 50(2): 212–5.

Commission on Money and Credit [1961]. *Money and Credit: Their Influence on Jobs, Prices, and Growth—The Report of the Commission on Money and Credit.* Englewood Cliffs, N.J.: Prentice-Hall.

Conard J.W. [1964]. The causes and consequences of inflation. In Commission on Money and Credit (Ed.) *Inflation, Growth, and Employment.* Englewood Cliffs, N.J.: Prentice-Hall: 1–102.

Cornwall J. [1963]. Three paths to full employment growth. *The Quarterly Journal of Economics* 77(1): 1–25.

Denison E.F. [1962]. How to raise the high-employment growth rate by one percentage point. *The American Economic Review* 52(2): 67–75.

Domar E.D. [1946]. Capital expansion, rate of growth, and employment. *Econometrica* 14(2): 137–47.

— [1947]. Expansion and employment. *The American Economic Review* 37(1): 34–55.

Dorrance G.S. [1966]. Inflation and growth: the statistical evidence. *Staff Papers – International Monetary Fund* 13(1): 82–102.

Dow J.C.R. [1964]. *The Management of the British Economy, 1945–60.* Cambridge: Cambridge University Press. National Institute of Economic and Social Research, *Economic and Social Studies*, N. 12.

Eckstein O. [1958]. Inflation, the wage-price spiral and economic growth. In Joint Economic Committee (Ed.) *The Relationship of Prices to Economic Stability and Growth: Compendium of Papers Submitted by Panelists Appearing before the Joint Economic Committee.* Washington, D.C.: United States Government Printing Office: 361–74.

Fellner W.J. [1960]. Rapid growth as an objective of economic policy. *The American Economic Review* 50(2): 93–105.

Fishman B.G. and L. Fishman [1958]. Economic stability, economic growth, and price stability. In Joint Economic Committee (Ed.) *The Relationship of Prices to Economic Stability and Growth: Compendium of Papers Submitted by Panelists Appearing before the Joint Economic Committee.* Washington, D.C.: United States Government Printing Office: 61–7.

Friedman M. [1958]. The supply of money and changes in prices and output. In Joint Economic Committee (Ed.) *The Relationship of Prices to Economic Stability and Growth: Compendium of Papers Submitted by Panelists Appearing before the Joint Economic Committee.* Washington, D.C.: United States Government Printing Office: 241–56.

— [1959]. Statement and testimony. In Joint Economic Committee (Ed.) *Employment, Growth, and Price Levels: Hearings Before the Joint Economic Committee Pursuant to S. Con. Res. 13, Part 9A, Constructive Suggestions for Reconcilling and Simultaneously Obtaining the Three Objectives of Maximum Employment, an Adequate Rate of Growth, and Substantial Stability of the Price Level, 86th Congress, 1st Session, 30 October 1959*, Washington, D.C.: U.S. Government Printing Office: 3019–53. Cited from documents provided by http://hoohila.stanford.edu/friedman/congress.php <http://0055d26.netsolhost.com/friedman/pdfs/congress/Gov.10.30.1959.pdf>.

— [1968]. The role of monetary policy. *The American Economic Review* 58(1): 1–17.

Godley W.A.H. and J.R. Shepherd [1964]. Long-term growth and short-term policy: the productive potential of the British economy, and fluctuations in the pressure of demand for labour, 1951–1962. *National Institute Economic Review* 29(1): 26–38.

Hagemann H. and H.-M. Trautwein [1998]. Cantillon and Ricardo effects: Hayek's contributions to business cycle theory. *The European Journal of the History of Economic Thought* 5(2): 292–316.

Harrod R.F. [1936]. *The Trade Cycle. An Essay.* Oxford: Clarendon Press.

— [1939]. An essay in dynamic theory. *The Economic Journal* 49(193): 14–33.

— [1948]. *Towards a Dynamic Economics: Some Recent Developments of Economic Theory and Their Application to Policy*. London: Macmillan.

— [1963]. Review of *Studies in an Inflationary Economy*. By F. W. Paish. *Economica* 30(117): 85–89.

— [1967]. *Towards a New Economic Policy: Lectures Given in the University of Manchester*. Manchester: Manchester University Press.

— [1969]. Review of *Why Growth Rates Differ: Postwar Experience in Nine Western Countries*. By E.F. Denison. *Economica* 36(143): 323–25.

Hayek F.A. [1931]. *Preise und Produktion*. Vienna: Julius Springer.

Hoover C.B. [1960]. Employment, growth and price levels: a review article. *The Quarterly Journal of Economics* 74(3): 374–92.

Jacoby N.H. [1957]. Thinking ahead. *Harvard Business Review* 35(3): 15–162.

— [1958]. Maintaining prosperity without inflation—objectives, problems, and policies. In Joint Economic Committee (Ed.) *The Relationship of Prices to Economic Stability and Growth: Compendium of Papers Submitted by Panelists Appearing before the Joint Economic Committee*. Washington, D.C.: United States Government Printing Office: 637–49.

Johansen L. [1959]. Substitution versus fixed production coefficients in the theory of economic growth: a synthesis. *Econometrica* 27(2): 157–76.

Johnson H.G. [1963a]. Economic growth and economic policy. In H.G. Johnson (Ed.) *The Canadian Quandary: Economic Problems and Policies*. Toronto: McGraw-Hill: 46–66.

— [1963b]. Objectives, monetary standards, and potentialities. *The Review of Economics and Statistics* 45(1): 137–44.

— [1963c]. An overview of price levels, employment, and the balance of payments. *The Journal of Business* 36(3): 279–89.

— [1963d]. A survey of theories of inflation. *The Indian Economic Review* 8(2) 29–69.

— [1964]. Discussion. *The American Economic Review* 54(3): 21–4.

— [1966]. Is inflation the inevitable price of rapid development or a retarding factor in economic growth? *The Malayan Economic Review* 11(April): 21–28.

Joint Economic Committee [1958]. *The Relationship of Prices to Economic Stability and Growth: Compendium of Papers Submitted by Panelists Appearing before the Joint Economic Committee.* Washington, D.C.: United States Government Printing Office.

— [1959]. *Staff Report on Employment, Growth and Price Levels.* Washington, D.C.: United States Government Printing Office.

Junankar P.N. [1970]. The relationship between investment and spare capacity in the United Kingdom, 1957–66. *Economica* 37(147): 277–92.

Kaldor N. [1959]. Economic growth and the problem of inflation. *Economica* 26(104): 287–98.

Kendrick J.W. [1964]. Concepts and measures of economic growth. In Commission on Money and Credit (Ed.) *Inflation, Growth, and Employment.* Englewood Cliffs, N.J.: Prentice-Hall: 231–88.

Kessel R.A. and A.A. Alchian [1960]. The meaning and validity of the inflation-induced lag of wages behind prices. *The American Economic Review* 50(1): 43–66.

Klein L.R. and R.G. Bodkin [1964]. Empirical aspects of the trade-offs among three goals: high level employment, price stability and economic growth. In Commission on Money and Credit (Ed.) *Inflation, Growth, and Employment.* Englewood Cliffs, N.J.: Prentice-Hall: 367–428.

Koopmans T.C. [1965]. On the concept of optimal economic growth. In *The Econometric Approach to Development Planning.* Amsterdam: North-Holland: 225–87.

Leeson R. [1997]. The trade-off interpretation of Phillips's dynamic stabilization exercise. *Economica* 64(253): 155–71.

Lewis J.P. [1958]. Pricing for stability and growth. In Joint Economic Committee (Ed.) *The Relationship of Prices to Economic Stability and Growth: Compendium of Papers Submitted by Panelists Appearing before the Joint Economic Committee.* Washington, D.C.: United States Government Printing Office: 375–96.

Lipsey R.G. [1960]. The relation between unemployment and the rate of change of money wage rates in the United Kingdom, 1862–1957: a further analysis. *Economica* 27(105): 1–31.

— [1997]. Introduction: an intellectual autobiography. In R.G. Lipsey (Ed.) *Microeconomics, Growth and Political Economy – The Selected Essays of Richard G. Lipsey*, Volume 1. Cheltenham, UK and Lyme, US: Edward Elgar: ix–xxxvii.

— [2010]. Evolutionary economics and the disappearing NAIRU and Phillips curve. *Homo Œconomicus* 27(1/2): 145–76.

—, and W. Scarth [2011]. Introduction: the history, significance and policy context of the Phillips curve. In R.G. Lipsey and W. Scarth (Eds) *Inflation and Unemployment: The Evolution of the Phillips Curve*, Volume 1. Cheltenham, UK and Northampton, MA, USA: Edward Elgar: xiii–xxxvii.

Long C.D. [1960]. Prosperity unemployment and its relation to economic growth and inflation. *The American Economic Review* 50(2): 145–61.

Minsky, H.P. [1961]. Employment, growth and price levels: a review article. *The Review of Economics and Statistics* 43(1): 1–12.

— [1968]. The crunch of 1966. Model for new financial crises? *Trans-action* 5(4): 44–51.

Musgrave, R.A. [1958]. The optimal mix of stabilization policies. In Joint Economic Committee (Ed.) *The Relationship of Prices to Economic Stability and Growth: Compendium of Papers Submitted by Panelists Appearing before the Joint Economic Committee.* Washington, D.C.: United States Government Printing Office: 597–609.

National Economic Development Council [1963a]. *Conditions Favourable to Faster Growth.* London: Her Majesty's Stationery Office.

— [1963b]. *Growth of the United Kingdom Economy 1961–1966.* London: Her Majesty's Stationery Office.

— [1964]. *The Growth of the Economy.* London: Her Majesty's Stationery Office.

Nelson R.R. [1966]. Full employment policy and economic growth. *The American Economic Review* 56(5): 1178–92.

Newman H.E. [1958]. Full employment as a goal of public policy. *American Journal of Economics and Sociology* 17(3): 237–48.

Nutter G.W. [1962]. *Growth of Industrial Production in the Soviet Union.* Princeton, NJ: Princeton University Press. *National Bureau of Economic Research General Series* N. 75.

Paish F.W. [1958]. Inflation in the United Kingdom, 1948–1957. *Economica* 25(98): 94–105.

— [1962]. *Studies in an Inflationary Economy: The United Kingdom 1948–1961.* London and New York: Macmillan & St. Martin's Press.

— [1968]. How the economy works. *Lloyds Bank Review* (April), 1–30.

Phelps E. [1961]. The golden rule of accumulation: a fable for growthmen. *The American Economic Review* 51(4): 638–43.

— [1967]. Phillips curves, expectations of inflation and optimal unemployment over time. *Economica* 34(135): 254–81.

Phillips A.W.H. [1954]. Stabilisation policy in a closed economy. *The Economic Journal* 64(254): 290–323.

— [1957]. Stabilisation policy and the time-forms of lagged responses. *The Economic Journal 67*(266), 265–277.

— [1958]. The relation between unemployment and the rate of change of money wage rates in the United Kingdom, 1861–1957. *Economica* 25(100): 283–99.

— [1961]. A simple model of employment, money and prices in a growing economy. *Economica* 28(112): 360–70.

— [1962]. Employment, inflation and growth. *Economica* 29(113), 1–16.

— [1968]. Economic policy and development. In R. Leeson (Ed.) *A.W.H. Phillips: Collected Works in Contemporary Perspective.* Cambridge: Cambridge University Press, 2000: 224–30. Handwritten seminar presentation.

Ramsey F.P. [1928]. A mathematical theory of saving. *The Economic Journal* 38(152): 543–59.

Reuber G.L. [1962]. *The Objectives of Monetary Policy.* Working paper prepared for the Royal Commission on Banking & Finance. Ottawa: Queen's Printer.

— [1964]. The objectives of Canadian monetary policy, 1949–61: empirical "trade-offs" and the reaction function of the authorities. *The Journal of Political Economy* 72(2): 109–32.

Rostow W.W. (1960). The problem of achieving and maintaining a high rate of economic growth: a historian's view. *The American Economic Review* 50(2): 106–18.

Samuelson P.A. [1955]. The new look in tax and fiscal policy. In W.L. Smith and R.L. Teigen (Eds) *Readings in Money, National Income, and Stabilization Policy*. Homewood, Ill.: Richard D. Irwin, Inc. 1965: 334–39. First published in *Federal Tax Policy for Economic Growth and Stability* (Joint Committee on the Economic Report, 84th Cong., 1st sess.), Washington, D.C.: U.S. Government Printing Office, 1955: 229–34.

— [1957]. Full employment versus progress and other economic goals. In M.F. Millikan (Ed.) *Income Stabilization for a Developing Democracy: A Study of the Politics and Economics of High Employment Without Inflation* (2nd ed.). New Haven and London: Yale University Press and Oxford University Press: 547–80.

—, and R.M. Solow [1960]. Analytical aspects of anti-inflation policy. *American Economic Review* 50(2): 177–94.

Scitovsky T. and A. Scitovsky [1964]. Inflation versus unemployment: an examination of their effects. In Commission on Money and Credit (Ed.) *Inflation, Growth, and Employment*. Englewood Cliffs, N.J.: Prentice-Hall: 429–70.

Scott R.H. and J.R. McKean [1964]. A "cross-section" look at employment, growth, and inflation. *Western Economic Journal* 3(1): 1–6.

Smith W.L. [1957]. Monetary-fiscal policy and economic growth. *The Quarterly Journal of Economics* 71(1): 36–55.

— [1960]. Monetary policy, 1957–1960: an appraisal. *The Review of Economics and Statistics* 42(3): 269–72.

Smithies A. [1958]. Price policy and economic growth and stability. In Joint Economic Committee (Ed.) *The Relationship of Prices to Economic Stability and Growth: Compendium of Papers Submitted by Panelists Appearing before the Joint Economic Committee*. Washington, D.C.: United States Government Printing Office: 611–5.

Solow R.M. [1956]. A contribution to the theory of economic growth. *The Quarterly Journal of Economics* 70(1): 65–94.

— [1957]. Technical change and the aggregate production function. *The Review of Economics and Statistics* 39(3): 312–320.

— [1960]. Investment and technological progress. In K.J. Arrow, S. Karlin, and P. Suppes (Eds) *Mathematical Methods in Social Sciences, 1959. Proceedings of the first Stanford Symposium.* Stanford: Stanford University Press: 89–104.

Sumner M.T. [1968]. The costs of Professor Paish. *Bulletin of the Oxford University Institute of Economics & Statistics* 30(4): 299–313.

Swan T.W. [1956]. Economic growth and capital accumulation. *Economic Record* 32(2): 334–61.

Tobin J. [1964]. Economic growth as an objective of government policy. *The American Economic Review* 54(3): 1–20.

Turner R.C. [1958]. Relationship of prices to economic stability and growth: a statement of the problem. In Joint Economic Committee (Ed.) *The Relationship of Prices to Economic Stability and Growth: Compendium of Papers Submitted by Panelists Appearing before the Joint Economic Committee.* Washington, D.C.: United States Government Printing Office: 671–84.

Turnovsky S.J. [2000]. Bill Phillips' contribution to dynamic stabilisation policy. In R. Leeson (Ed.) *A.W.H. Phillips: Collected Works in Contemporary Perspective.* Cambridge: Cambridge University Press: 296–303.

Wilson T. [1961]. Inflation and growth. *The Three Banks Review* 51(September): 3–21.

— [1963]. The price of growth. *The Economic Journal* 73(292): 603–17.

STABILIZATION POLICIES AND BANKING BEHAVIORS: A REREADING OF MINSKY'S CONCEPTION OF BUSINESS CYCLES

Eric Nasica[1]

The aim of this paper is to add to current debates on the efficiency of economic stabilization policies through an analysis of the conception of business cycles developed by Minsky in his earliest work at the end of the 1950s.

The argument is developed in three steps. First, how Minsky's conception of business cycles is influenced by the nonlinear models with floors and ceilings developed by Hicks in the 1950s is discussed. These models provide a relevant theoretical framework for Minskyan analysis of stabilization policies which act as 'thwarting systems' and whose purpose is to counteract and contain the naturally explosive amplitude of economic fluctuations. They allow a better understanding of his theory of financial instability. Contrary to the generally widespread interpretation, the Minskyan Financial Instability Hypothesis cannot be reduced to an endogenous and financial conception of economic fluctuations founded only on the behavior of private economic agents: public authorities, through their stabilization policies, also play a central role in explaining the form of business cycles (Section 2).

Second, the central role played by banks in Minsky's analysis of fluctuations is highlighted. We emphasize that the behavior of banks is guided essentially by a permanent quest for profit opportunities in the tradition of such authors as Tobin and Schumpeter. This feature is crucial for understanding Minsky's conception of business cycles since it provides an explanation for how banks' behaviors undermine the efficiency of stabilization policies, and therefore the form of economic fluctuations (Section 3).

The third step (Section 4) is an assessment of the relevance of Minsky's approach for understanding recent pre- and post-crisis stabilization policies.

Keywords: Minsky, financial instability hypothesis, business cycles, stabilization policies, monetary policies, fiscal policy.

JEL classification: B22, B26, B41, E12, E32, E52, E63, G01, G21

---

1. University of Nice Sophia-Antipolis–ISEM. E-mail: Eric.Nasica@unice.fr

Politiques de stabilisation et comportements bancaires : une relecture des cycles d'affaires chez Minsky

Cet article se veut une contribution aux débats actuels sur l'efficience des politiques de stabilisation économique à travers l'analyse de la conception de Minsky des cycles d'affaires dans ses tout premiers travaux à la fin des années 1950. Le propos de l'article se décline en trois étapes. Premièrement, il s'est agi de déterminer comment la conception des cycles économique chez Minsky a été influencée par des modèles non linéaires avec plancher et plafond développés par Hicks dans les années 1950. Nous pensons que ces modèles fournissent un cadre théorique adéquat à l'analyse minskyenne des politiques de stabilisation qui agissent comme des « systèmes de régulation » dont le but est de contrecarrer et contenir l'amplitude naturellement explosive des fluctuations économiques. De surcroît, ils permettent une meilleure compréhension de sa théorie de l'instabilité financière. Contrairement à l'interprétation largement répandue, l'hypothèse de l'instabilité financière de Minsky ne peut se réduire à une conception endogène et financière des fluctuations économiques fondée uniquement sur le comportement des agents économiques privés : les pouvoirs publics, à travers les politiques de stabilisation, jouent aussi un rôle central dans l'explication de la forme des cycles économiques (section 2).

Deuxièmement, le rôle central joué par les banques dans l'analyse des fluctuations chez Minsky est souligné. Nous mettons l'accent sur le fait que le comportement des banques est essentiellement guidé par une recherche permanente d'opportunités de profit dans la tradition d'auteurs comme Tobin et Schumpeter. Cet aspect est primordial pour comprendre la conception des cycles d'affaires de Minsky puisqu'il fournit une explication de la manière dont les comportements des banques affaiblissent l'efficience des politiques de stabilisation et, en conséquence, la forme des fluctuations économiques (section 3).

La troisième étape (section 4) évalue la pertinence de l'approche de Minsky pour comprendre les récentes politiques de stabilisation pré- et post-crise.

Mots clefs : Minsky, hypothèse d'instabilité financière, cycles économiques, politiques de stabilisation, politiques monétaires, politique fiscale.

1. Introduction

Starting in the mid 1950s, and continuing over the succeeding 40 years, Hyman P. Minsky developed his original business cycle theory based on his financial conception of economic fluctuations, more specifically, his 'Financial Instability Hypothesis' (FIH) [Minsky, 1975; 1982; 1986]. This theory is based mainly on two successive phases in the business cycle: a process of transition toward greater financial fragility, which builds up in the expansionary phase; and the transition from a financially fragile situation to a situation of recession and then major economic crisis.

Minsky's commentators usually point to two central features characterizing his business cycle theory. First, his approach is considered a continuation of the theory of economic fluctuations developed by Keynes in his *General Theory* [Keynes, 1936] and synthesized in *Quarterly Journal of Economics* article published in 1937. In Minsky's approach one can recognize the main themes developed by Keynesian fundamentalists: the role of uncertainty and the behaviors it generates, the dynamic instability of market economies, the role of money and liquidity preference. The second feature is the endogenous nature of his fluctuations approach. For most commentators, the FIH is based on the behaviors of private economic agents which endogenously create processes of financial and economic instability, and unsurprisingly, most recent models 'à la Minsky'[1] are founded on this idea. The main characteristic of these models is that they introduce financial structure variables (such as indebtedness ratios chosen by private agents) into Keynesian or Kaleckian macroeconomic frameworks. These financial variables are at the origins of unstable endogenous dynamics and produce fluctuations analogous to those studied by Minsky. It should be noted also that Minsky also developed an interest in non-linear models,[2] able to generate endogenous cycles and complex dynamics. Indeed, 'these non-linear models are not vulnerable to the criticism that endogenous business cycles are too regular' [Ferri and Minsky, 1992: 82]. Moreover, they explain the observed dynamics of market economies which, for Minsky, are not 'necessarily nice: monotonic

1. Arena and Raybaut [2001]; Delli Gatti et al. [1993a; 1993b]; Delli Gatti and Gallegati [2000], Asada [2001], Charles [2008], Isaac and Kim [2012], Lima and Meirelles [2006], Sasaki and Fujita [2012]. For models *à la Minsky* which explicitly integrate stabilization policies, see e.g. Keen [1995] and Nasica and Raybaut [2005].

2. See Ferri and Minsky [1992] which explicitly refer to Day's models [1982; 1986].

explosive, explosive amplitude cycles and even chaotic cycles are possible paths through time' [Ferri and Minsky, 1989: 137].

The aim of this paper is to show that this traditional interpretation of Minsky's business cycles theory is at least incomplete. However undeniable the influence of the ideas he inherited from Keynes, other theoretical schools and individual authors left their marks on his writings. As a result, these Minsky cycles cannot be considered a purely mechanical and endogenous succession of phases induced by the behaviors of private agents. Other economic agents, such as public authorities through their stabilization policies, also play a key role in the form of economic fluctuations described by the FIH.

The argument in this paper is developed in three steps. First, we show that Minsky's conception of business cycles is influenced by nonlinear models with floors and ceilings developed by Hicks in the 1950s. These models provide a relevant theoretical framework for a Minskyan analysis of stabilization policies which act as 'thwarting systems' whose purpose is to counteract and contain the naturally explosive amplitude of economic fluctuations (Section 2).

Second, the central role played by banks in Minsky's analysis of fluctuations is highlighted, and the behavior of banks guided essentially by a permanent quest for profit opportunities is emphasized, in the tradition of authors such as Tobin or Schumpeter. This feature is crucial for understanding Minsky's conception of business cycles since it describes how banks' behaviors undermine the efficiency of stabilization policies, and therefore the form of economic fluctuations (Section 3).

Section 4 briefly assesses the relevance of Minsky's approach for understanding recent pre- and post-crisis stabilization policies, and concludes the paper.

2. Reinterpreting growth models with ceilings and floors: The Hicks-Goodwin tradition revisited

In the late 1950s, Minsky[3] proposed business cycle models that drew heavily on the multiplier and accelerator interaction models developed several years earlier by Hicks [1950]. Hicks was well aware of both the

3. Minsky [1957a; 1959].

inherent limits of linear macroeconomic models of the type proposed by Samuelson, and the fundamentally non-linear nature of economic activity. For this reason his business cycle models incorporated constraints, whose role was to act as boundaries to expansion or depression.

The main assumptions underlying these models can be briefly restated. They are usually composed of a consumption function of the form, $C_t = aY_t - 1$ (where a is the average and marginal propensity to consume), and an induced investment function of the form, $I_t = b(Y_t - 1 - Y_t - 2)$ (where b denotes the accelerator). When introduced into the equilibrium condition, $Y_t = C_t + I_t$, these relations yield a second-order difference equation:

$$Y_t = (a + b)Y_{t-1} - bY_{t-2} \tag{1}$$

Equation (1) means that when the value of the reaction coefficients a and b and the values of the initial conditions, Y_{t-1} and Y_{t-2}, are known, it is possible to determine recursively any solution Y_n to the system. In addition, we know that the second-order difference equation (1) solves for:

$$Y_t = A_1U_1^t + A_2U_2^t \tag{2}$$

where U_1 and U_2 are the roots of the associated characteristic equation $U^2 - (a + b)U + b = 0$, and A_1 and A_2 are constants depending on the value of parameters a and b and on the initial conditions.[4]

Solving equation (2) yields different types of dynamics depending on the value of the parameters, namely: (a) monotonic convergence of the income level towards a stable level (if the roots are real and of absolute values of less than unity); (b) damped fluctuations, the system is stable and converging towards the long-term equilibrium level by values that are alternately less than and greater than the equilibrium output level (if the roots are complex and their modulus is less than unity); (c) explosive fluctuations, the amplitude of fluctuations of national output around the long-term equilibrium level increasing in each period (if the roots are complex and their modulus is greater than unity); (d) instability in the form of monotonic divergence or regular explosive growth, the national

4. If m is the effective growth rate of income, then for any two successive dates chosen as initial conditions, $Y_1 = mY_0$. This therefore gives (since $Y_1 = A_1U_1 + A_2U_2$ and $Y_0 = A_1 + A_2$: $A_1 = [(m - U_2) + (U_1 - U_2)]Y_0$ and $A_2 = [(U_1 - m)/(U_1 - U_2)]Y_0$. Assuming that values a and b are such that $U_1 > U_2 > 1$ (i.e. in the case of explosive time series in an unconstrained system), it follows that: $U_1 > U_2 > m$, therefore $A_1 < 0$ and $A_2 > 0$; whereas $U_1 > m > U_2$ implies that $A_1 > 0$ and $A_2 > 0$.

product diverging increasingly from its equilibrium level (if the roots are real and greater than unity in absolute value).

Unlike Samuelson's [1939] analysis, which investigates the whole range of solutions set out above, Hicks [1950] concentrates exclusively on parameter values which, when combined, give either accelerated growth or amplified fluctuations – cases (c) and (d). Hicks therefore situates his approach in a configuration such that both roots U_1 and U_2 are greater than unity, with $U_1 > U_2 > 1$. He further assumes that the economy exhibits a maximum growth rate, a ceiling, which we will denote g. Therefore, $Y_t = Y_0 e^{gt}$ when the ceiling is effective. In addition, the dominant root U_1 is very much greater than the growth rate of the income ceiling. Finally, both roots U_1 and U_2 are such that $U_1 > U_2 > g > 1$.

Under these assumptions, the economy evolves as follows. Let us suppose that the economy is initially defined such that it generates two consecutive incomes Y_0 and Y_1 ($Y_1 > Y_0$), and such that both these incomes are less than their corresponding ceilings and $U_1 > Y_1/Y_0 > U_2$. These initial conditions determine the positive coefficients A_1 and A_2, A_2 being much greater than A_1, because U_1 is assumed to be much greater than g.[5] Then equation (2), which characterizes the dynamics of the system or rather its unconstrained dynamics, yields an explosive-type evolution over time. However, after a certain time, let us say in period n, income reaches a higher value than the ceiling corresponding to that period. At that point, the constraint becomes binding and the realized income is no longer determined by equation (2). For two successive periods income is determined by equation:

$$Y_1 = gY_0 \tag{3}$$

This takes us back to a situation where $Y_1/Y_0 = g < U_2$. The prominent feature here is that the sign of the coefficient A_1 of dominant root U_1 solving equation (2) becomes negative. This change of sign indicates the start of the rebound of the path against the ceiling, that is, the turning point in the cycle. A cumulative depression process follows and the

5. See fn. 2. This characteristic implies that during the early periods (t small), the weight of U_2 is predominant in determining the dynamic evolution, whereas during subsequent periods, it is the root U_1 that tends to dominate. It follows that the income growth rate converges towards U_1 when t tends towards infinity.

economy henceforth undergoes a downturn that is guided essentially by the negative term of increasing absolute value, $A_1(U_1)^t$.

This explosive downward movement of income will only slow if there is a lower limit, or floor that counters the process generated by the unconstrained dynamics, analogous to the effect of the ceiling examined above. The floor may consist of a maximum value set for firms' divestments. When this maximum value is reached, the realized value Y_t is different from that obtained with equation (2). A new equation determines the change taking place in the economy. It features a negative and comparatively large coefficient A_2 and a positive and comparatively small coefficient A_1. As in the previous case, there is a point where the cycle reverts. A new expansion phase begins, which initially is moderate and then is explosive. It continues until the economy rebounds at the ceiling, as described previously. And so on.

In the late 1950s, Minsky proposed business cycles models with the same general form as the Hicks model presented above. Like Hicks, Minsky opted to take non linearities into account by introducing constraints on booms and slumps, in the form of floors and ceilings. Beyond this apparent similarity, however, the interpretations differ insofar as these two economists do not attribute the same meaning to the constraints that stabilize the economy dynamics. In Hicks's model, common sense justifies the existence of these constraints: real investment cannot be negative, hence the existence of a floor, determined by the growth of autonomous investment and the size of the investment due to depreciation. In addition, output, consumption, and investment are limited by the available amounts of natural resources and labor, as well as by the size of the gains in productivity. Hence, the existence of a ceiling.

However, although Minsky does not deny the influence of these constraints on the level of economic activity, he does not consider them essential for explaining the cyclical dynamics observed in market economies. He argues that floors and ceilings primarily reflect the set of institutional mechanisms put in place by public authorities in order to confine the amplitude of economic fluctuations within reasonable limits. Thus, Minsky terms these institutional arrangements 'thwarting systems' [Ferri and Minsky, 1992].

The original idea developed by Minsky is that the main purpose of these thwarting systems is to modify the initial conditions governing time series during phases of explosive expansion or cumulative depression. As already mentioned, these new initial conditions have the effect of inverting the sign of the dominant root of the oscillator model solution equation. As a result movement in the economy eventually slows and reverses. Depression (or deflation) is thus converted by an institutional-type floor into a moderate and then explosive recovery which in turn, comes up against an institutional ceiling. The time series observed then is the outcome of incessant rebounds between the ceilings and floors, generated by institutional thwarting mechanisms introduced into the economy.

Minsky's constrained linear model is interesting in more than one respect. First, unlike Samuelson's oscillator-type unconstrained linear model, it accounts for the complexity of change affecting capitalist economies over time. Evolution takes the form of 'steady growth (when $U_1 > g > U_2$), cycles (when $U_1 > U_2 > g > 1$), booms, or depressions when ($g > U_1$)' [Minsky, 1959: 134]. In other words, Minsky's model 'exhibits the features of chaotic models, including the sensitivity of the time series that is generated to initial conditions' [Ferri and Minsky, 1989: 138]. Second, unlike Hicks's non-linear model, which ignores institutional thwarting systems, this model accounts for the effect of institutional change and interventions by public authorities on economic dynamics. In Minsky's model the dependence of floors and ceilings on policy and institutional arrangements can be made quite precise.

The 'incoherence' of economic trajectories – in particular the occurrence of explosive, amplified change leading to either very large (even infinite) values or to negative values of economic magnitude – inherent in unconstrained linear models, can thus be countered by the incorporation of institutional thwarting mechanisms. Under these circumstances, 'business cycles can result either from the values of the "*U*'s" being complex, from regular interventions that contain the economy between "floors and ceilings" if the "*U*'s" are greater than one, and from introductions of energy from outside if the "*U*'s" are less than one' [Ferri and Minsky, 1989: 137].

In Minsky's approach, stabilizing economic activity, that is, setting new initial conditions in order to contain the amplitude of time series, is essentially the concern of government, and the Central bank.[6]

Minsky views budget deficits and central bank interventions as lender-of-last-resort actions and extremely effective instruments for stabilizing economic fluctuations. Even if full employment is not achieved, these instruments help to limit the drop in income and in liquidity during economic recessions and the onset of financial crises.

First, let us consider the role of budget deficits. In Minsky's theory, investment is the essential determinant of economic activity. Investment is influenced largely by aggregate profits (realized or anticipated).[7] Minsky argues, that it follows that 'a main aim of policy is to constrain the variability of profits' [Fazzari and Minsky, 1984: 107]. Also, Minsky reminds us that in a closed economy aggregate profits are equal to the sum of investment and the budget deficit, as expressed by Kalecki's [1971] accounting identity.[8] Consequently, a deficit, by upholding aggregate demand when private investment flags, establishes a lower limit, a floor, to profits, wages, and current production prices. In other words, 'policy will be stabilizing if a shortfall of private investment quickly leads to a government deficit, and a burst of investment quickly leads to a budget surplus' [Fazzari and Minsky, 1984: 107]. Such stabilization of actual and expected profits is crucial for ensuring the continuity of the economic system. It is utilized in particular to maintain the viability of debt structures, and therefore the level of private investment. In fact 'once rational bankers and business men learn from experience that actual profits do not fall when private investment declines, they will modify their preferred portfolios to take advantage of the stability of profits' [Minsky, 1992: 12]. This means in particular that, encouraged by increased confidence in future profits, banks are likely to raise their estimates of the maximum levels of indebtedness (in proportion to the value of the assets

6. In a few papers, Minsky examines other thwarting systems such as labor market institutions and market power. See e.g. Ferri and Minsky [1992] where the authors study these stabilizing mechanisms in some length.

7. See in particular Minsky [1986: Ch. 7 and 8].

8. If Y represents the national income, C the total consumption, W total wages, I the investment, Π the aggregate profits, G the government spending and T the taxes, we have: $Y = C + I + G$ and $Y = W + \Pi + T$. If, as Kalecki does, we suppose that $C = W$, we obtain: $\Pi = I + G - T$.

both they and potential borrowers hold) to which it is prudent to agree, and will tend to make more loans to businesses.

The importance of "Big Government" (i.e. a public sector that constitutes a significant share of aggregate demand) in economic dynamics is so fundamental for Minsky that he divides the performance of the U.S. economy into two periods: a "small government" era from the end of the American Civil War to the Depression, and a "big government" era dating from World War II (Minsky, 1986). He provides a detailed analysis of how the deficit of "Big Government" was crucial for maintaining profits during the 1974-75 recession [Minsky, 1986: ch. 2]. He points out that the annualized rate of contraction of the economy during the first two quarters of 1975 rivaled that of the worst rate of decline that occurred during the Great Depression. But big government's deficits prevented profits from declining and set the stage for recovery in the second part of the year.

Thus, the presence of a 'big government' whose fiscal policy is very sensitive to variations in overall profits improves the stability of the economy. Nonetheless, an isolated policy of this sort may prove insufficient in periods of economic turmoil. True public deficits partly offset the reduction in profit flows resulting from a fall in investments, and maintain current production prices and consumer goods prices. However, during an economic crisis, deficits cannot directly counteract the drop in another type of price, and one that is essential in Minsky's investment theory, the price of capital assets. This price is dependent upon the amount of money in circulation but also on more subjective variables such as liquidity preference, the debt level that is judged acceptable, or the profits economic agents expect.[9] It is necessary, as a supplementary step, to turn then toward a second type of institutional thwarting mechanism, the role of the Central bank as the lender of last resort.

The main purpose of this type of intervention is to offset debt-deflation phenomena or the different forms of financial instability that market economies experience.[10] For Minsky, these phenomena emphasize the need

9. Minsky [1975; 1986].

10. In the case of the U.S., to which Minsky gives precedence, he observes that the Fed's function as lender-of-last-resort has extended constantly to new institutions and new instruments. At the end of the 1960s the Fed intervened to sustain the municipal bonds market. In 1970 it acted in order to avoid the collapse of the commercial paper market. In the 1980s it stepped in during the foreign debt crisis, the Continental Illinois bankruptcy crisis, and the financial market crash. In each of these events the Fed

for an extended interpretation of the role of lender of last resort. Thus, he distinguishes three aspects of this type of intervention [Minsky, 1986]. First, when funds are lacking in the money market (a situation generally synonymous with substantial falls in the value of the claims agents exchange for liquidity), the Central bank must intervene by increasing the amount of money in circulation. Second, during the period of financial restructuring that follows a crisis, the Central bank must take care to favor recourse to long-term rather than short-term borrowing by acting on interest rates accordingly. Finally, the Central bank is responsible for guiding the development of the financial system, through both regulation and banking system surveillance, in order to restrain speculative banking (excessive reliance on liability management in particular).

Including the role of institutional mechanisms implies that Minsky's theory does not simply describe the cycle as an endogenous mechanical phenomenon, as a succession of the following types of phases: increased financial fragility → financial crisis → gradual return to more safe and sound finance. We saw that this is because Minsky considers that financial crises thwarted by institutional mechanisms fail to develop all their effects (debt-deflation, widespread bankruptcies, disappearance of agents with the most fragile financial structures, etc.). In the financially sophisticated economies that Minsky scrutinizes, the natural tendency to generate periods of great instability may be partly offset by thwarting systems.

3. "Active" banking and difficulty in stabilizing an unstable economy.

In this section we investigate another central idea in Minsky's approach: that the efficiency of the thwarting systems implemented by public authorities depends strongly on the more or less active behavior of commercial banks. Active behaviors are exemplified by the various practices banks use to modify their balance sheet structure, both the asset and the liabilities sides, and also their capacity to create or to favor the processes of financial innovation. The general idea Minsky develops is that if banks are passive, then they can be ignored in the theoretical reasoning: they do not influence the efficiency of the stabilization policies. On the

(believed, as it was, to be following a monetarist policy) provided liquidity and was compelled to validate to some extent many risky financial practices.

other hand, if banks are active, then the efficiency of these policies can be questioned.

Now, a key idea of Minsky's analysis is that banks are indeed active economic agents because (i) their behavior is guided essentially by the permanent quest for profit opportunities, and (ii) they are also entrepreneurial organizations striving to innovate in order to generate capital gains. The first feature illustrates the influence of Tobin's analysis, the second feature refers to the influence of Schumpeter's approach.

Minsky's view lessens to a great extent the distinction between banks, other financial institutions, and non-financial agents. Indeed, 'the line between commercial banks, whose liabilities include checking deposits, other depository thrift institutions, miscellaneous managers of money (like insurance companies, pension funds and various investment trusts), and investment bankers is more reflective of the legal environment and institutional history than of the economic function of these financial institutions' [Minsky, 1986: 223]. For similar reasons the distinction between financial institutions and non-financial agents seems not to be crucial for him: 'banks and bankers are not passive managers of money to lend or to invest; they are in business to maximize profits. They actively solicit borrowing customers, undertake financing commitments, build connections with business and other bankers, and seek funds' [ibid.: 229–30].

This aspect of Minsky's theory is reminiscent of the approach developed in 'Commercial Banks as Creators of Money' [Tobin, 1963], an article where Tobin contrasts the 'old view' on banking with the 'new view'. Like Minsky, Tobin and the supporters of the new view make no clear distinction between banks and other financial institutions, or between what Gurley and Shaw call the 'monetary system' – comprising the commercial banks and the Fed – and the 'other financial intermediaries' [Gurley and Shaw, 1955: 260–1]. All these financial agents are 'financial intermediaries' whose main and characteristic function is to 'satisfy simultaneously the portfolio preferences of...borrowers [and] lenders' [Tobin, 1963: 274].

Moreover, Minsky insists that banks are entrepreneurial firms whose innovations allow greater profits: new financial instruments, new financial procedures and new financial institutions in particular are created by innovative bankers who receive monopoly rents that disappear as innovations diffuse [Minsky, 1990; 1993]. This view is akin to

Schumpeter's analysis of banking. According to the Austrian author, in a capitalist environment, bankers perform an entrepreneurial function, which is in no way less important than that of business entrepreneurs for economic development: creation and destruction occur in the field of finance, as well as innovation - whether in the form of new products, processes or new organization, and whether it involves incremental or radical change. Moreover, new types of financing media may emerge and thereby trigger further process and product innovations.[11]

Like Schumpeter, Minsky considered that financial systems evolve not only in response to demands of business firms and individual investors but also as a result of the innovative activity of profit-seeking entrepreneurial financial firms.

The relationship between "active" banks' behaviors and the efficiency of stabilization policy was analyzed by Minsky in his first published article, 'Central Banking and Money Market Changes' [1957b]. This article highlights the entrepreneurial and innovative behavior of commercial banks, and the effects such behavior has on the efficiency of a monetary policy.

In this article, Minsky analyzes the case of the Central bank implementing a restrictive monetary policy to prevent an inflationary process during an economic expansion [Minsky, 1957b: 171–3]. This policy causes an increase in the interest rate owing to 'a vigorous demand for financing relative to the available supply' [ibid.: 163]. Two possibilities are considered by Minsky. The first consists of reasoning within a stable institutional environment, one where 'a tight money policy will be effective and the interest rate will rise to whatever extent is necessary in order to restrict the demand for financing to the essentially inelastic supply. This can be represented as a positively sloped curve between velocity and the interest rate' [ibid.: 172].

However, institutional stability is not Minsky's main focus. At the beginning of the 1950s changes began affecting the money market as the

11. Though rarely stressed by commentators, this feature of bankers was emphasized by Schumpeter. He noted that 'financial institutions and practices enter our circle of problems in three ways: they are "auxiliary and conditioning"; banking may be the object of entrepreneurial activity, that is to say, the introduction of new banking practices may constitute enterprise; and bankers (or other "financiers") may use the means at their command in order to embark upon commercial and industrial enterprise themselves (for example John Law).' [Schumpeter, 1947: 153] See also Festré and Nasica [2009].

markets for Federal funds and for repurchase agreements emerged and expanded. For Minsky these evolutions simply reflected the existence of a form of institutional instability governed by the profit-seeking and innovative behavior of commercial banks.

The process described in the 1957 article unfolds as follows. Rising interest rates act as a signal which private market operators interpret as new profit opportunities. Higher interest rates imply that greater opportunity costs affect the excess reserves held by commercial banks. Their incentive is therefore to lend these reserves to the Federal funds market. Also, Minsky observes [1957b: 164], the Federal funds rate is always lower than the discount rate b. This is a circumstance that banks short of reserves will exploit. Greater reliance of banks on the market for Federal funds allows a larger volume of demand deposits for a given amount of Central bank money. '[A] given volume of reserves now supports more deposits' [Minsky, 1957b: 171] because now the excess reserves of some banks are available to support the deposits of deficit banks which then are not forced to borrow from the Federal Reserve Bank or to sell securities.

Rises in interest rates also affect behaviors – and balance-sheet structures – of non-financial firms. The latter are guided away from non-interest-bearing demand deposits toward more profitable investments. New holdings can take the form of short-term liquid assets such as Treasury bills or repurchase agreements issued by government bond houses. [12] Government bond houses will be further induced to borrow from non-financial firms through the issue of repurchase agreements if the interest rates on these instruments fall below the discount rate charged by the Federal Reserve and the interest rates charged by commercial banks.

An important consequence of this potential shift of Treasury bills and of lending to government bond houses from commercial banks to nonfinancial firms is that bank resources are freed to finance other activities: for a given volume of deposits, the share of loans to firms in banks assets is likely to increase.

At the same time, this process can cause a decrease in the liquidity of the economy as illustrated by the following example.

12. Government bond houses are private financial institutions that invest their funds in government debt (Treasury bills, longer-term government debt). They finance their position partly by their own resources, and partly through borrowing from commercial banks, the Federal Reserve, and non-financial firms.

Consider a very simplified monetary system composed by a bank B, a non-financial firm F, and a government bond house GBH.

The government bond house holdings are composed of Treasury bills (TB) and longer-term government debt ($LTGD$). These assets are financed by their own capital (C), sales and repurchase agreements with firms (RA_F,) sales and repurchase agreements with the Federal Reserve System, at the discount rate, (RA_{Fed}), and finally loans from commercial banks (L_B). The holdings of the non-financial firm F are made up of demand deposits (DD), Treasury bills, and sale and repurchase agreements with government bond houses ($RA_{GBH} = RA_F$). The assets of the commercial bank B are made up of Treasury bills, loans to the non-financial firm (L_F), and loans to the government bond house ($L_{GBH} = L_B$).

Initially, balance-sheets take the following form:[13]

B	
TB	
L_F	
L_{GBH}	

F	
DD	
TB	
RA_{GBH}	

GBH	
TB	C
$LTGD$	RA_F
	RA_{Fed}
	L_B

Suppose a situation similar to the one prevailing in the US money market from 1954 to 1957. During this period the following two phenomena are observed [Minsky, 1957b: 163 and 167–8]: (a) The interest rate pattern relevant to the operations of GBH becomes $TB < RA_F < RA_{Fed} < LTGB < L_B$; (b) Short-term interest rates rise.

These changes appear as new profit opportunities for private economic agents which react by modifying their balance-sheets as follows:

B	
$TB - 50$	
$L_F + 100$	
$L_{GBH} - 50$	

F	
$DD - 150$	
$TB + 50$	
$RA_{GBH} + 100$	

GBH	
TB	C
$LTGD$	$RA_F + 100$
	$RA_{Fed} - 50$
	$L_B - 50$

The GBH reacts to this new interest pattern by increasing its borrowings from the non-financial firm, that is, by issuing more (+100) repurchase agreements. Simultaneously, the GBH decreases both its bank

13. Here we ignore the liability of banks and firms whose potential changes are not central to the current reasoning.

and Federal Reserve borrowings by 50.[14] This is facilitated especially because rises in short-term interest rates lead the firm to move away from non-interest-bearing demand deposits (which decrease by 50) and to invest its cash in Treasury bills (which increase by 50) and repurchase agreements issued by the *GBH* (which rise by 100). These changes to the firm's and the GBH balance sheets in turn affect the portfolios of the commercial banks and Treasury bills (−50) and loans to the GBH (−50) are replaced by loans to firms (+100).

The above example highlights an important outcome of the profit-seeking behavior of economic agents. Liability and asset management induced by changes in the interest rate pattern generate a greater risk of illiquidity in the economy since both financial (commercial banks) and non-financial (firms) agents now have less liquid assets in their portfolios.

The institutional changes in the money market, and the behaviors of private economic agents in this market, induce another central result: they increase the lending ability of commercial banks. Indeed, for a given quantity of reserves and money, the amount of loans to firms that can be supplied by commercial banks tends to increase. In other words, the process of institutional innovation tends to increase the velocity of the circulation of money. This results in rightward shifts in the interest rate–velocity curve. An upward-stepped curve obtains, similar to the curve depicted in the figure 1.

Fig. 1. Active commercial banks and the efficiency of monetary policy

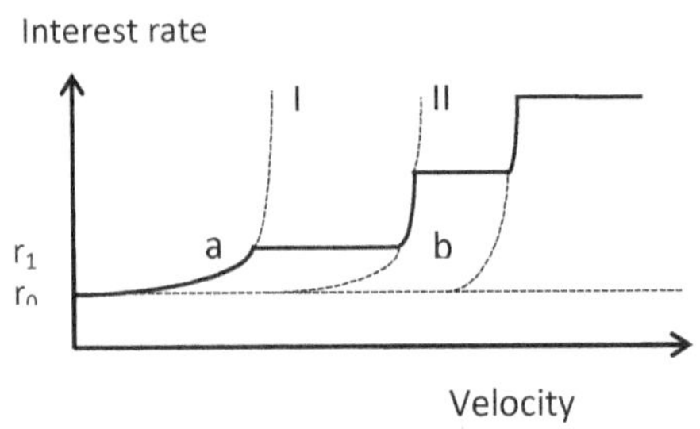

14. As Minsky explains, non-financial firms became the main source of finance for government bond houses in mid 1956.

The increasing portions of the curve describe the effect of a restrictive monetary policy on the interest rate when the institutional environment remains stable. However, these increases are not permanent; an increase in the interest rate (for instance, from r_0 to r_1) creates profit opportunities, money market innovations and thus institutional instability, as described by the curve shift from I to II. A plateau, *a–b*, is reached, which characterizes the period during which institutional innovation is spreading.

During this plateau period, the impact on the interest rate of a restrictive monetary policy is completely counteracted, while the velocity of circulation and the lending ability of commercial banks appear to be infinitely elastic. As stressed by Minsky, in such a context the effectiveness of monetary policy based on the surveillance of monetary aggregates weakens, with the result that, in order to fight inflation, the Central bank has no choice but to act directly on the liquidity of commercial banks. The Central bank will try to diminish their reserves to an extent great enough to compensate for the increase in velocity. This reaction to the profit-seeking and innovative behavior of commercial banks then has the effect of pushing interest rates up even more, thus recreating the conditions for the whole process to recur. Hence, the succession over time of the increasing and horizontal portions of the curves represented in the figure.

To sum up, Minsky's first published article is very instructive as to his conception of the ability of a monetary policy to be an efficient thwarting system.

The efficiency of a restrictive monetary policy aimed at fighting inflation during a period of boom is severely reduced by the behavior of commercial banks because they are not only eager (because of profit opportunities), they are also able (thanks to asset management and innovation) to respond to firms' larger credit demands.

This is not to say that such a policy is a totally inefficient tool to curb inflation. The upper turning point in Minsky's cycle is explained partly by the increases in interest rates induced by a restrictive monetary policy: 'in terms of the financing of investment . . . an infinitely elastic supply of finance will exist if and only if the banking system is *willing* and *able*, to finance any amount of investment . . . at unchanging interest rates. For a variety of reasons –the limited equity base of banks, internal and foreign drains of bank reserves and, in modern times, Central bank (Federal Reserve) actions to restrain the money supply – the supply of finance from banks eventually becomes less than infinitely elastic' [Minsky, 1986: 195 – emphasis in original]. This implies that a restrictive monetary policy contributes to the existence of a ceiling to aggregate activity. However, the main message in Minsky's approach is that this policy is relatively inefficient during a boom phase if implemented in isolation. As underlined above, to be a really efficient thwarting system, such a policy must be complemented by other types of Central bank actions bank (such as prudential regulation) and by an active anti-cyclical fiscal policy with a government budget that goes quickly into surplus when investment, debt, and inflation are high.

Another consequence is that a restrictive policy may also be destabilizing since, as we have seen, it generates a greater risk of illiquidity in the economy when liquidity-decreasing money-market innovations occur. In other words, the innovative process described earlier is likely to lead to a situation where the economy becomes less liquid although the quantity of credit supplied to firms is rising. Minsky [1957b: 173] describes it thus: 'the reverse side of the coin to the increase in velocity is that every institutional innovation which results in both new ways to finance business and new substitutes for cash assets decreases the liquidity of the economy'.

4. Concluding comments

For more than two centuries, there have been two opposing conceptions of the evolution of economic activity. In his memorial to Wesley Mitchell, Schumpeter [1951: 252] distinguishes between those economists who consider that 'the economic process is essentially non-oscillatory and that the explanation of cyclical as well as other fluctuations must be sought in particular circumstances (monetary or other) which disturb that even flow' and those who believe that the 'economic process itself is essentially wave-like – that cycles are the form of capitalist evolution.'

The analysis developed by Minsky in his earliest works, while not questioning this distinction, shows that it must nevertheless be reconsidered if institutions are to be embodied explicitly within business cycle analysis. More precisely, his approach highlights that taking into account the interactions between public (government and Central bank) and private institutions (commercial banks) opens space for a third family of business cycle theories. Fitting somewhere in between purely exogenous conceptions and endogenous explanations of business cycles, it depicts the economic process as not "essentially non-oscillatory" just as it is not "essentially wave-like" to use Schumpeter's terms. This approach encompasses both steady growth and regular business cycles as possible transient features of an economic time series but it also does not exclude the emergence of the potentially unstable dynamics resulting from the interactions between private and public institutions.

Thus, Minsky's conception of business cycles in the 1950s revives the treatment of the relations that arise between public institutions and economic fluctuations. In traditional macroeconomic models, it is often assumed that economic policies are totally exogenous and public institutions can only disturb the operations of markets that otherwise clear through the interplay between supply and demand. In contrast, Minsky's approach shows that the public authorities react in an endogenous fashion to the behavior of private agents. Thus, they participate in creating a genuinely institutional dynamics that interwines with the real and the financial dynamics of the economy and modifies the unconstrained outcomes that would occur in the absence of institutional thwarting systems.

Finally, scrutiny of Minsky's earliest works provides a better understanding of his vision of an efficient stabilization policy as necessarily based upon an active anti-cyclical fiscal policy. This is considered necessary (in the tradition of Kalecki) to avoid the economy sinking into a never-ending depression because budget deficits increase global profits and validate the financial structure of private economic agents. To be efficient, this stabilization policy has to be associated with a monetary policy that remains relatively accommodative to whatever economic situation in order to maintain interest rates at a low level, and to stabilize asset prices. The efficiency of other kinds of monetary policies aimed at regulating economic activity, is very weak in a context where banks adopt active and innovative behaviors which annihilate a great part of the Central bank's actions.

The conclusions reached by Minsky in the 1950s appear relevant today; only recall the inability of the Fed to prevent financial instability problems during the 2000-2007 pre-crisis period, because of the active behaviors of U.S. banks. Although the Fed succeeded in maintaining inflation stability, it failed to prevent the rise of financial fragility and instability induced by innovative and riskier banking behaviors.[15]

15. Innovations took different forms: securitization, CDO, CDS, prime brokerage operations while banks' leverage strongly increased during this period.

The same reasoning can be applied to the current post-crisis situation in Europe where commercial banks have huge excess reserves at their disposal thanks to the very low interest rate three-year loans granted by the European Central Bank (ECB) in December 2011. However these reserves are not being activated by the banks: crisis-hit euro zone banks are parking record amounts of cash in the ECB for overnight storage, despite low interest rates. In normal times, banks shy away from depositing cash at the ECB, preferring to lend any overnight surplus to other banks and earn a higher rate of return. But the crisis has spawned a lack of trust among the banks with the result that they are opting to store their money with the ultra-safe ECB rather than take the riskier route of lending it to counterparts. So, commercial banks which are adopting behaviors founded on a greater liquidity during the current post-crisis period are tending to privilege more liquid and less risky assets. In doing so, they are contributing to reducing the quantities of money and credit in circulation and reducing the efficiency of the monetary policy, just as Minsky described more than 50 years ago.

References

Arena R. and Raybaut A. [2001]. On the foundations of Minsky's business cycles theory: an interpretation. In R. Bellofiore, and P. Ferri P. (ed.) *The Legacy of P.H. Minsky*, volume 2. Cheltenham, UK: Edward Elgar: 113–32. not in text

Asada T. [2001]. Nonlinear dynamics of debt and capital: a Post-Keynesian analysis. In Y. Aruka, (ed.) *Evolutionary Controversies in Economics*. Tokyo: Springer Verlag: 73–87.

Charles S. [2008]. Corporate debt, variable retention rate and the appearance of financial fragility. *Cambridge Journal of Economics* 32(5): 781–95.

Day R.H. [1982]. Irregular growth cycles. *American Economic Review* 72: 406–14.

— and Shafer W. [1986]. Keynesian chaos. *Journal of Macroeconomics* 7(2): 277–95.

Delli Gatti D. and Gallegati M. [2000]. Financial instability revisited: aggregated fluctuations due to changing financial conditions of heterogeneous firms. In R. Bellofiore, and P. Ferri (eds.) *The Legacy of H.P. Minsky*, volume 2. Cheltenham, UK: Edward Elgar: 185-200.

— and Gardini L. [1993a]. Complex dynamics in a simple macroeconomic model, with financing constraints. In G. Dymski and R. Pollin (eds.) *New Perspectives in Monetary Macroeconomics, Explorations in the Tradition of Hyman Minsky*. Ann Arbor: The University of Michigan Press, 51–76. not in text

— and Gardini L. [1993b]. Investment confidence, corporate debt and income fluctuations. *Journal of Economic Behavior and Organization* 22: 161–87. not in text

Fazzari S. and Minsky H.P. [1984]. Domestic monetary policy: if not monetarism, what? *Journal of Economic Issues* 18: 101–16.

Ferri P. and Minsky H.P. [1989]. The breakdown of the IS-LM synthesis: implications for Post-Keynesian economic theory. *Review of Political Economy* July:123–41.

— [1992]. Market processes and thwarting systems. *Structural Change and Economic Dynamics* 3(1): 79–91.

Festré A. and Nasica E. [2009]. Schumpeter on money, banking and finance: an institutionalist perspective. *European Journal of the History of Economic Thought* 16(2): 325–56.

Franke, R. and Semmler, W. [1992]. Expectation dynamics, financing of investment, and business cycles. In D. Papadimitriou (ed.) *Profits, Deficits and Instability*. London: Macmillan: 330-48.

Goodwin, R. [1951]. The non-linear acceleration and the persistence of business cycles. *Econometrica* 19(1):1–17.

Gurley J. and Shaw E. [1955]. Financial aspects of economic development. *American Economic Review* 45(4): 515–38.

Hicks J.R [1950]. *A Contribution to the Theory of the Trade Cycle*. Oxford: Clarendon Press.

Isaac A.G. and Kim, Y.K. [2012]. Consumer and corporate debt: a neo-Kaleckian synthesis. *Metroeconomica*, doi: 10.1111/meca.12005.

Kalecki M. [1971]. *Selected Essays on the Dynamics of the Capitalist Economy, 1933-1970*. Cambridge: Cambridge University Press.

Keynes J.M. [1936]. *The General Theory of Employment, Interest and Money*, reprinted in *The Collected Writings of John Maynard Keynes*, Vol. VII. London: Macmillan, 1973.

— [1937]. The general theory of employment. *Quarterly Journal of Economics*, 51(2): 209–23; reprinted in *The General Theory and After*, Part 2: *Defence and Development*, *The Collected Writings of John Maynard Keynes*, Vol. XII. London: Macmillan, 1973: 109–23.

Keen S. [1995]. Finance and economic breakdown: modeling Minsky's financial instability hypothesis. *Journal of Post Keynesian Economics* 17(4): 607–35.

Lima G.T. and Meirelles A.J.A. [2006]. Debt, financial fragility and economic growth: a post Keynesian macromodel. *Journal of Post-Keynesian Economics* 29(1): 93–115.

Minsky H.P. [1957a]. Monetary systems and accelerator models. *American Economic Review* 47(6): 860–83.

— [1957b]. Central banking and money market changes. *Quarterly Journal of Economics* 71(2): 171–87.

— [1959]. A linear model of cyclical growth. *Review of Economics and Statistics* 41(2): 133–45.

— [1975]. *John Maynard Keynes*. New York: Columbia University Press.

— [1982]. *Can "It" Happen Again?* Armonk, New-York: M.E. Sharpe.

— [1986]. *Stabilizing an Unstable Economy*. New Haven, CT: Yale University Press.

— [1990]. Schumpeter: finance and evolution. In A. Heertje and M. Perlman (eds) *Evolving Technology and Market Structures: Studies in Schumpeterian Economics*. Ann Arbor: The University of Michigan Press: 51–74.

— [1992]. Profits, deficits and economic instability: a policy discussion. In D. Papadimitriou (ed.) *Profits, Deficits and Instability*. London: MacMillan: 11–22.

— [1993]. Schumpeter and finance. In in S. Biasco, A. Roncaglia and M. Salvati (eds) *Markets and Institutions in Economic Development : Essays in honour of Paolo Sylos Labini*. New York: St Martin's Press: 103–15.

Nasica E. and Raybaut A. [2005]. Profits, confidence and public deficits: modeling Minsky's institutional dynamics. *Journal of Post Keynesian Economics* 28(1): 136–54.

Samuelson P.A. [1939]. Interactions between the multiplier analysis and the principle of acceleration. *The Review of Economics and Statistics* 21: 75–8.

Sasaki H., Fujita S. [2012]. The importance of the retention ratio in a Kaleckian model with debt accumulation. *Metroeconomica* 63 (3): 417–28.

Schumpeter J.A. [1947]. The creative response in economic history, *Journal of Economic History* 7(2): 149-159. Reprinted in R.V. Clemence (ed) *Essays on Entrepreneurs, Innovations, Business Cycles and the Evolution of Capitalism*. New Brunswick and Oxford: Transaction Publishers, 1989, 221–31. Originally published in 1951 by Addison-Wesley.

— [1951]. *Ten Great Economists: From Marx to Keynes*. New York: Galaxy Press.

Tobin J. [1963]. Commercial banks as creators of 'money'. In Dean Carson (ed.) *Banking and Monetary Studies*. for the Comptroller of the Currency, U.S. Treasury, Richard D. Irwin, 1963: 408–19; reprinted in *Essays in Economics, Volume 1: Macroeconomics*. Cambridge: The MIT Press, 1987.

Repenser les biens communs

Sous la direction de

B□atrice Parance et Jacques de Saint Victor

L'eau, l'air, les ressources naturelles et les fonds marins, certains médicaments, le spectre hertzien, le numérique… peuvent être analysés comme des « biens communs ». Nécessaires à tous, il convient d'en offrir l'usage à chacun. Mais par quels outils ?

Le droit moderne occidental a fait de la propriété, publique ou privée, la pierre angulaire de tous les rapports entre les personnes et les choses. Après la chute du Mur, la privatisation des biens a même fini pour devenir le dogme, avec parfois des dérives dramatiques.

Comment régler les droits d'accès et la protection de certains biens que l'on considère comme essentiels pour la survie de l'espèce ? Le droit doit, de toute urgence, se réinventer.

ISBN : 978-2-271-08006-6

Format: 15 x 23

314 pages

25 €

CNRS EDITIONS

15, rue Malebranche 75005 Paris

Tél : 01 53 10 27 00 - Fax : 01 53 10 27 27

Mail : cnrseditions@cnrseditions.fr—www.cnrseditions.fr

14

REVUE FRANÇAISE DE SOCIO-ÉCONOMIE

SECOND SEMESTRE 2014

Rfse

Recruter : les enjeux de la sélection

Le recrutement constitue un objet frontière qui se prête à des regards disciplinaires croisés. Pourtant, il reste relativement peu exploré. Ainsi, l'attention des économistes a davantage été retenue par les mécanismes de marché ou par les décisions de volumes d'embauches des entreprises que par l'instant où se réalisent l'achat et la vente de la « marchandise-travail ». Les sociologues, de leur côté, s'interrogent sur l'autonomie de cette scène qui n'est pas réductible à des enjeux marchands et sélectionne autant qu'elle socialise. De fait, le moment de cette transaction ne doit pas faire oublier que le travail est inséparable de la personne du travailleur, que les échangistes sont socialement situés et que leur rencontre s'inscrit dans une histoire et une temporalité plus dilatées qu'il n'y paraît. Entre transaction économique et « fait social total », le recrutement met en branle un grand nombre d'institutions, qui structurent, organisent et légitiment des opérations de sélection qui se déroulent à de multiples niveaux, au risque de se contredire. Les contributions retenues dans ce numéro permettent précisément d'éclairer tant la sélectivité des pratiques en vigueur que les risques de discrimination et d'exclusion dont elles sont porteuses, sans oublier les formes de valorisation qui sont à l'œuvre au cours des opérations plurielles dont se composent les processus de recrutement.

Éditorial. De quoi les pénuries de main-d'oeuvre sont-elles le nom ?
Marc Zune

Prix des doctoriales GDR « Économie et Sociologie » et RFSE

Le recrutement des figurants de l'audiovisuel. L'ANPE Spectacle, un intermédiaire public sur le marché des images
Luc Sigalo Santos

DOSSIER

Introduction au dossier Recruter : les enjeux de la sélection
Guillemette de Larquier, Sylvie Monchatre

Le recrutement du médecin en Unité de Soins Palliatifs. Sélections, désignation et habilitations
Florent Schepens

L'alternance au risque de la sur-sélectivité
François Sarfati

Quand les entreprises font leur marché : canaux et sélection sur les marchés du travail
Guillemette de Larquier, Géraldine Rieucau

La méthode de recrutement par simulation de Pôle Emploi : un « produit » à placer ?
Jean-Marie Pillon

La « professionnalisation du recrutement » au prisme des dispositifs de sélection
Yannick Fondeur

Entretien avec François Eymard-Duvernay et Emmanuelle Marchal

HORS DOSSIER

Comment les professionnels appréhendent-ils leur marché ? L'exemple de l'industrie des articles de sport
Samuel Julhe, Marina Honta

Le rôle de la confiance dans les relations d'échange : le cas du marché de poisson de Kribi
François Tiotsop, Patrice Guillotreau, Juliette Rouchier

Un regard sur la qualité de l'emploi après le chômage
Laurence Lizé, Nicolas Prokovas

NOTES CRITIQUES

COMPTES RENDUS D'OUVRAGES

COMPTES RENDUS DE THÈSES SOUTENUES

ISBN 978-2-7071-8332-3 25 €

L'Harmattan
Édition -Diffusion
5-7, rue de l'École Polytechnique 75005 Paris

Tél. 01 40 46 79 20 (comptoir et renseignement libraires)
Tél. 01 40 46 79 14 (manuscrits et fabrication)
Tél. 01 40 46 79 22 (service de presse)
Fax 01 43 25 82 03 (commercial)
Fax 01 43 29 86 20 (manuscrits et fabrication)

BULLETIN DE REABONNEMENT POUR LA REVUE « **CAHIERS D'ECONOMIE POLITIQUE** » (n°s 66 à 67)

NOM : ....

ADRESSE : ....
....

Tarif pour envois en France : 44 €

Je joins un chèque de .... € à l'ordre de l'Harmattan. Pour l'étranger, merci de régler en euros sur banque domiciliée en France, par virement sur notre CCP 23 625 44 N Paris ou par carte bancaire VISA n°................................ date d'expiration........................

BULLETIN DE REABONNEMENT POUR LA REVUE « **CAHIERS D'ECONOMIE POLITIQUE** » (n°s 64 à 65)

NOM : ....

ADRESSE : ....
....

Tarif pour envoi à l'étranger : 47 €

Je joins un chèque de .... € à l'ordre de l'Harmattan. Pour l'étranger, merci de régler en euros sur banque domiciliée en France, par virement sur notre CCP 23 625 44 N Paris ou par carte bancaire VISA n°................................ date d'expiration........................

Relevé d'identité postale 20041 00001 2362544 N 020 11 PARIS / RC 75 B 3599
SIREN 311 023 121 / SIRET 00024 - APE 221 A TVA FR 88 311 023 121

Cahiers d'économie politique

Bon de commande

à retourner à

Éditions L'Harmattan, 5-7 rue de l'École Polytechnique, 75005 Paris

Tél: 01.43.54.79.10, **Télécopie**: 01.43.25.82.03

Page Web (commande en ligne): http://www.editions-harmattan.fr

	Prix en euros	Nb	Montant en euros
N°26	21,34		- - - - -
Nos27-28 Le libéralisme à l'épreuve : de l'empire aux nations		- -	- - - - -
(Adam Smith et l'économie coloniale)	24,39	- -	- - - - -
N°29	13,72	- -	- - - - -
Nos30-31: Keynes, économie et philosophie	27,44	- -	- - - - -
N°32	16,77	- -	- - - - -
N°33	21,34	- -	- - - - -
N°34 Qu'a-t-on appris sur la relation salaire-emploi depuis Keynes ?	22,87	- -	- - - - -
N°35	13,72	- -	- - - - -
N°36	16,77	- -	- - - - -
N°37 Qu'a-t-on appris sur la concurrence imparfaite depuis Cournot ?	28,96	- -	- - - - -
N°38	18,29	- -	- - - - -
N°39 J.R. Hicks, Une œuvre multi-dimensionnelle	21,35	- -	- - - - -
N°40-41 Lectures de J.R. Commons	25,90	- -	- - - - -
N°42	18,00	- -	- - - - -
N°43	17,50	- -	- - - - -
N°44 Qu'a-t-on appris sur les institutions ?	20,50	- -	- - - - -
N°45 Qu'a-t-on appris sur le prêteur en dernier ressort ?	25,00	- -	- - - - -
N°46	17,50	- -	- - - - -
N° 47 Les économistes et la démocratie. Qu'a-t-on appris depuis Schumpeter		- -	- - - - -
?..	22,00	- -	- - - - -
N°48	21,00	- -	- - - - -
N°49 L'agent économique : théorie et histoire	21,00	- -	- - - - -
N°50..	22,00	- -	- - - - -
N°51 Les économistes autrichiens 1870-1940	27,50	- -	- - - - -
N°52	18,50	- -	- - - - -
N°53 Rousseau : philosophie et économie..................................	17,50	- -	
N°54	20,00		- - - - -
N°55 David Ricardo 199 ans après	16,50	- -	- - - - -
N°56	22,00	- -	- - - - -
N°57 Éditer des économistes	28,50	- -	- - - - -
N°58	21,00	- -	- - - - -
N°59 Pauvreté et misère dans l'histoire de la pensée économique.........	25,00	- -	- - - - -
N°60	22, 50	- -	- - - - -
N°61 Qu'a-t-on appris sur la répartition du revenu en macroéconomie		- -	- - - - -
depuis les années de haute théorie ?..................................	24,50	- -	- - - - -
N°62	24,40	- -	- - - - -
N°63 De la concurrence parfaite : définitions, usages et			- - - - -
fondements..	25,00	- -	
N°64	32,00		- - - - -
N°65 Philosophie économique..................................	26,00	- -	- - - - -
N°66	30,00	- -	- - - - -
CES PRIX DOIVENT ETRE MAJORES DE 4 € POUR FRAIS DE PORT			....
		TOT.	

Économie et Entreprise aux éditions L'Harmattan

Dernières parutions

BIORAFFINERIE 2030
Une question d'avenir
Schieb Pierre-Alain, Lescieux-Katir Honorine, Thénot Maryline, Clément-Larosière Barbara
Cette étude de la bioraffinerie intégrée de Bazancourt-Pomacle, en Champagne près de Reims, met en exergue le potentiel de la bioéconomie industrielle à réaliser une substitution de ressources fossiles (charbon, pétrole, gaz naturels) par des ressources tirées de la biomasse (agro-ressources principalement) dans des conditions plus durables tout en étant performantes sur le plan économique et social. Un enjeu majeur du XXIe siècle.
(27.00 euros, 256 p.)
ISBN : 978-2-343-04458-3, ISBN EBOOK : 978-2-336-35816-1

EXPLOITATION (L') DU GAZ DE SCHISTE EN FRANCE
Entre enjeux et opportunités
Thévenet Florentin
Le gaz naturel devrait jouer un rôle croissant dans la balance énergétique globale des années à venir, en particulier grâce à l'exploitation du gaz de schiste. Que cache cette nouvelle énergie ? Au-delà des aspects purement financiers ou environnementaux, l'exploitation du gaz de schiste est-elle une fin en soi ou peut-elle être utilisée comme pilier d'une transition énergétique qui se fait attendre ?
(Coll. Géoéconomie et Géofinance, 21.00 euros, 204 p.)
ISBN : 978-2-343-04399-9, ISBN EBOOK : 978-2-336-35934-2

SCIERIE (LA) FRANÇAISE ET LA PRODUCTIVITÉ
Chalayer Maurice
Préface de Christian Senegas ; postface d'Yves Poss
Après un état des lieux du secteur, l'Observatoire du métier de la scierie trace trois scénarios de développement en termes de productivité et d'augmentation de volume de sciages. Une étude des tendances centrées sur la construction et l'emballage permet de dessiner des perspectives d'adaptation des scieries à l'horizon 2020.
(17.00 euros, 170 p.)
ISBN : 978-2-343-04316-6, ISBN EBOOK : 978-2-336-35726-3

INNOVATION (L'), ÉLAN DU XXIe SIÈCLE
Innover dans l'économie de la connaissance et des services
Mathe Hervé, Pavie Xavier
La réflexion et l'action de l'Institute for Strategic Innovation and Services, créé en 2004, s'articulent autour de la promotion et l'émergence de l'innovation dans l'économie de la connaissance et des services du XXIe siècle. Cet ouvrage reprend les idées développées ces dernières années qui s'articulent autour de trois grandes parties : «Stimuler l'innovation», «Innover dans les services : défis et perspectives» et «La responsabilité au cœur de l'innovation».
(45.00 euros, 402 p.)
ISBN : 978-2-343-02923-8, ISBN EBOOK : 978-2-336-35875-8

GUERRE (LA) DES BREVETS
D'Edison aux frères Wright
Une comparaison franco-américaine
Mangolte Pierre-André
Avant 1914, les industries françaises du cinéma et de l'aviation dominent le monde. La cause de cette situation ? La guerre des *patents* déclenchée aux États-Unis par Edison et les frères Wright. Le patent américain, à la différence du brevet d'invention français, donne la possibilité de produire des brevets larges, dans le but de contrôler tout ou partie d'une industrie. Face à l'enjeu, les propriétaires des titres finiront par former différents pools de brevets pour signer enfin la «paix des patents».
(Coll. Chemins de la Mémoire, série Histoire économique, 25.00 euros, 242 p.)
ISBN : 978-2-343-03734-9, ISBN EBOOK : 978-2-336-35951-9

TAILLE (LA) CRITIQUE DES BANQUES FRANÇAISES
Santenac René - Préface d'Emmanuel Okamba
On oublie trop souvent que les banques sont des entreprises et que, de ce fait, elles obéissent aux logiques de rentabilité et de performance. Les banques françaises ont développé des stratégies de concentration, ce qui a eu des effets sur leur taille. Dans quelle mesure la taille peut-elle influencer les banques dans leur développement ? Quel modèle élaborer pour optimiser la taille critique ?
(Coll. Entreprises et Management, 25.50 euros, 246 p.)
ISBN : 978-2-343-03746-2, ISBN EBOOK : 978-2-336-35796-6

REGARDS CROISÉS SUR LE CODESIGN
L'expérience du codesign dans trois écoles d'ingénieurs de Lille
Sous la direction de Roche Claude
Le codesign est une pratique de conception collaborative apparue récemment dans l'univers de l'innovation. Il promeut une approche transdisciplinaire de la conception, permettant notamment de confronter les expertises pointues à la vision des simples usagers. Cet ouvrage répond à plusieurs interrogations : comment concevons-nous le codesign et son animation, comment les étudiants ont-ils vécu cette expérience, quels en sont les effets sur la formation et au-delà leur impact prévisible en entreprise ?
(31.00 euros, 308 p.)
ISBN : 978-2-343-03761-5, ISBN EBOOK : 978-2-336-35142-1

POUR UNE POLITIQUE DU RISQUE
Comprendre et agir
Sous la direction de Bernard Guillon
Les contributions ici réunies portent attention à de nouveaux secteurs comme à des initiatives proactives dans l'univers particulier du risque. Que l'on ait à faire à des entreprises privées, à des groupes liant les sociétés aux structures publiques ou encore à des collectivités territoriales, ces travaux montrent la nécessité d'adopter une vision managériale des problèmes ouvrant la voie à de réelles opportunités.
(Coll. Recherches en Gestion, 37.00 euros, 360 p.)
ISBN : 978-2-343-03780-6, ISBN EBOOK : 978-2-336-35267-1

GÉOSTRATÉGIE DES ENTREPRISES
Propositions pour la zone OHADA
Garrier Claude
Préface Mamadou Koulibaly
L'auteur montre aux entrepreneurs africains que l'étatisme français est préjudiciable à la croissance de leur activité. Les propositions pour la zone OHADA sont aussi nécessaires pour les PME d'Europe souvent plus grosses que leurs cousines africaines et d'autant plus en mesure de «monter à l'assaut» commercial de la planète. L'ouvrage expose les modes de raisonnement du géo-stratège et présente divers outils juridiques.
(Coll. Le droit en marche, 38.00 euros, 378 p.)
ISBN : 978-2-343-03376-1, ISBN EBOOK : 978-2-336-35230-5

DIRIGEANT (LE) DE SOCIÉTÉS COMMERCIALES (Tome 1)
Le dirigeant sociétal officiel
Ayangma Ayangma Joseph - Préface de Jean Gatsi
Le véritable dirigeant n'est pas nécessairement celui qui trône au sommet de la pyramide sociétale. Le dirigeant connu, dont il est question dans ce premier tome, est simplement un manager officiellement consacré et, par voie de corollaire, hissé au sommet de la pyramide sociétale. Il est légalement et solennellement le gestionnaire sociétal et engage éventuellement, en cette qualité, sa responsabilité.
(Coll. Harmattan Cameroun, 33.00 euros, 328 p.)
ISBN : 978-2-343-02509-4, ISBN EBOOK : 978-2-336-35205-3

DIRIGEANT (LE) DE SOCIÉTÉS COMMERCIALES (Tome 2)
Le dirigeant sociétal effectif
Ayangma Ayangma Joseph
Préface de Jean Gatsi
Le véritable dirigeant de la société commerciale, c'est-à-dire celui qui détient le pouvoir et l'exerce directement ou indirectement dans la société commerciale, serait le dirigeant le dirigeant effectif ou «en veilleuse». Il décide et fait prévaloir sa rationalité au dirigeant officiel, qui se charge de l'appliquer. Celui-ci devient une sorte d'agent d'exécution, à défaut d'être spectateur de l'exercice du pouvoir managerial. Pourtant, le dirigeant en veilleuse n'a pas toujours recours à un pouvoir de fait pour s'imposer dans la gestion.
(Coll. Harmattan Cameroun, 37.50 euros, 372 p.)
ISBN : 978-2-336-30128-0, ISBN EBOOK : 978-2-336-35206-0

COMMENT (RE)FAIRE DE LA FRANCE UN PAYS ENTREPRENANT ?
Daniel Laurent, Lirzin Franck - Préface de Claude Bébéar ;
avec la collaboration de Hubert Lévy-Lambert
Comment relancer l'économie française et en exploiter le formidable potentiel ? Le pays a déjà été confronté à des situations semblables à la fin du XIXe siècle ou après 1945, et chaque fois il a su se réinventer. Après Friedman et Keynes, voici venu le temps de Schumpeter et de la «destruction-créatrice». Loin du déclinisme actuel, ce livre montre au travers d'exemples précis que les initiatives se multiplient pour créer un nouveau «modèle français», original et performant.
(19.00 euros, 184 p.)
ISBN : 978-2-343-00992-6, ISBN EBOOK : 978-2-296-53749-1

FILIÈRE (LA) PORCINE EN FRANCE
Le porc français a-t-il un avenir ?
Marzio Antoine
Consommerons-nous encore du porc français dans dix ans ? Et de quelle qualité ? Après une visite détaillée de la filière, ce livre analyse la question environnementale, du bien-être animal, des surconsommations vétérinaires, de l'hyperconcentration des élevages en Bretagne, et propose des solutions axées sur le redéploiement géographique, la diversification des races de porcs et des techniques d'élevage et la montée en gamme.
(23.00 euros, 232 p.)
ISBN : 978-2-343-00634-5, ISBN EBOOK : 978-2-296-53791-0

ÉCONOMIE (L') SOCIALE ET SOLIDAIRE ET LE TRAVAIL
Sous la direction de Patrice Braconnier et Gilles Caire
Dans un contexte où l'accès à l'emploi se fait toujours plus difficile et où les conditions de travail se durcissent, l'économie sociale et solidaire est-elle en mesure de proposer des façons de «travailler autrement» ? Existe-t-il une spécificité de l'emploi et de l'organisation du travail dans le champ de l'ESS ? Entre travail et bénévolat, entre salariat et entrepreneuriat, entre employeurs et employés, les frontières au sein de l'ESS sont floues. Mais peut-elle encore proposer de nouvelles utopies en matière de travail ?
(Coll. L'esprit économique, série L'économie formelle, 26.00 euros, 252 p.)
ISBN : 978-2-343-00563-8, ISBN EBOOK : 978-2-296-53764-4

ART (L') DE LA CRISE
Prévenir, contenir et sortir d'une situation sensible
Fusalba Thierry
L'objectif de cet ouvrage est de proposer aux organisations prises dans le maelström des événements une méthode fiable et performante qui leur permette d'avoir des points de repères solides afin d'élaborer une stratégie de sortie de crise efficace. L'auteur propose une réflexion sur la stratégie, sur l'organisation et l'entraînement des cellules de crises, sur l'exploitation des enseignements ainsi que sur le management et la communication de crise.
(34.00 euros, 332 p.)
ISBN : 978-2-343-00042-8, ISBN EBOOK : 978-2-296-53717-0

CONTRÔLE (LE) DES CONCENTRATIONS TRANSNATIONALES
Burnier Da Silveira Paulo
Préface de Bruno Lasserre ; avant-propos de Vinicius Carvalho
Les concentrations transnationales augmentent et les systèmes de contrôle des concentrations se multiplient. Alors que les enjeux économiques revêtent désormais une dimension internationale, les mécanismes juridiques de régulation demeurent cantonnés à une échelle nationale ou régionale. Le risque : être confronté à des décisions contradictoires ou incohérentes rendues par différentes autorités de la concurrence... Des mécanismes de régulation s'imposent, ainsi que l'adoption par l'OMC de règles contraignantes.
(39.00 euros, 406 p.)
ISBN : 978-2-336-29198-7, ISBN EBOOK : 978-2-296-53776-7

DES HOMMES ET DES RISQUES
Le rôle des assurances dans la construction des sociétés humaines
Nabeth Marc
Préface de Jean-Hervé Lorenzi - Postface de François-Xavier Albouy
Il est difficile d'imaginer un monde sans assurance ni protection sociale de nos jours. Pourtant, pour plus de 80% de la population des pays en développement, l'absence d'assurance est une réalité tangible. Les témoignages que ces personnes nous livrent sur leur perception des risques et leur créativité pour y faire face démentent de nombreux préjugés religieux, sociaux et culturels. L'enjeu est stratégique : il révèle le rôle essentiel de l'assurance dans la construction des sociétés humaines.
(Coll. Affaires stratégiques, 20.00 euros, 194 p.)
ISBN : 978-2-343-00120-3, ISBN EBOOK : 978-2-296-53744-6

INTELLIGENCE STRATÉGIQUE ET ÉNERGIE : UN TANDEM INDISSOCIABLE AU SERVICE D'UNE NOUVELLE GÉOPOLITIQUE
Du Castel Viviane
Voici un éclairage sur les enjeux énergétiques de demain, à travers la grille de lecture que propose l'intelligence économique et stratégique. Celle-ci permet, grâce à ses capacités d'analyse et d'investigation, de se projeter dans l'avenir, d'anticiper les évolutions et de se positionner en leader sur le marché international de l'énergie.
(Coll. Intelligence stratégique et géostratégie, 28.00 euros, 276 p.)
ISBN : 978-2-336-00726-7, ISBN EBOOK : 978-2-296-53876-4

DES MARCHÉS SANS FOI NI LOI
Bensebaa Faouzi, Boudier Fabienne
Tout est vendable, tout est échangeable, tel est le credo des « drôles de marchés ». Parmi eux, les « marchés sans foi ni loi ». Jetant aux orties le sacré, contournant la règle ou profitant de ses imperfections, ils sont peu visibles du grand public. Pourtant, les pratiques que l'on y découvre sont inédites et permettent souvent à des acteurs situés à la marge du système de se rencontrer. Ces « marchés sans foi ni loi » peuvent tout aussi bien être facteurs de désordre et de transgression que sources de créativité.
(Coll. Drôles de Marchés, 14.00 euros, 132 p.)
ISBN : 978-2-343-00469-3, ISBN EBOOK : 978-2-296-53537-4

L'HARMATTAN ITALIA
Via Degli Artisti 15; 10124 Torino

L'HARMATTAN HONGRIE
Könyvesbolt ; Kossuth L. u. 14-16
1053 Budapest

L'HARMATTAN KINSHASA
185, avenue Nyangwe
Commune de Lingwala
Kinshasa, R.D. Congo
(00243) 998697603 ou (00243) 999229662

L'HARMATTAN CONGO
67, av. E. P. Lumumba
Bât. – Congo Pharmacie (Bib. Nat.)
BP2874 Brazzaville
harmattan.congo@yahoo.fr

L'HARMATTAN GUINÉE
Almamya Rue KA 028, en face
du restaurant Le Cèdre
OKB agency BP 3470 Conakry
(00224) 657 20 85 08 / 664 28 91 96
harmattanguinee@yahoo.fr

L'HARMATTAN MALI
Rue 73, Porte 536, Niamakoro,
Cité Unicef, Bamako
Tél. 00 (223) 20205724 / +(223) 76378082
poudiougopaul@yahoo.fr
pp.harmattan@gmail.com

L'HARMATTAN CAMEROUN
BP 11486
Face à la SNI, immeuble Don Bosco
Yaoundé
(00237) 99 76 61 66
harmattancam@yahoo.fr

L'HARMATTAN CÔTE D'IVOIRE
Résidence Karl / cité des arts
Abidjan-Cocody 03 BP 1588 Abidjan 03
(00225) 05 77 87 31
etien_nda@yahoo.fr

L'HARMATTAN BURKINA
Penou Achille Some
Ouagadougou
(+226) 70 26 88 27

L'HARMATTAN SÉNÉGAL
10 VDN en face Mermoz, après le pont de Fann
BP 45034 Dakar Fann
33 825 98 58 / 33 860 9858
senharmattan@gmail.com / senlibraire@gmail.com
www.harmattansenegal.com

L'HARMATTAN BÉNIN
ISOR-BENIN
01 BP 359 COTONOU-RP
Quartier Gbèdjromèdé,
Rue Agbélenco, Lot 1247 I
Tél : 00 229 21 32 53 79
christian_dablaka123@yahoo.fr

Achevé d'imprimer par Corlet Numérique - 14110 Condé-sur-Noireau
N° d'Imprimeur : 114674 - Dépôt légal : décembre 2014 - *Imprimé en France*